Why Plato Wrote

Blackwell-Bristol Lectures on Greece, Rome and the Classical Tradition

Current Series Editor: Neville Morley

The Bristol Institute of Greece, Rome and the Classical Tradition promotes the study of Greco-Roman culture from antiquity to the present day, in the belief that classical culture remains a vital influence in the modern world. It embraces research and education in many fields, including history of all kinds, archaeology, literary studies, art history and philosophy, with particular emphasis on links between the ancient and modern worlds. The Blackwell Bristol lectures showcase the very best of modern scholarship in Classics and the Classical Tradition.

Published

Why Plato Wrote
Danielle Allen

Tales of the Barbarians: Ethnography and Empire in the Roman West
Greg Woolf

BLACKWELL BRISTOL
LECTURES ON
GREECE, ROME
AND THE CLASSICAL
TRADITION

Why Plato Wrote

Danielle S. Allen

A John Wiley & Sons, Ltd., Publication

This paperback edition first published 2013
© 2013 Danielle S. Allen

Edition history: Blackwell Publishing Ltd (hardback, 2010)

Blackwell Publishing was acquired by John Wiley & Sons in February 2007. Blackwell's publishing program has been merged with Wiley's global Scientific, Technical, and Medical business to form Wiley-Blackwell.

Registered Office
John Wiley & Sons Ltd, The Atrium, Southern Gate, Chichester, West Sussex, PO19 8SQ, UK

Editorial Offices
350 Main Street, Malden, MA 02148-5020, USA
9600 Garsington Road, Oxford, OX4 2DQ, UK
The Atrium, Southern Gate, Chichester, West Sussex, PO19 8SQ, UK

For details of our global editorial offices, for customer services, and for information about how to apply for permission to reuse the copyright material in this book please see our website at www.wiley.com/wiley-blackwell.

The right of Danielle S. Allen to be identified as the author of this work has been asserted in accordance with the UK Copyright, Designs and Patents Act 1988.

Wiley also publishes its books in a variety of electronic formats. Some content that appears in print may not be available in electronic books.

Designations used by companies to distinguish their products are often claimed as trademarks. All brand names and product names used in this book are trade names, service marks, trademarks or registered trademarks of their respective owners. The publisher is not associated with any product or vendor mentioned in this book. This publication is designed to provide accurate and authoritative information in regard to the subject matter covered. It is sold on the understanding that the publisher is not engaged in rendering professional services. If professional advice or other expert assistance is required, the services of a competent professional should be sought.

Library of Congress Cataloging-in-Publication Data

Allen, Danielle S., 1971–
  Why Plato wrote / Danielle S. Allen.
    p. cm. – (Blackwell-Bristol lectures on Greece, Rome and the classical tradition)
  Includes bibliographical references and index.
  978-1-4443-3448-7 (hardcover : alk. paper) ISBN 978-1-1184-5439-8 (pbk. : alk. paper)
  1. Plato. 2. Authorship–Psychological aspects. I. Title.
  B395.A53 2010
  184–dc22
                                                          2010027875

A catalogue record for this book is available from the British Library.

Cover design by Nicki Averill
Set in 10/12pt Sabon by Thomson Digital, Noida, India
Printed in Malaysia by Ho Printing (M) Sdn Bhd
1   2013

For *all my teachers and students*

ἔνθα πολιτείας μὲν οὐχ ἥψατο, καίτοι πολιτικὸς ὢν ἐξ ὧν γέγραφεν.

And in his own city he did not meddle with political affairs, although he was a politician or political leader to judge from his writings. (Diog. Laert. 3.23)

Contents

Acknowledgments

This book grew from the four Bristol-Blackwell lectures that I gave at the University of Bristol in May 2008. First and foremost I owe thanks to the hosts of that event: Al Bertrand, Gillian Clark, Bob Fowler, Charles Martindale, and Neville Morley. I am grateful too to their colleagues, all such warm hosts also: Chris Bertram, Terrell Carver, Sarah Hitch, Kurt Lampe, Nico Momigliano, and Giles Pearson. The 2009 Lionel Trilling Lecture at Columbia University, a Friday night lecture at St. John's College, and the 2010 Benedict Lectures at Boston University provided the opportunity to summarize the book's argument before engaged and challenging audiences. I am particularly grateful to the respondents on those occasions, including Nadia Urbinati, Katja Vogt, Amelie Rorty, David Roochnik, and Mitch Miller for trenchant commentary.

Two decades of conversation have gone into this book. I'd like to thank the students in seminars I taught at the University of Chicago on Plato's *Menexenus*, *Republic*, and *Theaetetus*, colleagues in the "Moral Authority of Nature" working group at the Max Planck Institute for the History of Science in Berlin and in the Language, History, and Political Thought group at the University of Chicago as well as audiences at Baylor University, Bryn Mawr College, Cambridge University, Columbia University, Harvard University, the Institute for Advanced Study, University of Michigan, Princeton University, the University of Southern California, and several American Political Science Association annual meetings.

The research conclusions of several former dissertation students are assimilated here, as indicated in the notes, particularly those of Brendan Boyle, Alex Gottesman, Hugh Liebert, Jennifer London, Emily Nacol, John Paulas, Daniela Reinhard, and Neil Roberts. Working with each was a great joy.

This book has also benefited tremendously from exchanges with William Allen, Graham Burnett, Caroline Bynum, James Conant, Lorraine Daston,

Mary Dietz, Jimmy Doyle, Peter Euben, Chris Faraone, Simon Goldhill, Kevin Hawthorne, Bonnie Honig, Leslie Kurke, Gabriel Lear, Jonathan Lear, Patrick McGuinn, Maureen McLane, Patchen Markell, Eric Maskin, Sara Monoson, Mary Nichols, Jennifer Pitts, Robin Osborne, Malcolm Schofield, Melissa Schwartzberg, Rick Schweder, Joan Scott, Kendall Sharp, George Shulman, Laura Slatkin, Marc Stears, Lisa van Alstyne, Robert von Hallberg, John Wallach, and Michael Walzer. Special thanks go to those who read the whole manuscript in draft, saw beyond where I had gotten, and inspired me to the final phase of this work: Paul Cartledge, John Cooper, Jill Frank, Richard Kraut, Melissa Lane, and Josh Ober.

Errors are mine.

The author and publisher gratefully acknowledge the permission granted to reproduce the copyright material in this book:

Reprinted by permission of the publishers and the Trustees of the Loeb Classical Library from *Plato*: Volume IX, translated by R. G. Bury, Loeb Classical Library Volume 234, pp. 486, 488–490, 494–496, 498, 512–514, 516–518, 528, 530–534, 538–540, 552, 562, Cambridge, MA: Harvard University Press, Copyright (c) 1929 by the President and Fellows of Harvard College. The Loeb Classical Library® is a registered trademark of the President and Fellows of Harvard College.

G. R. F. Ferrari, *Plato: The Republic*, translated by Tom Griffith, 2000, © in the translation and editorial matter Cambridge University Press 2000, reproduced with permission.

The information used to generate the map on p. 96 comes from R. Ginouvès and M. Hatzopoulos, eds. 1994. *Macedonia from Philip II to the Roman Conquest*. Princeton, NJ: Princeton University Press, 48–49.

Abbreviations

Aes.	Aeschines
Ath. Pol.	Aristotle, *Constitution of the Athenians* (*Athênaiôn politeia*)
Dem.	Demosthenes
Diels–Kranz	*Die Fragmente der Vorsokratiker*, ed. Hermann Diels and Walther Kranz. Zurich: Weidmann, 1985
Diog. Laert.	Diogenes Laertius
Din.	Dinarchus
Diod.	Diodorus
F. Gr. Hist.	*Fragmenta historicorum graecorum*, ed. K. Muller. Paris: Didot, 1851
Hyp.	Hyperides
Kassel–Austen, *PCG*	*Poetae comici graeci*, ed. R. Kassel and C. Austin. Berlin and New York: W. de Gruyter, 1983–
Kock, *CAF*	*Comicorum atticorum fragmenta*, ed. T. Kock. 3 vols. Leipzig: Teubner, 1880–1888
IG	*Inscriptiones Graecae*
LSJ	*A Greek–English Lexicon*, ed. H. G. Liddell and R. Scott, revised and augmented by Sir Henry Stuart Jones. 9th edn. Oxford: Oxford University Press, 1996 [1940]
Lyc.	Lycurgus
Meineke, *CGF*	*Fragmenta comicorum graecorum*, ed. A. Meineke, vols. 1–3. Berlin: Reimer, 1840
Paus.	Pausanias

Plato works:

Apol.	*Apology*
Def.	*Definitions*
Prot.	*Protagoras*
Rep.	*Republic*
Symp.	*Symposium*
Plut.	Plutarch

Plutarch works:

Dem.	*Demosthenes*
Mor.	*Moralia*
Phoc.	*Phocion*
Thuc.	Thucydides
TLG	*Thesaurus linguae graecae.* Available online at http://www.tlg.uci.edu/
Tod	*Greek Historical Inscriptions from the Sixth Century* BC *to the Death of Alexander the Great*, ed. M. N. Tod. Chicago: Ares, 1985
SEG	*Supplementum epigraphicum graecum*

Prologue
Why Think about Plato?

Why write about Plato nearly 2400 years after his death? Don't we understand him by now?

We do and we don't. But more important than whether humanity's
collective knowledge about Plato, built up over centuries, includes mastery
of his systematic philosophy is whether our generation understands Plato
at all.

The grand total of human knowledge might be conceived in either of two
ways. One might think of it as the sum of all the intellectual material in all the
books in all the libraries of the world; this mountain of text would include
everything that has already been said about Plato, or any other subject, from
the beginning of time. On this conception, each scholarly project on Plato
rolls one more small stone up onto the accumulated pile of human contributions to interpreting his works; one would imagine that each contribution
would yield smaller and smaller returns and that humanity would eventually
exhaust the subject.

But one might rather conceive of human knowledge as the sum of what all
human beings currently alive know and understand. Everyone starts life with
little knowledge or understanding; everyone dies with a lifetime's treasury. On
this conception, the sum of human knowledge is what each generation wins for
itself between birth and death. To some extent, any given generation can speed
up its self-education by teaching itself what earlier generations have already
discovered; to some extent, any given generation must discover things for
itself. On this second conception of the sum of human knowledge, a scholarly
project on Plato lights up yet again, for this generation, as earlier scholars have
for their own generations, a range of questions and ideas significant to human
life. Sometimes one manages to light up questions that have been dark for a
long time.

Why Plato Wrote   Danielle S. Allen. © 2010 Danielle S. Allen

I prefer this second conception of human knowledge. After all, if all the books in the world contained the secret of life, but no one had read them, how much actual knowledge about the secret of life would be alive in the world? Humanistic scholarship activates knowledge and understanding here and now – both by reclaiming things that have been known by earlier generations and by asking and introducing, where necessary, fresh questions and new ideas. Nor does reclaiming past intellectual gains require agreement with them. They are a valuable property, an inheritance, because they help us grasp the conceptual alternatives that frame human life; but we will agree with some and disagree with other ideas from earlier generations. The project of coming to understanding *now* is a matter of deciding for ourselves where to agree or not.

This book both reclaims what has been known and understood about Plato by earlier generations and introduces new ideas.

So how can it happen that a person might have a new idea about a subject as long-lived as Plato's philosophy? Reactivating older bodies of knowledge for present use often seems also to spur discovery. Why is that?

Human knowledge is inevitably partial, by which I mean both incomplete and situated: the combined total of human knowledge emanates from hundreds of billions of individuals each situated in a specific place and time and with individualized curiosities, preoccupations, and desires. As we ourselves learn what our predecessors have known, we discover not only their successes – ideas worthy of being relit – but also their limits – conceptual points where corrections, revisions, subtractions, or additions are necessary. Our own views will have similar blemishes; we should never pretend otherwise.

In my own case, some accidental discoveries, made meaningful by technological contingencies, led me to question how earlier scholars had interpreted Plato's view of the relation between philosophy and politics.

What were the accidental discoveries? And what do I mean by "technological contingencies"?

About fifteen years ago, when I was working on my dissertation on the politics of punishing in democratic Athens of the fourth century BCE, I noticed that some of Plato's philosophical vocabulary appeared in speeches given by Athenian politicians. Some of Aristotle's vocabulary showed up too. But this wasn't supposed to happen. Hadn't the execution of Socrates by the Athenians caused Plato such disillusionment with his home city that he had turned his back on politics? And since Aristotle wasn't even a citizen, his political engagement had been entirely with the Macedonians, principally as tutor to Alexander the Great, no? Students are told year after year that in Athens after the death of Socrates philosophy and politics lived separate lives.[1] They learn that during the fourth century BCE an ideal of contemplation took hold; philosophy became identified with time spent away from practical realities in peaceful retreats where ceaseless conversation could be oriented toward securing knowledge, not society's daily needs. What, then, were these fragments of philosophical vocabulary doing in political speeches?

I was not the first scholar to notice that, for instance, a speech by the politician Lycurgus, which charges a citizen named Leocrates with treason, was remarkably full of Platonic vocabulary.[2] But was I the first to notice that a key term in Aristotle's ethical theory, *prohairesis*, which means "deliberated commitment," turned up frequently in late fourth-century Athenian political speeches? Maybe.[3] Whatever the case, once I had noticed the migration of these concepts from philosophy to politics, I was able to do something earlier scholars couldn't: I ran the terms through a computer database of Greek texts to see whether patterns emerged in their usage.[4] Were these two examples one-offs? Or could one spot some more systematic movement of philosophical concepts into politics?

As we shall see in chapter 6, patterns did emerge. First, the relevant terms (*prohairesis* and also the word *kolasis*, which refers to a reformative approach to punishment) seem genuinely to have originated with Plato and/or Aristotle; they were largely unused by earlier writers. Second, the political use of these and related terms had a distinct chronological pattern; the terminological migration seems to have begun in the 350s BCE. Third, some politicians took up the philosophical vocabulary more eagerly than others; and at least one politician actively resisted at least the Platonic vocabulary. What was one to make of these facts, newly visible thanks to technological contingency? It has taken more than a decade to answer that question.

I was not alone in my confusion over how to understand the relationship between philosophical ideas and political events. If anything, social scientists freely admit uncertainty with regard to this question.[5] In 1936 the economist John Maynard Keynes wrote: "The ideas of economists and political philosophers, both when they are right and when they are wrong, are more powerful than is commonly understood."[6] Three decades later, another economist, Albert O. Hirschman wrote the following about the decline in the seventeenth century of a heroic ethos and rise of a valorization of commercial activity: "This astounding transformation of the moral and ideological scene erupts quite suddenly, and the historical and psychological reasons for it are still not wholly understood."[7]

What are the processes by which intellectuals' ideas come to shape a community's values? When non-philosophers adopt concepts from philosophers, getting them partly wrong and partly right, using and abusing them to particular, strategic ends, how should we think about the degree of "influence" on social events wielded by those philosophers and their concepts? In what sense might the ideas of economists and political philosophers be "powerful," as Keynes put it? Why isn't the role of ideas in politics well understood, as both Keynes and Hirschman indicate? Although these questions are old, and even trite, we still don't have good answers. As I pondered the movement of terms like *kolasis* (reformative punishment) and *prohairesis* (deliberated commitment) from philosophical to political argument, versions of these questions, linking Plato and Aristotle to Athenian politics, preoccupied me.

About half way through the period of my consternation and confusion, it suddenly occurred to me to ask the question: Why did Plato write anyway? His teacher, Socrates, had not done so. Socrates had insisted on philosophy as an oral practice directed toward the examination of self and other. If anything, he appears to have disdained writing. Why, then, should his ardent disciple have pursued an altogether different way of life? I soon realized that asking and answering the question, "Why did Plato write?" might provide us with philosophical and historical treasure.

Plato wrote, but he never wrote to speak in his own voice. He wrote dialogues representing conversations among various casts of characters. Very often, but not always, Socrates played the lead role. Socrates' opinions (at least as represented by Plato) are therefore those one most immediately takes from any given Platonic dialogue as the main ideas. This has led to the perennial question of how one can distinguish the ideas and opinions of teacher and pupil. What did Plato think, actually, if we hear, in his dialogues, only ever from Socrates? It occurred to me that, since Plato had chosen to write, when Socrates had not, if we could figure out *why* Plato wrote, we would know something fundamental about the philosophical differences between him and Socrates.[8]

Happily, this question, "Why did Plato write?" turned out also to be the key to the appearance of Platonic formulations in the mouths of Athenian politicians. Plato wrote, among other purposes, to effect political change. Yes, Plato was the world's first systematic political philosopher, using text to record technical philosophical advances, but he was also, it appears, the western world's first think-tank activist and its first message man.[9] He wrote – not solely but consistently – to change Athenian culture and thereby transform Athenian politics.[10] As Diogenes Laertius, one of the most important biographers of Plato, put it, "in his own city Plato did not meddle with political affairs, although he was a politician or political leader [*politikos* in the Greek], to judge from his writings" (*entha politeias men ouch hêpsato, kaitoi politikos ôn ex hôn gegraphen*).[11]

But the question of "Why Plato wrote" and the answer that he wrote as a politician raise the further question of who would have read Plato's dialogues. Historians concur that in the fourth century most male Athenian citizens would have had the basic literacy necessary for the city's political business, which involved written laws, decrees, and lists of names identifying who was obligated to serve in particular capacities.[12] But such citizenly literacy would have developed into higher forms only for a smaller circle of elites who received formal education.[13] But we know that, as far as this social group was concerned, Plato's books did travel. We hear that one woman, Axiothea of Philesia, was drawn from her Peloponnesian city to Athens to study with Plato on account of having read the *Republic*.[14] Some range of elite Athenians (and foreigners) would have had access to Plato's written texts. Perhaps even some non-elite citizens would have too: Socrates, in Plato's *Apology*, remarks that Anaxagoras' books were easily available to anyone in the market-place for a drachma (*Apol.* 6). But then again, a drachma would have been the better part of a day's wage for a laborer.[15]

While it is unlikely that Athens achieved general literacy for citizens during Plato's lifetime, one of his characters advocated such a goal in the *Laws* (810a).[16] In the ideal city described in that dialogue, all citizens would be able to read books like Plato's. This means Plato could imagine a general reader for his dialogues, and my argument in this book is that he developed a mode of philosophical writing that anticipated such readers even in advance of their general emergence.

Reading was not, however, the only way to learn about philosophy in Athens. Plato gave at least one public lecture, and Aristotle gave several. The subject of Plato's lecture was "the good," while Aristotle's public lectures were about rhetoric. We can't help but notice that the subject of Plato's lecture was also the subject of the middle books of the *Republic*. All we know about his lecture, though, is that attendees complained that it had too much to do with mathematics. Curiously, this complaint is also familiar to anyone who has tried to teach the middle books of the *Republic*.[17] It's plausible that some of what Plato said in that lecture would have overlapped with what he wrote. Whatever the case, since Plato did give this public lecture, and Aristotle too gave public lectures, we know that the circle of Athenians exposed to Plato's ideas, and philosophy generally, extended beyond the students enrolled in his school, the Academy.

In fact, that circle also stretched to include the tens of thousands of citizens who attended the comic theater. Just as toward the end of the fifth century Aristophanes had mocked Socrates with a real understanding of Socrates' ideas, so too later comic poets seemed to get Plato.[18] Thus, Theopompus mocks: "'For one thing is no longer only one, but two things now are scarcely one,' as Plato says."[19] Theopompus is clearly jabbing at the importance to Plato of the idea of number, as well as at Plato's commitment to the unity of the good. Word had spread broadly enough about Plato's ideas, then, including even the metaphysical ones, for them to be the basis for jokes meant to be accessible to the ordinary, even minimally literate, Athenian citizen. And those who didn't get the joke at least learned that Plato was up to some funny business with numbers. Plato's written dialogues would, though, have anchored these alternative forms of dissemination through the lectures and plays.

Importantly, to identify Plato as a message man is not to diminish his status as a philosopher. First, these were and are not mutually exclusive roles, and Plato pursued both.[20] Second, Plato's pursuit of language that might shift cultural norms was itself philosophically grounded, as we shall see. The effort to answer the question, "Why did Plato write?" leads us deep into his philosophy of language, which in turn provides at least provisional answers to the sorts of questions raised by Keynes, Hirschman, and others in the social sciences about how ideas intersect with social life. Most importantly, Plato's philosophy of language indicates that the route to explaining the relation between ideas and events requires bringing together the resources of multiple disciplines: linguistics, psychology, and sociology, at least.

In his dialogues, Plato offers an argument about the linguistic, psychological, and social processes by which ideas gain a hold on the human imagination. Like the linguist and cultural theorist George Lakoff, he makes a case for the powerful effects of metaphor and allegory on the dissemination of concepts, information, and evaluative schema. Like the father of psychoanalysis, Sigmund Freud, he analyzes how the proximity of mothers to children, the charisma of paternal authority, and the fear of death generate psychological phenomena in individuals that anchor their moral values. Like the French historian and theorist of power, Michel Foucault, he argues that social norms are disseminated not only through texts and other media of verbal communication but also through material realities themselves; like Foucault, he understood that human beings build their worlds – including their social practices and material objects – around their core values, with the result that those social practices and material objects themselves convey dominant social norms.[21]

On Plato's account, the social power of ideas arises from how well their verbal expression exploits the resources of metaphor, how closely they respond to psychic structures arising from maternal proximity, paternal authority, and the fear of death, and how available they are for transformation into rules of action that generate concrete practices and material effects. Speakers and writers who mobilize any of these sources of power inherent in language seek to acquire a surplus of linguistic power (or social influence) beyond the average quantities available to each of us every day in ordinary talk.[22]

In writing his dialogues, Plato, I will argue, sought to generate exactly such surplus linguistic power as a means to acquire social power within his own city, ancient Athens of the fourth century BCE. As a part of explaining how philosophers' ideas can have power, he makes the strongest possible case that I know of for language as a potential cause of social and political change. His argument is not, however, that somehow philosophers' ideas – their reigning concepts – are transmitted whole (unchanged and unadapted) to their publics, with political consequences flowing immediately out from those ideas. He recognizes the anarchic structure of the lives of human beings in language. As words and concepts move from person to person, there are myriad forms of slippage, misapprehension, metonymic extension, and Freudian replacement, not to mention the constantly trailing shadow of the antitheses of the concepts under discussion. Plato's argument is therefore not that any given author can finally control how her ideas are taken up and used but that an author can at least dramatically increase the likelihood that her ideas *will be* taken up and used. And the more likely that an author's ideas are to be used, the greater the number of that author's ideas that are likely to circulate broadly. Finally, Plato also seems to have thought that, whenever an author's ideas are systematically linked to each other through metaphorical structures and as the number of such linked concepts that are taken up by other users increases, the less will the new uses of those concepts deviate from the author's own original conceptual schema. It is when we can see sets of linked concepts that appeared in the work of a philosopher appearing again in social discourse, still linked in the same ways, that we can say not merely that people have begun to use these new concepts but also that the thinker who produced them has had an influence. And when we can see that people are using such sets of linked concepts to define decisive political choices for themselves, we can say that the philosopher has had an influence on politics.

Many people reading this book will think that Plato's view of the quantities of social power available to be tapped through the careful use of language is optimistic in the extreme, and even inclines to folly. Indeed, Plato seems to have thought that the kinds of linguistic power that he analyzed, developed, and propounded, particularly in the *Republic*, which lays out the structure of a utopian city, depended for their full effects on operating within a homogeneous community. His political thought included an argument for a sort of ethno-nationalism, and in the *Republic* Socrates argues that the disintegration of the utopian city will begin when the city ceases to provide its young with the right sort of education in symbols, a failure that is cast as simultaneous to a breakdown of the utopia's eugenic match-making practices.[23] A homogeneous community can maintain a more stable linguistic universe over time; communications among its members should transpire with a higher ratio of signal to noise than in contexts of diversity.[24] Plato's theory of linguistic power, and his press to maximize such power with his own texts, would be blunted in a world of diversity where the anarchic structure of the lives of human beings in language is heightened.

Yet this does not mean that we, living with diversity of necessity and by choice embracing it (I hope), should disregard Plato's arguments about how the work of intellectuals affects social life. There is something right about his theory of the power of metaphor, of the psychological consequences of maternal proximity, paternal charisma, and the fear of death, and of the discursive basis of our material lives. He hasn't gotten the whole story right – about how ideas come to have social power and effects – but he has gotten *something* right. If we wish to understand the role played by ideas in social processes, we could profit from taking Plato's account seriously. Once we have understood it, we can proceed to revise it, or to build an alternative.

The primary focus of this book, then, is on Plato and on answering the question, Why did Plato write? – but the answer requires beginning to identify the theoretical positions outlined just above. For the time being, I can make only a beginning of the latter work. A full account of Plato's theory of language and its usefulness for understanding the relationship between ideas and events, or discourse and structure, will have to wait. My hope, though, is that this book, in addition to answering the question of why Plato wrote, will mark trailheads that might be pursued toward the goal of answering our long-lived questions about the relationships between ideas and events.

Part I
Why Plato Wrote

1

Who Was Plato?

When Plato, son of Ariston and Perictione, was born to an aristocratic family in Athens in 424/3 BCE, he had two elder brothers, Adeimantus and Glaucon, roughly eight and five years older. Glaucon, at least, would soon be an aspiring politician.[1] Plato also had two uncles, Critias and Charmides, who were intensely involved in Athenian politics and who, in 404/3 BCE, joined a group of aristocrats in an oligarchic take-over of the democratic city.[2] It seems they invited young Plato to join them. He was then just twenty, the age at which young Athenian men usually got involved in politics, but he declined the invitation. Some years earlier his life had already taken an interesting turn; he had met the famous wise man Socrates, who lived from 469 to 399 BCE. Now, at age twenty, he began to follow Socrates formally.

The word philosopher wasn't yet much in use during the years that Socrates frequented the Athenian city center and market-place or *agora*; Socrates would generally have been called a *sophistês*.[3] This word literally means "wise man" but came to have the negative connotation of "sophist," a person who fast-talks his way out of moral, intellectual, and practical quandaries or trickily leads others into them. Plato probably met Socrates in his early or mid-teens, and even then earned the older man's admiration; he would have been sixteen in 408–407 BCE, which appears to have been the year that Socrates undertook to educate Plato's older brother Glaucon in wise political leadership, a conversation that both Xenophon and Plato record.[4] Xenophon represents Socrates as having struck up the conversation with Glaucon as a favor to Plato, so the latter must by then already have been a regular associate of Socrates.[5]

Plato's record of such a conversation occurs, of course, in the very famous dialogue, *The Republic*, in which Socrates leads Glaucon (and Adeimantus too) through an answer to the question, "What is justice?" Over the course

Why Plato Wrote   Danielle S. Allen. © 2010 Danielle S. Allen

of the conversation, Socrates builds an argument for a utopia led by philosopher-kings and queens and protected by a class of guardian-soldiers, including both men and women, who hold their property in common, have egalitarian gender relations, and enjoy open marriages. But the historian Xenophon also records a conversation between Socrates and Glaucon about political leadership. In a book called *Reminiscences of Socrates*, Xenophon represents the conversation between Socrates and Glaucon as having been unextraordinary (*Mem.* 3.6.1 ff.). According to Xenophon, the wise man asked Plato's brother questions like: "Tell us how you propose to begin your services to the state"; "Will you try to make your city richer?"; "In order to advise the city whom to fight, it is necessary to know the strength of the city and of the enemy ... tell us the naval and military strength of our city, and then that of her enemies." Although the questions are conventional, Glaucon fares poorly. So Socrates admonishes him: "Don't you see how risky it is to say or do what you don't understand?"

Plato's involvement with Socrates ended prematurely – even before Plato was out of his twenties. In 399 BCE, the citizens of Athens condemned his teacher to death. Why? Five years earlier, in 404 BCE, the group of oligarchs, among whom Plato's uncles numbered, had taken over the city in an oligarchic coup; Socrates was associated with several of the participants. Within a year, the democratic resistance had in turn overthrown the oligarchs. Admirably, the reinstated democratic citizenry sought reconciliation among different factions in the city and issued a broad amnesty (for all except the leaders of the coup) in which the citizens swore not to remember past events.[6] Yet despite this amnesty, some legal cases continued to emerge from the controversies. The plausibility to the Athenians of the charges against Socrates – of impiety and of corrupting the youth – is generally thought to have depended on the preceding political turmoil.[7]

Both Plato and Xenophon wrote accounts of Socrates' trial and speeches, each titled *The Apology*. In the original Greek the word, "apology" simply meant "a defense speech," and Socrates was not the only citizen to have to deliver a highly politicized one in 399 BCE. In the same year, the orator Lysias wrote an apology for an anonymous citizen who had been charged with subverting the democratic constitution. And these were just two out of six major public trials in the year 400/399 BCE that somehow related to the previous events.[8] Nor was Socrates the first philosopher to be brought to trial in Athens. Approximately thirty years earlier, at the beginning of the Peloponnesian War, another time of political stress in the city, the Athenians reportedly prosecuted Anaxagoras.[9] Late in the fourth century, they would go after philosophy again, as their subjection to Macedon was becoming permanent. They would prosecute (and acquit) Theophrastus sometime between 317 and 307 BCE and then directly legislate against philosophy in 307 BCE.[10]

How did Plato react to the judgment and execution of his teacher? He attended the trial and wrote himself into his account of Socrates' defense speech. In his *Crito*, he represents himself as having offered to put up money so that Socrates could pay his penalty with a fine rather than with his life. This is the only place in his dialogues that Plato himself shows up. But versions of Plato's life story, which help answer the question of how he reacted to Socrates' death, appear in several other texts, among them an allegedly autobiographical letter dating to 354 BCE. Plato supposedly wrote this letter to a group of politicians in Syracuse on the island of Sicily, where he had spent considerable time, but scholars now generally agree that Plato did not himself write this letter. Whoever did, though, knew Plato's dialogues well and wrote from close proximity to him; the author was probably someone involved in Syracusan politics.[11] We can therefore take seriously what this letter – called the *Seventh Letter*, as one of thirteen attributed to Plato – tells us about his life.

According to the *Seventh Letter*, the death of Socrates changed Plato's life. Having thought that he wished to enter Athenian politics, he abandoned that path and sought philosophical associates instead. He moved to Megara, on the border of Attica, where a community of philosophers, who had left Athens in the trial's wake, had gathered. Then Plato appears to have traveled more widely, arriving in Syracuse in 384/3 BCE, where he became involved with the family of the Syracusan tyrant, Dionysius I, as a teacher and political advisor. Plato's first stay at Syracuse was brief. By 383 BCE he had returned to Athens and opened his philosophical school, the Academy, just outside the city center of Athens.[12] This means that within two decades of Socrates' death, Plato had already written dialogues important enough to generate a philosophical reputation that could justify opening a school; these dialogues would have included the *Apology*, *Gorgias*, *Symposium*, and Book 1 of the *Republic*.[13] Plato's time of travels had also been time to write. He then spent the rest of his life at the Academy but for two more stints in Syracuse (in 367 BCE and 361 BCE), where he was again politically entangled. By the time of his second visit in 367 BCE, he had finished the *Republic* and three other major dialogues. And by the time he died in Athens in 348/7 BCE at the age of seventy-six, he had written, over roughly fifty years, more than two dozen dialogues. Plato, in contrast to his teacher, had lived a writer's life.

One might think that, with all those books by Plato to consult, scholars would long ago have come up with settled answers to the questions of what Plato thought and what his relationship to Athenian politics was. Yet these two questions have been continually vexing. After all, although Plato wrote more than two dozen dialogues, he speaks in his own voice in none. And since Socrates is often the central character in the dialogues, we are constantly confronted with the difficulty of distinguishing Socratic from Platonic elements in them. The second question – about Plato's relation to Athenian politics – flows pretty directly from the first. Because of the great difficulty in identifying what Plato himself thought, scholars are at a loss for how to interpret the relation of his richly elaborated political theory to actual politics. Indeed, scholars have taken quite opposing positions on how Plato expected his theory to relate to practice.

At one extreme, some scholars have seen the arguments in the *Republic* as a straightforward constitutional blueprint that Plato hoped to see implemented. Those adopting this view have seen Plato as a would-be totalitarian advocating the creation of a fascist state.[14] At the other end of the spectrum, scholars have seen the arguments of the *Republic* – and particularly the arguments for the equality of women and communistic property arrangements – as so obviously laughable (as the comic playwright Aristophanes made similar ideas in comedies like *The Assemblywomen*) that the dialogue must be making a point of their impossibility, not their desirability.[15] These scholars see Plato as arguing against any pursuit of radical change in the structure of human life. On this view, the conversion of Plato's theory into a practical politics mainly entails educating moderate, conservative rulers whose respect for philosophy will help them steer their societies along moderate, conservative courses.[16]

The *Seventh Letter*, which ruminates in Plato's name on why the philosopher engaged with Syracusan politics, provides support for both positions. The letter claims that Plato desired to see his theoretical plans made real: "If anyone ever was to attempt to realize these principles of law and government, now was the time to try, since it was only necessary to win over a single man and I should have accomplished all the good I dreamed of" (328b–c).[17] Yet the advice given by Plato to the Syracusans does not directly mirror the blueprint provided in the *Republic*. For instance, in the *Republic*, Socrates argues that the construction of a utopian city requires first banishing everyone over the age of ten; the philosopher-rulers need a clean slate from which to start work. But in Syracuse, according to the *Seventh Letter*, Plato eschewed such political violence. He always sought, the *Letter* insists, repeating the point three times, to bring about "a blissful and true life" without resorting to massacres, murders, and exiles (327d, 331d, 351c).

Indeed the *Seventh Letter* describes Plato as pursuing a blissful and true life for Syracuse mainly through the education of its young ruler, Dionysius II, into a love of philosophy. This provides some support to those scholars who see Plato's relation to politics as resting primarily on his interest in educating elites. But neither the view that Plato's theoretical ideas provided a blueprint for political change nor the view that he sought primarily to educate elites helps us understand his relationship to politics in Athens. After all, we have no evidence that he worked in legislative arenas to change Athenian institutions in the directions described in the *Republic*; nor in Athens did he have occasion to educate a tyrant or monarch, or even a closed and controlling political elite, as he had had in Syracuse. Yes, he educated elites but not an oligarchical elite.

A third account of how Plato thought his philosophy related to politics focuses on Plato's role as a critic in Athens. His dialogues are full of probing commentary on Athenian culture and political leaders as well as being full of metaphors, for instance from the theater and practices of spectatorship, that themselves emerged from Athenian culture. These facts are the basis for an argument that Plato, through his dialogues, acted on Athenian politics as a constant critic showing up its defects.[18] Again, the *Seventh Letter* provides some support. According to the *Letter* Plato believed that "if to the man of sense his state appears to be ill governed he ought to speak, if so be that his speech is not likely to prove fruitless nor to cause his death" (331cd). Since Plato managed to publish texts critical of Athens over the course of his entire life without suffering punishment, he must be recognized as having succeeded at just such a project of sustained dissent.[19]

But what about all the positive arguments in his dialogues for an alternative set of political ideals? Plato's project was not merely critical but also constructive. Some scholars have recognized this, focusing in particular on Plato's use of the dialogue form to enact an open-ended, and therefore (on their argument) democratic method of engaging with important questions thrown up by democratic life.[20] But how did Plato's investigations of political questions (whether tending in an anti-democratic or democratic direction) feed back into Athenian politics? How did he hope they might feed back? These scholars do not ask or answer this question. And neither the blueprint theory nor the theory about the education of elites fully explains how Plato's positive project related to Athens. Each of the three existing scholarly accounts of how Plato related to Athenian politics gives us a spark of truth, but the matter isn't yet fully illuminated. This is because we have not yet asked and answered the fundamental question: Why did Plato write? The fact that Plato wrote distinguishes him absolutely from Socrates. If we can discover why Plato wrote, we will have identified a cornerstone of his philosophy.[21]

Figuring out why Plato wrote is a tricky operation. In general, pursuing an author's intentions is unfashionable but even if it were a more conventional undertaking, it also remains, simply, difficult. After all, Plato did not invent the concept of the Socratic dialogue; more than a dozen of Socrates' students (or students of his students) wrote them.[22] How could we distinguish Plato's intentions from those of any other writer of dialogues? And even Socrates seems to have engaged in some literary experimentation, at least at the end of his life.

In the *Phaedo*, the dialogue in which Plato recounts Socrates' last days, we hear that in prison Socrates has been busily writing a hymn to Apollo. When asked by his student Cebes, why the aged wise man who had never composed poems should spend his final days versifying, Socrates answers:

> I composed these verses not because I wished to rival [the poet] Evenus or his poems, for I knew that would not be easy, but because I wished to test the meaning of certain dreams, and to make sure that I was neglecting no duty in case their repeated commands meant that I must cultivate the Muses in this way. They were something like this. The same dream came to me often in my past life, sometimes in one form and sometimes in another, but always saying the same thing: "Socrates," it said, "make music and work at it." And I formerly thought it was urging and encouraging me to do what I was doing already and that just as people encourage runners by cheering, so the dream was encouraging me to do what I was doing, that is, to make music, because philosophy was the greatest kind of music and I was working at that. But now, after the trial and while the festival of the god delayed my execution, I thought, in case the repeated dream really meant to tell me to make this which is ordinarily called music, I ought to do so and not to disobey. For I thought it was safer not to go hence before making sure that I had done what I ought, by obeying the dream and composing verses. So first I composed a hymn to the god whose festival it was; and after the god, considering that a poet, if he is really to be a poet, must compose myths and not speeches, since I was not a maker of myths, I took the myths of Aesop, which I had at hand and knew, and turned into verse the first I came upon. (60d–61b)

This passage reveals Socrates to have experimented with poetry after a lifetime of avoiding it. Importantly, though, it does not in fact reveal him to have written his poems: the verbs for writing are never used in this passage; Socrates is described simply as composing (*poieô*) poems. Even at the end of his life Socrates seems to hold back from putting his words into durable material form. Yet this passage does reveal that Socrates was self-conscious about the genre of communication that he had employed throughout his life and thought that the divine spirit guiding him wished to direct him specifically to one or another form of communication. The questions of how to communicate, of whether to write, of what to write, if one wrote, were clearly fraught for Socrates and his students.

Another Platonic dialogue, the *Theaetetus*, does actually describe Socrates as contributing to the writing of a dialogue. The dialogue begins when its narrator, Eucleides, offers to have a slave read out a text recording a conversation between Socrates and Theaetetus. Eucleides reports that when he visited Socrates in prison during the wise man's final days, Socrates recounted to him this conversation from years earlier; once he was home, Eucleides wrote it down in order to remember it better; and then, on his subsequent visits to Socrates, Socrates read and corrected his text until they had recorded the conversation accurately. Plato, in other words, fictionally attributes the written production of the text of the *Theaetetus* not only to Eucleides but also to Socrates (142a–143c). This is the nearest we come to seeing Socrates himself write a dialogue. According to Diogenes Laertius, who wrote his biography of Plato some time between the third and fifth centuries CE, Plato, like Eucleides, also read out a dialogue to Socrates. But that reading, of the *Lysis*, supposedly elicited from Socrates not editorial collaboration but criticism: "O, Hercules! what a number of lies the young man has told about me!" (Diog. Laert. 3.24). Was Plato writing different kinds of dialogues than Eucleides?

Whatever the case, from Plato's account of the genesis of the *Theaetetus* we learn that Socrates was understood to have endorsed some writing projects, despite not undertaking any of his own. In particular, Socrates is represented as a willing supporter of a student who wished to produce a text to aid efforts to remember a Socratic conversation. We can't know, though, what Socrates really thought about Plato's dialogues or even whether Plato had started writing before Socrates' death.[23] Yet Socrates' general position toward the efforts of his students to write dialogues must have been affirmative, since so many made the effort. The restraint required of Socrates – of not writing – appears not to have been required of anyone else.

One scholar has made the helpful point that in the *Apology*, when Socrates describes the life of philosophy, he actually presents not one but two philosophical projects, one for himself, which can be called missionary philosophizing, and one for everyone else, which can be called lay philoso-phizing.[24] Socrates' missionary philosophizing was a duty owed to the god and required that he question people to the point of irritating them. Lay philosophizing, in contrast, is motivated not by an external obligation to a divinity but only by each individual's internal desire to pursue her full flourishing. Lay philosophizing requires each individual to seek to know herself but does not require her to force others into self-awareness too. The basic idea is that there must have been a well-understood distinction between philosophy as Socrates had to practice it, because of his divine injunction, and philosophy as everyone else should practice it. This is surely right. The fact that while Socrates did not write so many of his students did is enough to indicate that his philosophical life and theirs were fundamentally different.

But if so many of Socrates' students wrote, why should we expect to learn anything special from an understanding of why Plato in particular chose to write? Let's go back again to the conversation between Socrates and Cebes about Socrates' eleventh hour versifying.

That exchange reveals that Socrates' followers were engaged in explicit dis-cussion of which modes of literary activity were appropriate to philosophy. Cebes does not merely on his own account ask why Socrates has now taken up versifying. Cebes has already heard others talking about this change and, for that matter, another friend has also asked him to ask Socrates about it.

Plato, in other words, presents a picture of Socrates' followers as trying, even on the eve of his death, to understand why he values or criticizes one or another form of discourse. Since Cebes was self-conscious about the sorts of discourse and intellectual production that Socrates might or might not endorse, it makes sense that Plato, who polished the dialogue form, would be *at least* as self-conscious as Cebes. Indeed, his dialogues, and the *Seventh Letter* too, regularly thematize the relative value of oral and written forms of discourse.

Even more importantly, Plato chose not merely to write but even to live a life of writing. The sheer volume of his literary production makes this clear, and his choice must have been ultra serious, since Socrates considered the question of how best to make philosophical music a theological matter. Given the decisiveness of Plato's methodological break from his mentor and the background conversation clearly under way about the value of different kinds of literary project, we can assume that Plato's decision to write was not simply deliberate but, more important, philosophically serious. To ask the question of why Plato wrote is to recognize the philosophical seriousness of his choice.

So why did Plato write? The dialogues contain arguments both for and against philosophical writing; these arguments are placed in Socrates' mouth. Socrates argues *contra* at the end of the *Phaedrus* and *pro* in the *Republic*.[25] When Socrates of the *Republic* argues against Socrates of the *Phaedrus*, we are presented with the structure of the argument about philosophical writing that must have lain behind Plato's decision to choose a writer's life. Since we have no reason to doubt that Plato genuinely revered Socrates, he must have given Socrates the strongest possible arguments on each side of the case. We will have to turn to these two dialogues, then, to answer the question of why Plato wrote. The answer will be very rich, and will lead us to answers to both our central questions: Who was Plato? And what was his relationship to Athenian politics?

Yet these philosophical arguments *pro* and *con* writing, placed in the mouth of Socrates, are not our only resource for analyzing Plato's decision to write. In the *Republic*, through Socrates, Plato offers very precise analyses and moral evaluations of different formal techniques used by poets and story-tellers.[26] How do Plato's own dialogues fare on the rubrics he proposes? After we consider the arguments for and against writing, we can learn still more about why and how Plato wrote by testing the dialogues against his own criteria of literary evaluation, the very ones elaborated in the *Republic*. When we do, we see that his works exemplify just the kinds of writing endorsed there by Socrates. Since Plato's writerly actions harmonize with Socrates' arguments in the *Republic* in favor of philosophically serious writing, we can confirm that those arguments are intended to provide an account of Plato's decision to write. They are not meant ironically.

This book therefore proposes a rereading of the *Republic* to make an argument for a fourth way of understanding the relation between Plato and Athens specifically, and between philosophy and politics generally. What is political in the *Republic*, and the rest of the dialogues, is not Plato's creation of a utopian plan but his effort to refashion Athenian political language.[27] The utopian image is a tool used for the latter purpose. Because Plato not only made an argument about the role of language in politics, but also tested his theory by writing his dialogues, we can in turn test the value of this theoretical argument by considering how well the particular ways in which Plato influenced Athenian politics align with his theory about the kind of influence his dialogues ought to have had. For have an influence on Athens Plato most certainly did. Traditionally, scholars have thought that in fourth-century Athens philosophy and politics lived lives apart.[28] In fact, as I have indicated, distinctively Platonic (and Aristotelian) political vocabulary migrated into Athenian politics in the late fourth century; at least a few Platonic institutions followed thereafter; and at least two orators, as we shall see, considered these changes revolutionary. This book will first answer the question of why Plato wrote and then consider the nature of his influence on Athens, as a way of testing his claims about the power of the philosophical language that he had designed.

But there is more too. As I argued in the Prologue, Plato's decision to write flowed from a comprehensive analysis, presented in the *Republic*, of the role of language in politics. Plato's analysis is comprehensive – that is, it takes within its purview language as a total phenomenon – because he considers questions that are now conventionally distinguished from one another as philosophical, psychological, or sociological.[29] Plato considers how language functions as a system of meaning – a philosophical question; he explains how human cognitive capacities relate to language's functioning – a psychological question; and he analyzes how culture, or systems of value shared by any particular community, are built out of and disseminated through language – a sociological (or anthropological) question. This comprehensive theory of language provides the basis not for Plato's anti-democratic political argument, which has a metaphysical foundation, but for the conversion of his metaphysical commitments into an enacted anti-democratic politics. Most interpretations of the *Republic* focus on Plato's metaphysical arguments and on the ethical and political commitments that flow from them. These arguments establish the ends toward which Plato directed his political activity. By focusing instead on Plato's theory of language, and the question of why Plato wrote, I focus on the means by which he expected to conduct political activity. I have a view about the ends Plato sought, and that will become clear, too, over the course of the following chapters, but I will not be arguing here for that view because my present focus is on the methods, not the ends.

This focus on Plato's political methods has an important consequence for our understanding of what kind of philosopher he was and of his philosophical contributions. By scrutinizing his comprehensive theory of language, we will see that Plato conjoined metaphysics and pragmatism. This claim should come as a surprise, since pragmatism is usually described as setting itself against just the sort of metaphysical stance taken by Plato. By pragmatism I mean something like the philosophical approach made famous in the late nineteenth and early twentieth centuries by the American philosophers Charles Peirce and William James. James describes the core ideas of pragmatism thus:

> To attain perfect clearness in our thoughts of an object, then, we need only consider what conceivable effects of a practical kind the object may involve – what sensations we are to expect from it, and what reactions we must prepare. Our conception of these effects, whether immediate or remote, is then for us the whole of our conception of the object.[30]

In order for this description to fit Plato's work, we need to modify it in two modest ways. First, we need to strike the "only" in the first sentence. For Plato, this pragmatic method is not the only way to achieve truth but just one, and the inferior, of two possible ways, with the second being dialectic, or oral examination in search of the truth, for those who are able to practice it.[31] Although Plato does, it is true, see the pragmatic method as inferior to metaphysics, it will be important to recognize that he does nonetheless consider it an additional method of ascertaining the truth content of beliefs. The pragmatic method does some of the same work as metaphysics, if not as well.

Second, we need to revise the phrase "our conception of these effects is the whole of our conception of the object" to "our conception of these effects is a necessary but partial component of our conception of the object." In Plato's argument understanding the effects of a concept must be combined with metaphysical analysis of it. But the need for metaphysical analysis does not actually invalidate pragmatic analysis or make it superfluous, and vice versa.[32]

As we will see, Plato was very concerned to understand how people's beliefs shape their actions. His focus on the relation between belief and action leads him ultimately to the conclusion that by shifting beliefs philosophers can also shift action and so politics. That is, Plato took an insight, that we more typically designate as a pragmatist insight, about the relation between effects and concepts and, by establishing the reverse direction for the relationship, made it the basis for an instrumentalist account of how language or concepts can have political effects.

As a consequence, Plato's pragmatism is ultimately very cynical. As we shall see, he will argue that an idea does not need to be true, in metaphysical terms, to be effective and therefore valuable, or true, in pragmatic terms. Plato captures this idea of the union of pragmatic truth with metaphysical falsehood with the idea of a "noble lie" or *pseudos gennaion*. An utterance can be metaphysically false – a *pseudos* – but also "noble" or "true to its birth," the core meaning of *gennaios*, provided that it leads people to act more or less as they would act if they knew the truth.[33] We will see exactly what this means in chapter 4, but here it is worth noting that this is a very dark idea. On its basis, Plato becomes an advocate of deception.

In the *Republic* he has Socrates argue that philosopher-rulers must be expert in the production of fictions:

> "Help! I exclaimed. We're going to need some extremely expert rulers, my dear friend" ...
> "... But why do they have to be expert?"
> "Because they are going to have to use some pretty strong medicine," I replied ... "The probability is that our rulers will need to employ a good deal of falsehood and deception for the benefit of those they are ruling. And we said, if I remember rightly, that useful things of that kind all came in the category of medicine." (459b–d)

The Greek word used here for "medicine" is *pharmakon*. Our words "pharmacy" and "pharmacology" come from it. In Greece, a *pharmakon* was a drug or potion of some sort that could be used either as medicine in order to cure someone or as poison in order to kill. Sometimes, in tragedy for instance, one character would use a *pharmakon* to kill another character in an act of revenge that would be as much cure to the killer as final destruction for the victim. What sorts of medicines or *pharmaka* do the philosopher-rulers dispense?

In particular, Socrates argues, the philosopher-rulers will have to develop the fiction, conventionally identified as "the noble lie," that the citizens of Kallipolis, the ideal city of the *Republic*, were all born with one of four metals in their souls: gold, silver, iron, or bronze. Those with gold in their souls become members of the guardian class; those with silver, merchants; and those with iron or bronze, farmers or craftsmen. Citizens are to be taught this story to reinforce and naturalize the city's social hierarchy. Philosopher-rulers will generate other fictions too; they are to be experts at it. Plato refers to their misrepresentations as "some pretty strong medicine."[34]

The medical writer Hippocrates defines medications or *pharmaka* simply and broadly as things that shift the present state of things (*ta metakineonta to pareon*). *Pharmaka* are sources of change.[35] I will therefore say, a little whimsically, that the study of change might be called pharmacology.[36] I risk this flight of fancy partly to underscore our absence of a term to capture the study of social change but mainly to indicate that Plato, as a student of *pharmaka*, was an analyst of social change. As Plato presents the discipline of "pharmacology," it entails above all understanding how abstract concepts and their rhetorical conveyance, whether in images or stories or poems or even dialectical argument, shift the horizons of understanding and expectation and the normative commitments both of the individual and of the social group with consequences for lived experience.[37] Once one accepts the pragmatist's understanding of the relation between belief and action, one must recognize philosophers – who work on our beliefs – as being also "pharmacologists," whose expertise contributes to social change.

That Plato was a pragmatist philosopher, as well as a metaphysician, provides us with a fourth way of understanding his relation to Athenian politics. Plato's acceptance of core elements of pragmatism led, I will argue, to the decisive break with Socrates manifest in the decision to write. Plato saw writing as the better instrument for fulfilling the pragmatist functions of the work of philosophy.

But in advocating deception, Plato pushed a pragmatist understanding of the work of philosophy well beyond any limits that I (or any philosopher conventionally identified as a pragmatist) would endorse. In order to get at his distinctive combination of metaphysics and pragmatism, we will have to ask and answer the question: "Why did Plato write?" And as we answer this question, we will also need to separate what is valuable from what is dangerous in Plato's account of the role of language and philosophy in politics.

If we can do this, however, we will find a very powerful theory of language that explains how beliefs and actions come to be so tightly bound to each other and therefore also why the core pragmatist theses are correct. Seeing the value in Plato's theory of language will require holding the theory apart from the ends to which he applied it.

Where to, then?

We must turn now to chapters 2, 3, and 4 to take up the arguments for and against philosophical writing. We will begin with the *Phaedrus* and Socrates' argument against writing. Then we will turn to the *Republic* and Socrates' argument for writing. In chapter 5, "What Plato Wrote," we will evaluate Plato's dialogues against the literary standards set by Socrates in the *Republic* in order to figure out what Plato might have thought of his own dialogues as literary products. As we shall see, the answer to the question of why Plato wrote will also lead us to an account of the methods Plato developed for engaging with Athenian politics. And once we have a clear view of the method of engagement that Plato crafted for himself, we will have a fuller understanding of the arguments and consequences of his political theory. In chapter 6, "How Plato Lived," we will return to the *Seventh Letter* to see whether it provides support for this fourth account of how Plato understood his relation to politics. Then, in Part II (chapters 7, 8, and 9), "What Plato

Did," we will be able to test Plato's hypotheses about the role of language in politics generally and about the role of his own language in Athenian politics specifically. We will ask the question of whether his dialogues worked on the Athenian polity as he thought that writing of his kind should. The book then concludes with an epilogue, "And to My Colleagues," which summarizes the scholarly contributions that I hope result from this effort to explain why Plato wrote.

To quote Diogenes Laertius again: "in his own city [Plato] did not meddle with political affairs, although he was a politician or political leader, a *politikos*, to judge from his writings" (Diog. Laert. 323). The Greek word *politikos*, which I have here translated as "politician or political leader," had a semantic range running from "politician" to "statesman." Plato wrote for political purposes, for other purposes too (as chapter 5 makes clear), but certainly for these. This book is an exercise in understanding that interpretation of Plato as a *politikos* and its philosophical significance.

2

The Importance of Symbols
in Human Life

2.1 Introduction

So why did Plato write? The dialogues contain arguments both for and against philosophical writing; each case is placed in Socrates' mouth. He argues *contra* at the end of the *Phaedrus* and *pro* in the *Republic*, so in the controversy between Socrates of the *Republic* and Socrates of the *Phaedrus*, we can see the structure of the argument about philosophical writing that must have lain behind Plato's decision to choose a writer's life.[1] Since we have no reason to doubt that Plato genuinely revered Socrates, he must have given Socrates the strongest possible arguments on each side of the case.

We will have to turn to these two dialogues, then, to answer the question of why Plato wrote. The argument *against* writing is simpler, so we will begin with that in the first half of this chapter. In the second half, we'll tackle the arguments *in favor of* writing, but it will take us two additional chapters (chapters 3 and 4) to get to the bottom of them. This work will pay off. Laying out the arguments against and in favor of writing will lead us to answers to both our central questions: Who was Plato? And, what was his relationship to Athenian politics?

First, then, to the *Phaedrus* and the argument against writing.[2]

2.2 Against Writing

The core of Socrates' argument at the end of the *Phaedrus* is as follows: Writing is like painting (*zōgraphia*). It produces "creatures like living beings, but if one asks them a question, they preserve a solemn (*semnos*) silence"

Why Plato Wrote   Danielle S. Allen. © 2010 Danielle S. Allen

(275d). Since a written text cannot answer back to questions, it cannot engage a reader in dialectic. Without engagement in dialectic, there is no true possibility of knowledge. Since the philosopher should be concerned only with the pursuit of knowledge, she should prefer oral dialectic to writing. Moreover, oral discourse can be adapted to the soul of the listener so that the philosopher will offer "to the complex soul elaborate and harmonious discourses and simple talks to the simple soul" (277bc). A written text, of course, is static.

After this clear prioritization of oral above written communication, Socrates makes two exceptions. These, however, merely reinforce the superiority of oral discourse. First, a philosopher might write to provide himself with "reminders" and amusements for his old age. Socrates argues:

> He who has knowledge of the just and the good and beautiful … will write, when he writes, to treasure up reminders for himself, when he comes to the forgetfulness of old age, and for others who follow the same path. (276cd, cf. 275cd)

Second, a person who writes poetry, speeches, or laws, "with knowledge of the truth" and who "is able to support [his writings] by discussion of that which he has written, and has the power to show by his own speech that the written words are of little worth should take his title not from his writings but from the serious pursuit that underlies them," namely philosophy (278c). This sort of writer, who can convey that written words are of little worth, may earn the title of philosopher. Any other writer of poems, speeches, or laws will be merely a poet, an orator, or a legislator. The written word is at best only an "image" (eidôlon) of "the living and breathing word of him who knows" (ton tou eidotos logon legeis zônta kai empsuchon, hou ho gegrammenos eidôlon an ti legoito dikaiôs) (276a).

Here in the Phaedrus, in his argument against writing, Socrates accepts some writing as philosophically defensible but only those forms that plainly declare their allegiance to live dialectic. A philosophically acceptable text is ideally a reminder not even of particular substantive arguments but of the practice of dialectic itself. Yet the argument that texts serve primarily as reminders itself reminds us of the theory of knowledge as recollection put forward in the Meno.[3] If learning is a form of recollection, then why don't texts, which can set someone on the road to recollection, have higher value for Socrates?

In explaining the difference between oral and written discourse, Socrates uses an image that introduces an alternative approach to learning and knowledge. He repeatedly compares discourse or logos, whether written or oral, to a seed planted in a recipient's mind. According to the logic of this image, the eventual growth of knowledge in a student depends on the combination of an external stimulus, the seed, or *logos* itself, which is to say, the concept or idea planted in the mind of the listener or reader, on the one hand, and, on the other, the quality of the soil in the student's mind or soul. Attention to this image of *logos* as seed will refine our understanding of the argument in favor of orality.

Here is the relevant passage:

SOCRATES: Now tell me this. Would a sensible husbandman, who has seeds which he cares for and which he wishes to bear fruit, plant them with serious purpose in the heat of summer in some garden of Adonis, and delight in seeing them appear in beauty in seven days, or would he do that sort of thing, when he did it at all, only in play and for amusement? Would he not, when he was in earnest, follow the rules of husbandry, plant his seeds in fitting ground, and be pleased when those which he had sowed reached their perfection in the seventh month?

PHAEDRUS: Yes, Socrates, he would, as you say, act in that way in earnest and in the other way only for amusement.

SOCRATES: And shall we suppose that he who has knowledge of the just and the good and beautiful has less sense about his seeds than the husbandman?

PHAEDRUS: By no means.

SOCRATES: Then he will not, when in earnest, write them in ink, sowing them through a pen [literally: a reed; *en hudati grapsei melani speirôn dia kalamou*] with words which cannot defend themselves by argument and which cannot teach the truth effectually. (276b–d)

When Socrates says that a written text can be no more than a reminder, he implies, despite the arguments about recollection elsewhere, that written texts cannot generate knowledge in a reader's mind; they cannot teach. Only oral discourse can do that. Oral discourse produces sturdy, healthy growths, whereas written texts initiate only short-lived and fragile growth. Socrates has a technical term for the quality of words that are capable of implanting themselves and coming to life in students' minds; they have *enargeia* or vividness (278a). The related adjective, *enargês*, or vivid, was used by Homer to describe the appearance of the gods in visible form.[4] With perfect clarity, the ideas and arguments of oral dialectic, like Homer's gods, are "set before our eyes," as if in flesh. Socrates' argument about the superiority of oral to written discourse hinges on an account of teaching and learning that turns the human imagination into a gardener's plot; things are not recollected there but come to life and grow.

Socrates' argument against writing is not wholly palatable to Phaedrus. When Socrates asks Phaedrus whether the philosopher will want to sow his words in ink through a pen, Phaedrus does not offer a simple negative. He says, "No, at least probably not." Similarly, when Socrates describes the writing of the philosopher who produces reminders for himself as amusements for his old age, Phaedrus surprises him by calling that endeavor a noble pastime. Socrates has to assert explicitly that dialectic is the far nobler undertaking.

Here is the exchange:

SOCRATES: Then he will not, when in earnest, write them in ink, sowing them through a pen with words which cannot defend themselves by argument and cannot teach the truth effectually.

PHAEDRUS: No, at least probably not.

SOCRATES: No. The gardens of letters [*tous en grammasi kêpous*] he will, it seems, plant for amusement and will write, when he writes, to treasure up reminders for himself, when he comes to the forgetfulness of old age, and for others who follow the same path, and he will be pleased when he sees them putting forth tender leaves ...

PHAEDRUS: A noble pastime, Socrates, and a contrast to those base pleasures, the pastime of the man who can find amusement in discourse, telling stories about justice, and the other subjects of which you speak.

SOCRATES: Yes, Phaedrus, so it is; but in my opinion serious discourse about them is far nobler, when one employs the dialectic method and plants and sows in a fitting soul intelligent words which are able to help themselves and him who planted them, which are not fruitless, but yield seed from which there spring up in other minds other words capable of continuing the process for ever, and which make their possessor happy, to the farthest possible limit of human happiness.

PHAEDRUS: Yes, that is far nobler. (276 c–d)

Socrates has a vision of the transmission of philosophy as proceeding one person at a time, through one-on-one conversations, delivering abundant happiness as it progresses along its very narrow path. Phaedrus agrees that this practice is fine but holds out hope that writing might be too. He seems to think more might be said on the subject. His hesitant agreement with Socrates' prioritization of oral above written discourse is our first sign of instabilities in Socrates' argument. Our second is that Socrates' dismissal of texts is conveyed to us in a text. The very fact of Plato's lifetime of written production would seem to tell against the arguments offered by Socrates in the *Phaedrus*.

For all its power, then, the argument against writing wobbles some; it can't be the whole story.

2.3 The Hole in the Argument

What arguments in favor of writing might meet the objections outlined in the *Phaedrus*? Before we begin to unravel the *Republic*, interpreting it broadly as a defense of philosophical writing, we should begin by noticing that the arguments of the *Phaedrus* leave open two possible routes for that defense.

First in Socrates' argument against writing in the *Phaedrus*, one requirement for the philosophical writing he admits as an exception is that it should constantly valorize oral dialectic. And isn't the dialogue form a vehicle for doing just that? This means that the argument on behalf of philosophical writing can develop its technical resources out of the Socratic critique of writing itself, thereby showing respect for it. By writing dialogues, a philosopher could, paradoxically, assimilate the critique of writing into his writerly project.

But this doesn't provide us with a justification of the decision to write in the first place.

The second route toward a more comprehensive defense of philosophical writing requires a break with the view presented in the *Phaedrus*, and a close look at that view reveals a hole in Socrates' argument, permitting that break. According to Socrates, a writer sows his seeds in the hot sun of the Garden of Adonis and sees fast propagation. Although the growth thus cultivated by writing, as described in the *Phaedrus*, is neither healthy nor durable, the image nonetheless suggests that written words or concepts do have some generative power of their own; to that degree, they are independent of speakers and any dialogic process. Is this power of no value?

Here the question of who is the target of each kind of discourse – oral dialectic and written texts – becomes relevant. A commitment to oral discourse directs and restricts the concepts of philosophy to the intellectually talented who have the capacity to engage in dialectic. By implicit contrast, the notion of sowing in the Garden of Adonis stands in for teaching the unlearned and less able. But what if a written text can convey an abstract concept to one of the unlearned or less able many? Even if the assimilation of concepts implanted in the unlearned by written texts were necessarily imperfect, even if it were quick and unsteady, what can justify withholding the power of true concepts[5] from this group?

A guiding principle of both Platonic and Socratic philosophy, as we understand them, is that leaving people with false ethical concepts, when one has the power to correct them, is to harm them.[6] Since one should cause no harm, a philosopher, if it is within his power to convey true concepts, not only to intellectually able students but also to the unlearned and intellectually weak, should do so. And if writing can convey true concepts to those who are unable to participate in dialectic, what can justify a decision not to write?

Even the Socrates of the *Phaedrus* admits that the seeds of the husband-man-writer have *some* generative power, if not of the same force and quality as inheres in dialectic. As we shall see, the argument for writing presented in the *Republic* rests on just this point: texts *can* successfully convey true concepts to the unlearned.[7]

2.4 Spotting the Defense of Philosophical Writing

Where does the defense of philosophical writing appear in the *Republic*? In the *Phaedrus* Socrates directly addresses the topic of writing at the end of the dialogue, but in the *Republic* the theme is in play throughout. It is, however, largely addressed through the famous critique of poetry.[8] Although the *Republic* is commonly and rightly read as harshly condemning of poetry, the argument about poetry is really just an opening for Plato to discuss the role of symbols and symbol-making in human life generally. By symbols, I mean perceptible signs (whether verbal, visual, or material) of things that are imperceptible. As we shall see, the *Republic* does not argue against all symbol-making, only against the symbols made by conventional poets.[9] And in the process of criticizing the traditional poets, Socrates lays out a positive argument for a type of symbol-making that should be embraced in the ideal city. This symbol-making will be the basis for philosophically acceptable writing.

Socrates' use of a discussion of poetry as a vehicle for defending philo-sophical writing has obscured the fact that Socrates does offer such a defense in the *Republic*. Equally distracting is the fact that Socrates' vocabulary for his discussion of symbol-making is primarily visual. Thus, his arguments about poetry develop a careful distinction between two different categories of image.[10] There are, on the one hand, shadows or *eidôla*, which are what poets produce.[11] Socrates repudiates these. But there are also useful and valuable images, which he endorses. Socrates refers to the latter with terms like: theoretical models (*paradeigma logôi*, 472c), paradigms (*paradeigmata*, 361b, 472c),[12] types (*tupos*, 443c),[13] images (*eikones*, 487e, 488a, 588bc[14]), paintings (*zôigraphiai* 472d, 488a, 501a–b), sculptures (*andriantopoioi*, 540c, also 420c–d), patterns after the divine pattern (*paradeigmata en ouranôi*, 592b), and diagrams (*diagrammata* 529d–e). Socrates himself produces these sorts of images and teaches his interlocutors to do so also.[15] But for all his emphasis on visuality, Socrates produces these images with words, as do the poets their shadows.

Think of all the famous word-pictures that Socrates generates in the *Republic*.[16] There are political images: the two ecphrastic pictures of the ideal cities – first, the original city of pigs, where simple residents live a simple, rural life, and, second, Kallipolis, urban utopia. There are ethical

images: the tyrannical man, the aristocratic man, the oligarchic man, and
the democratic man. There are also psychological images, for instance, the
soul as consisting of a man, a lion, and a many-headed hydra, where the
man represents reason; the lion, spirit; and the many headed-hydra, desire.
Of course, there are epistemological images such as the sun, the line, and
the cave. One could extend this list. Plato's Socrates is remarkably fertile
as a spawner of verbal images, and he uses his vocabulary of image-
making to analyze a practice of symbol-making that is primarily verbal.
Importantly, he uses very specific verbs to talk about his own production
of verbal images: they are *eikazein*, which means "to approximate" or
"guess at" with images; *plattein*, which means "to mold" or "to sculpt"
(our own word "plastic," comes from *plattein*); and *graphein* which
means not only "to paint" but also "to write" (488a).[17] When Socrates
discusses symbol-making in the *Republic*, he includes written symbol-
making in his analysis.

As we shall see, in the *Republic*, Socrates offers a defense of the kinds of
images or word-pictures that he himself makes. He makes clear that the
production of such word-pictures by philosophers, including in written form,
is philosophically defensible. If anything, he exhorts philosophers to take up
the project of writing philosophically defensible word pictures. But what is
his defense? What qualifies his images as philosophically defensible? The
answers to those questions provide the argument in favor of writing.

Those answers will turn out to have a sociological, psychological, and
epistemological component. Socrates analyzes the role of symbols – visual,
verbal, and material – in social life, showing how central symbols are to the
development of culture; he locates the power of symbols in basic psychological functions; and he then distinguishes between epistemologically defensible and epistemologically indefensible symbols, including verbal images,
even written ones. As we will see, he argues that some symbols provide those
who assimilate them with access to knowledge, whereas others lead people
only into falsehood. This distinction between epistemologically worthy and
epistemologically unworthy symbols (and particularly images), combined
with his account of their social and psychological importance, provides the
basis for an explanation of why philosophers may and should write. They
should write because only they, on Socrates' account, are capable of planting
healthy symbols in our fertile imaginations. Their obligation not to harm
others requires them to use writing to protect potential readers against false
concepts through the implantation of true ones.

But we are getting ahead of ourselves. We need to consider the argument
step by step, turning first to the sociological and psychological arguments
about the importance of symbols in human life and then, in the next chapter,
to the distinction between epistemologically valuable and epistemologically
pernicious symbols.

2.5 A Sociology of Symbols

Why does Socrates think symbols are so important? The *Phaedrus* banishes philosophical writing to a garden of letters occupied by an aging philosopher at leisure. The *Republic* imagines a very different literary garden. When Socrates introduces the idea of the garden in Book 3, he argues for its broad influence on society and proposes that philosophers and rulers must guide its cultivation. The garden image here bears a sociological point:

> Is it only the poets we have to keep an eye on, then, compelling them to put the likeness [*eikona*] of the good nature into their poems, or else go and write poems somewhere else? Don't we have to keep an eye on the other craftsmen as well and stop them putting what has the wrong nature, what is undisciplined, slavish or wanting in grace, into their representations [*eikosi*] of living things, or into buildings, or into any manufactured [*dêmiourgoumenôi*] object? Anyone who finds this impossible is not to be allowed to be a craftsman in our city. That way our guardians will not be brought up among images [*eikosi*] of what is bad, like animals put out to graze on a bad pasture. We don't want them browsing and feeding each day – taking a little here and a little there – and without realizing it accumulating a single large evil in their souls. No, we must seek out the craftsmen with a gift for tracking down the nature of what is fine, what has grace [*all' ekeinous zêtêteon tous dêmiourgous tous euphuôs dunamenous ichneuein tên tou kalou te kai euschêmonos phusin*], so that our young can live in a healthy environment, drawing improvement from every side, whenever things which are beautifully fashioned expose their eyes or ears to some wholesome breeze from healthy regions and lead them imperceptibly, from earliest childhood, into affinity, friendship, and harmony with beauty of speech and thought. (401b–d)[18]

Like poets, craftsmen make symbols. Their material artifacts, too, convey definitions of beauty, discipline, and freedom. Alongside the poets, they help construct culture, the network or system of symbols that educates those who live within it. Since language itself is built out of symbols and particular languages incorporate the symbolic systems of particular cultures, Socrates' image represents "the rise and role of organized language" in human life:[19] people build their material universe around their norms; their material universe therefore expresses those norms, both where they cohere and where they conflict; their material universe thus anchors their cultural ideals; and as people graze in a culture, bit by bit they assimilate concepts through symbolic communication that powerfully engages human cognitive capacities.[20] Socrates does not yet specify the nature of the communicative power which can implant concepts in people's minds by means of symbols, but he does suggest that poets, in particular, understand it.[21] One might wonder whether Socrates' argument in the *Republic* against poetry has only oral, not written, poetry in mind, but this passage makes clear that the concern is with durable cultural products.[22] And, remember, Socrates uses the verb *graphein*, which means "to write" (as well as "to draw" and "to paint"), to designate the image-making practice he will eventually endorse.[23] Contra the argument in the *Phaedrus* that written texts cannot establish permanent growth, Socrates here argues that the poets and other craftsmen disseminate their concepts broadly and effectively. The sociological points are that culture affects education and that poets and other craftsmen fabricate culture's durable content.[24]

But how does the educative power of symbols work? After having presented the garden of symbols and the regulation of symbol-makers as appropriate objects of philosophic and political concern, Socrates likens the educative experience of grazing among symbols to learning to read:

> "Aren't there two reasons, Glaucon, why musical and poetic education is so important? First because rhythm and mode penetrate more deeply into the inner soul than anything else; they have the most powerful effect on it, since they bring gracefulness with them. They make a person graceful, if he is rightly brought up, and the opposite, if he is not. And second because anyone with the right kind of education in this area will have the clearest perception of things which are unsatisfactory – things which are badly made or naturally defective ... It's just like learning to read ... We could do it as soon as we realized that there are only a few letters, and that they keep recurring in all the words which contain them. We never dismissed them as unworthy of our attention, either in short or long words, but were keen to recognize them everywhere, in the belief that we would not be able to read until we could do this."
> "True."
> "Well, then. We won't recognize images [*eikonas*] of the letters – were reflections of them to appear in water or a mirror – until we can recognize the letters themselves. Don't both involve the same skill and expertise?"
> "Of course they do."
> "And isn't it, as I say, exactly the same with musical and poetic education? There's not the remotest chance of becoming properly educated – either for ourselves or for the people we say we must educate to be our guardians – until we recognize the sort of thing self-discipline is. Likewise courage, liberality, and generosity of spirit, which keep recurring all over the place, plus all the qualities which are closely related to them, and their opposites. We must see the presence both of them and of their likenesses [*eikonas*] in all the things they are present in, and we must learn never to dismiss them, be the context trivial or important, but to regard them as part of the same skill and expertise. (401d–402c)[25]

Learning to read becomes here a metaphor for the process of coming to see the essential content of the virtues through attention to diverse concrete particulars. The cognitive processes involved in finding concepts in texts, by converting strings of particular letters into words, equally allow human beings to find concepts, like courage, liberality, and generosity of spirit, through consideration of the diverse particulars of material phenomena – both physical and textual. The critical point of the garden image is that the products of human culture – here the specific examples are buildings, material objects, and representations of living things, which would include poems, stories, and paintings – can implant concepts, including abstract concepts, in human minds through our "reading" of those objects.[26] Not dialectic but reading, not only of the natural world but also of texts, becomes in this argument basic to the formation of character, particularly for the young. Even the type of representation that is (as we shall see) least valid in epistemological terms – shadowy reflections in water or in a mirror – provides an opportunity for reading, and the philosopher should attend to what can be read out of even those shadows. In this image, reading becomes all-important to the formation of the human soul.[27]

Beyond merely attending to the meaning of the symbols in the garden, philosophers should wrest from poets power over the organization of language, Socrates argues. At the very least philosophers "must seek out the craftsmen with a gift for tracking down the nature of what is fine" in order to ensure that the garden of letters is filled with the right symbols. As we have already seen, Socrates will eventually argue that philosopher-rulers should themselves produce fictions. We now see that they also have another task. Founders of the city and philosopher-rulers must serve as critics and censors, establishing the rules to guide poets' work. These are not merely formal, though there are some of those. Instead, the argument preceding the introduction of the image of the symbol-garden concerns the thematic principles around which poets must build their tales. For instance, they are not permitted to tell stories that show the gods as changeable, or as evil-doers.[28] Instead all their poems must convey that the gods are perfect and unchanging, responsible only for good, never for evil.[29]

But why do symbols have so much power in human life?

2.6 The Psychological Power of Symbols

Socrates cares as much as he does about the concepts and ideas that are implanted in people's souls because, as he argues, we mold our characters around them. This is true regardless of whether we have taken them in wittingly. He uses metaphors from the domain of literary art to describe the formation of character (498e), and this indicates how far he has gone in arguing for a discursive basis to the human psyche. One example is his description of the philosopher's own self-fashioning. The project of the philosopher is as completely as possible to "match virtue in word and deed," to "as it were rhyme [parisômenon kai hômoiômenon] with virtue" (498e). The philosopher has the job of looking closely at divine order and then of "molding" (*plattein*) his own personality to that order, and "of trying to mold the personalities of others too" (500d).

Scholars have always been aware that the subjects of politics, psychology, epistemology, and poetics tightly intermesh in the *Republic*.[30] The relevance of these sub-disciplines to this dialogue, and of it to them, stems from the dialogue's grounding interest in the role of concepts, and of abstract concepts in particular, in human life, both individual and collective.[31] Right from the beginning of the dialogue, Socrates analyzes how abstract concepts – concepts for things that are without material existence and inaccessible to human perception – affect human experience.

Stories of the after-life, told in Book 1 by Cephalus, an elderly, wealthy owner of a shield factory, provide the first example of cognizable conceptions about imperceptible things; such conceptions have a controlling influence on human morality. Cephalus has invited Socrates to join his family and friends for conversation; Cephalus, as an older man, enjoys conversation more than ever. This confession leads to a conversation with Socrates about sources of contentment in a person's life. Cephalus makes a case for the prominence of good character in a peaceful, satisfied existence: the tragic playwright Sophocles, he says, has been his teacher on that. Socrates pushes him to admit that situational features of his life, for instance his wealth and residence in Athens, contribute to his well-being. Cephalus admits this but claims that they make only a minor contribution. Character is all.

He does admit, though, that wealth helps in one very particular way. As one faces the grave's unknown and feels fear of death, wealth provides peace of mind by ensuring that one can meet one's obligations before one's time comes. Socrates jumps on this connection between the fear of death and a desire to meet obligations and claims the issue at stake is whether Cephalus understands justice rightly. Socrates thus draws out a subtle point. When human beings begin to wonder whether stories about what happens at or after death are true, their minds also turn to questions of justice and injustice. The question of life after death raises the prospect of punishment after death. In the face of epistemological uncertainty about any afterlife, human beings lose hold of whatever peace of mind they may have achieved, the dialogue suggests. Cephalus clearly has only one resource to help him contemplate what happens at death: poetry. In mediating human beings' epistemological uncertainty about the after-life, poets establish the conditions for their beliefs about justice.[32]

Cephalus' invocation of the poets, his fear of the after-life, and the consequence of his epistemological uncertainty concerning justice are all bound together. The opening scene of the *Republic* thus presents poetry as dwelling in the cognitive space where human psychology and epistemology combine to generate metaphysical conclusions that sustain particular notions of justice.[33]

Just when Socrates challenges Cephalus on his definition of justice, Cephalus' son and heir Polemarchus jumps in to the conversation. At this point, Cephalus withdraws to his sacrifices; Polemarchus, Socrates says, has inherited the argument (331d–e). The argument that he has inherited began with the problem of desire, made a case for the value of good character as the route to peace of mind, connected the difficulty of achieving peace of mind to epistemological uncertainties about both death and justice, and, most importantly for our purposes, conceded the poets' power.

Notably, the *Republic* ends where it began: with stories of the after-life.[34] In the famous Myth of Er, which concludes the dialogue, Socrates tells the tale of Er, who either has a near-death experience or returns from the dead, but whatever the case has seen the other side, and is able to tell us what happens. He reports that we are reincarnated and that the life we have led in the here and now determines the sort of life we are likely to choose when the time comes for us to re-enter life in a new form. The Myth of Er displaces the conceptualization of the after-life that Cephalus had first offered. Even more importantly, the myth adheres to the principles of poetic composition articulated in Books 3 and 4, when Socrates lays down the rules for the kinds of stories that can be told about the gods. I will return to these points about the Myth of Er in the chapter 5. For now the relevant points are, first, that the inability of human beings to see or know what happens after death captures a key feature of our epistemological experience and, second, that this fact about knowledge bookends the dialogue.

Human beings develop concepts for things they cannot see, and these govern our lives. While the after-life will be the first and most powerful example of such a concept, this point also applies to the other ideas investigated in the dialogue: justice, courage, moderation, and wisdom. Symbols are tools used to convey these concepts.

Indeed, Socrates explicitly assigns philosophers the job of being symbol-makers with authority over just such ethical concepts. In the middle of Book 6, Socrates makes the case that the philosopher must be a "constitution-painter" (*zôgraphos politeiôn*) who will "work away with frequent glances back and forth. First toward what is in its nature just, noble, self-disciplined, everything of that sort, and then again toward what he is putting into mankind, mingling and blending institutions to produce the true human likeness based on that model which Homer called, when it appeared among mankind, a 'godlike form and likeness.'" (501b).[35] The philosopher's glance turns first toward the invisible, "what is in nature just, noble, and self-disciplined," and then to the visible realm of human-kind; somehow he works as a painter to connect these two realms. Socrates does not here tell us how the constitution-painter puts in human beings whatever he does put in them, but his status as a "painter" is surely relevant. He must be some kind of image- or symbol-maker, even if we don't yet know what kind. It will be by making symbols that he brings constitutions into being; they are his tools for cultivating particular states and dispositions in the souls of citizens.

Of course, Socrates most extensively discusses poets and painters and affirms the rightness of their exile from the ideal city in the dialogue's final book, Book 10. In order to understand what kind of symbol-maker the constitution-painter is, we'll have to ascertain how he differs from all the poets and painters that Socrates discusses and bans there.

Having begun the dialogue, then, by conceding the power of the poets, Plato structures Socrates' argument in the dialogue, from beginning to end, to counter that power. One can detail extensively how the theme of poetry is woven into the dialogue from start to finish. Suffice it to say that it never disappears: from the opening quotations of poets by multiple characters in Books 1 and 2 and the discussion of the poetic education of the guardian children in Books 3, 4, and 6 to the discussion of the use of the noble lie and even to the introduction of the Muses themselves, in Book 8, to explain the eventual disintegration of the ideal city that begins when the citizens of Kallipolis neglect poetic education (545d–546d). Book 10 does not, in short, change the subject but serves as the crowning conclusion of an argument about the ethical and political functions of abstraction. Its goal is to transfer authority from poets to "constitution-painters."[36]

But we still don't really know what kind of artist this so-called constitution-painter is, nor why the kind of symbol-making he does is acceptable when the work of the poets is not. After all, Socrates' proscription of poetry in the beginning of Book 10 appears pretty totalizing.

He begins the argument in that book saying:

> "There are many reasons," I said, "why I feel sure we have gone about founding our city in the right way, but I am thinking particularly of poetry."
> "What in particular about poetry?"
> "Our refusal to accept any of the imitative part of it [*autês hosê mimêtikê*]. Now that we have distinguished the parts of the soul from one another, it is clearer than ever [*enargêsteron*], in my view, that imitative poetry is the last thing we should allow." 595ab

On what grounds can the art of the constitution-painter survive? Socrates has said after all that the constitution-painter will

> work away with frequent glances back and forth. First toward what is in its nature just, noble, self-disciplined, everything of that sort, and then again toward what he is putting into mankind, mingling and blending institutions to produce the true human likeness [*to andreikelon*] based on that model, which Homer called, when it appeared among mankind, a "godlike form and likeness [*theoeides te kai theoeikelon*]." (501b)

Is such work not imitative? Is it not a version of *mimêsis*?

Socrates says at the start of Book 10 that the importance of the ban on *mimêsis* or "imitation" is obvious from what he and his interlocutors have recently worked out about the nature of the soul and its parts. He is referring to the famous division of the soul in Book 4 into reason, spirit, and desire but also, and even more directly, to the discussion at the end of Book 6 about the soul's several cognitive capacities. In order to understand what "mimetic poetry" is, as Socrates defines it in Book 10, and how it differs from the work of the constitution-painter, we must turn back to the epistemological discussions of Books 6 and 7. In his famous "line analogy," the most exciting, stunning part of the *Republic*, Socrates establishes critical distinctions between different kinds of image-making practice, some that are mimetic and some that are not.[37] These distinctions are the basis for Socrates' Book 10 arguments about *mimêsis*.

On the basis of a sociological and psychological argument, then, Socrates establishes that the production of durable symbols, including written ones, is vital to human life, and that philosophers should attend, like watchdogs, to their production for the sake of protecting people from unhealthy images, whether visual, verbal, or material. This is the first step of his argument in defense of philosophical writing.

But it is with an epistemological argument that Socrates will give philosophers their positive assignment as writers. We'll turn to this epistemological argument in the next chapter and, more specifically, to the famous line analogy. It will teach us the difference between epistemologically valuable and epistemologically pernicious symbols. This will also be a difference between "models" and "shadows." The constitution-painter is charged with producing the former.

3

The Philosopher as Model-Maker

3.1 Introduction

The most important step in Socrates' argument in defense of philosophical writing in the *Republic* comes in his epistemological arguments in Books 6 and 7. In these arguments he distinguishes among categories of symbol-making and argues that some symbols are epistemologically valuable while others are epistemologically pernicious. This is the purpose of the famous line analogy. The second step of Socrates' argument in favor of philosophical writing is thus to show that there are epistemologically valuable symbols, which it is appropriate and worthwhile for philosophers to produce, including in written form.

3.2 Discovering a Defensible Kind of Philosophical Writing

In Book 6, the description of the work of the philosopher as a constitution-painter provokes a conversation about how the philosopher will come to know, truly, what "just," "noble," and "self-disciplined" are in their nature. A constitution-painter needs this core competency for success.

The answer is straightforward, on one level. The potential philosopher will have to be educated through dialectic to understand the Forms. But before the discussion of dialectic can begin, Socrates must ensure that his interlocutors understand dialectic's purposes. Before his interlocutors can affirm its value, they need reason to believe in its function. They also will want to know *how* dialectic enables human beings, given their limited capacities, to cognize

---

Why Plato Wrote   Danielle S. Allen. © 2010 Danielle S. Allen

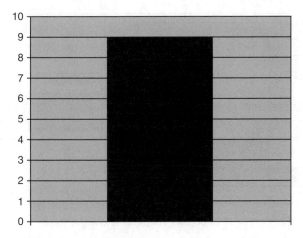

FIGURE 3.1. The line. *Republic* 509c–511e

truths about the good and just. This is the purpose of the epistemological discussion in the middle of the dialogue and of the images of the sun, the line, and the cave. Of these three images, the line image provides the basic account of how humans make cognitive use of images, including verbal ones.[1]

How does it go? Socrates posits a line of any length whatsoever. Figure 3.1 is a picture to clarify his example.

The line that I have modeled here happens to be nine units long and this model has perceptible width, but those features are arbitrary. Any model of a line would do. This particular model will, however, make it easier to see the consequences of Socrates' argument. Socrates will eventually use the line to represent the spectrum of types of human cognition, but first he performs a mathematical trick with it.

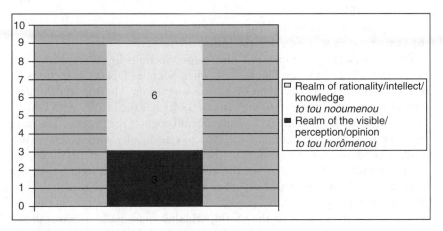

FIGURE 3.2. The line divided to show relative value of faculties

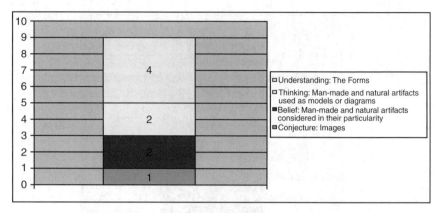

FIGURE 3.3. Relative value of objects cognized with each faculty

Socrates tells his interlocutors to imagine dividing the line into two parts of unequal length. For my example, I will divide the line into parts with one twice as long as the other (see Figure 3.2), but any unequal division will work for the argument that follows.

The longer and higher part of the line represents our superior faculties of intelligence (or *nous*), he says, and the lower and shorter part represents our weaker faculties of visual perception (*to horaton*) and opinion or belief. Intelligence produces greater clarity than mere perception.[2]

Importantly, in the domain of intelligence we conduct mental exercises on things that are unseen, which is to say, on ideas. In the domain of perception, we conduct mental exercises only on what we can actually perceive, which is to say on the natural and man-made artifacts of the material world.

Each resulting piece of the original line should then itself be divided and in the same ratio as was used for the initial division.

The result, in my example, is a line in four sections in the mathematical proportions $4:2:2:1$ (see Figure 3.3). Then Socrates labels the sections so that each one reflects one type of human cognition. The top and longest section represents "understanding" (*noêsis*) which is the faculty with which, Socrates argues, we participate in dialectic and cognize the Forms.[3] The next section represents thinking (*dianoia*), which is the faculty with which we use models or diagrams, for instance, those a mathematician produces, to cognize concepts. We cannot see the abstract concept of a right angle, for instance, but a mathematical diagram allows us to comprehend it.[4] That diagram is an image (or *eikôn*) of what truly is.[5] The third section of the line represents all the objects in the world, whether man-made or natural; we cognize these with a faculty of belief (*pistis*). And the bottom and shortest section represents shadows, for instance photographs and paintings. These are also images (again, *eikones*) but Socrates immediately particularizes them as shadows and phantasms (*skiai, phantasmata*) representing particular objects in the world.[6] The faculty that cognizes these is imagination or conjecture (*eikasia*).[7] When we see a tree trunk reflected in the water much distorted, but are unable to see the tree itself, we can conjecture what is causing the water's wavering pattern. We cannot be certain, though, that what we see is a tree, and we certainly could not identify the kind of tree we're seeing. In contrast, images in the domain of thought, such as a mathematical diagram, are props or crutches that provide access to concepts linked to the truth. But dialectic, the activity of the uppermost domain, is discussion about abstractions, that is, about the Forms, that proceeds without relying on any visualization whatsoever. This distinguishes the cognitive capacity used in the domain of true understanding from the other three. Only when we can think without images are we in the realm of truth.[8]

The higher up on the line the section is, the greater the value of the faculty. The greater the length of the section representing the faculty, the greater the value of the objects cognized by that faculty.[9] Value here signifies proximity to truth along two axes. The higher faculties have greater access to truth; and the objects they cognize are themselves also closer to the truth.

Now if you look closely at these sections of the line, you'll notice that Socrates has played an interesting trick. The middle two sections of the line are equal in length; this means the objects being cognized in each of these domains must be of equal value. In fact, not only are they equal in value; they are even the same set of objects. All the world's material artifacts, which are available to be cognized in the domain of belief, are also available to be cognized in the domain of thinking.[10]

What does this mean exactly?

In the domain of thinking we work with models and diagrams, for instance, a mathematician's diagram of a square to teach us about right angles. But in addition to two-dimensional diagrams, three-dimensional models can also serve. A model of a cube would help us understand right angles just as well as a diagram of a square. And here Socrates converts the mathematical into a philosophical trick. Not only the objects we already call models but also all the material objects that fill our world turn out to be three-dimensional models.

Take a die as an example. Or the box a television set comes in. They too are models of right angles and cubeness. I don't need to make a model to understand those abstract concepts. I can just hold up a die or point to an appropriate box. The diagram and the die itself, taken this way, have equal status as objects of cognition. They both convey independently imperceptible but nonetheless real phenomena: right angles, equality of length, and so on.

We can "use" the material objects of our world, Socrates says, "as images or *eikones*." Suddenly, it appears that all the material objects in our world, which are the objects of cognition in the realm of belief, are *also* objects of cognition in the realm of thought. How can they belong to both domains? They shift domains depending on our cognitive relation to them.[11]

When I consider the die immediately before me, I may be trying to come to know this die here, which, for instance, happens to be green with gold spots. Or I may be trying to understand cubeness itself. Am I using the die to develop beliefs about concrete particulars or to access general concepts? The cognitive and intellectual effort directed toward the object determines its epistemological status. Thus, we can say that man-made and natural material artifacts, *qua* themselves, are the objects of cognition in the realm of belief, while man-made and natural material artifacts, *qua* three-dimensional models of concepts or principles, are objects of cognition in the realm of thinking. The concepts or principles for which the stuff of our world serves as three-dimensional models are true if they derive from (or better, "participate in," see appendix 1) the Forms.[12] Dialectic helps us climb from a concept, which is symbolically conveyed, to the Forms, for which we need no visual aids. The two middle portions of the line are the same length because they are populated by the same sets of objects. Those objects are categorized in two different ways, though, because we can cognize them in either of two ways, and as we cognize them differently their status as objects shifts.

Let me use one more example to make sure that we are achieving clear understanding of these four categories of cognition and its objects. Let's take houses as our example. A photograph of a house belongs in the domain of the imagination or conjecture. From a photograph we can imagine what the house in the picture is really like, although we will not achieve a full understanding of it; we won't even have a strong opinion about it. We certainly wouldn't want to buy the house based on one photo or even a few. Nor does the photo allow us to conjecture about what "houseness" itself really is; we wouldn't know how to build another house by virtue of looking at this single photo. Now consider the house itself, of which we have the photograph. We can visit the house itself during a Sunday open house and take a full tour for the sake of developing a solid opinion about, and perhaps buying, this particular house. We are operating, in this instance, in the domain of belief. Alternatively, we may be a student of architecture. We may be hoping to build a house. We may tour the same house during a Sunday open house in order to think about how it is put together; we may take an architectural blueprint along to help us think through the principles of engineering that allow the house to stand. Both the house, our three-dimensional model, and our blueprint, the diagram, allow us to operate in the realm of thinking and to begin to achieve some conception of what "houseness" itself is, so that we might go off and build another house that would be different from this particular house that we are visiting, but no less a house for that difference. The house itself, just like an architectural blueprint, is an instance or a version of "houseness." Or, finally, we might bump into Socrates after a tsunami has just destroyed all the houses in our region, and as we work on determining where to spend the night and what to plan to construct the following day, he might engage us in a dialectical discussion of "houseness" in order that we might be fully prepared on the following morning to build a house without the help of any visual aid whatsoever. In that conversation with Socrates, in order to understand what "houseness" is, we would operate in the realm of the Forms.[13]

Now consider again the bottom and smallest section, representing the realm of conjecture, where shadows and reflections are cognized, and also the second section, representing the realm of thinking where diagrams and 3-D models are cognized. The objects in both categories are images or *eikones*; but these two sets of images have each a very different epistemological status. The images or shadows that occupy the realm of conjecture do not provide access to what really is or to truth; the images or models in the realm of thinking do, so long, that is, as they are correct. We can begin to climb from them toward the Forms, kicking away our symbols as we make the ascent. Images in this latter category are clear; they are *enargês* and are specifically valued (*tetimêmenois*) for their clarity (511a).[14]

Each type of image is also the product of a different activity: the clear images of the mathematician result from model-making; the shadowy images of the lowest realm are the products of imitation or *mimêsis* (509d–510e). Importantly, one can imitate only what one can perceive. In the domain of conjecture, artists make images by imitating things just as they appear to us, which means, just as our senses are able to grasp them. Precisely because the realms of understanding and thought are concerned with concepts that are in themselves inaccessible to sense perception, those concepts are also not available to be imitated. Images in the domain of thought work instead as *visualizations* that provide access to those independently imperceptible concepts. (The contemporary use of visualization in sciences like astrophysics functions in just this way.) Hence the importance of Socrates' insistence that in the realm of *dianoia* or "thought" mathematicians "use" models and objects "as images" (*hôs eikosi chrômenê*, 510b). This vocabulary of "using images" distinguishes model-making from imitation. Socrates carefully employs this terminology whenever he wishes to insist that the particular images under discussion do not fall into the category of "imitative art."

Importantly, this distinction between categories of image and of image-making also yields two types of visual expert. There are people who work in the realm of thought (*dianoia*) and make models via the activity of visualization. And then there are the people who work in the realm of conjecture (*eikasia*) and make shadows via the activity of imitation. These latter image-makers are the imitators banned in Book 10; the former model-makers are represented in Book 6 by mathematicians. But by now it should be clear that the philosopher too can work with images; he too, like the mathematician, can be a symbol-maker – provided he has learned how to be a model-maker. The experts at model-making will include the constitution-painter.

We are now in a position to understand the Book 10 proscription against imitative poetry and to provide a more complete account of the difference between imitators and constitution-painters. Let us return to Book 10, then, so that we can finalize our understanding of the constitution-painter's art, as distinct from imitation.

3.3   Imitators vs. Constitution-Painters

I will anticipate the conclusion. Book 10 does not, as is commonly thought, conclude the *Republic* by rejecting all poetry and poets indiscriminately but instead definitely distinguishes good from bad poetry, a distinction we have been edging toward throughout the dialogue.[15] The value of different kinds of poetry – that is, of distinct types of symbol-making – turns on the critical difference between models and shadows developed in the discussion of the line analogy. The "mimetic artists" who are banned in Book 10 are poets and artists who imitate only concrete objects that presently exist in the world and which are accessible to our senses; they do not attend to what really is. In contrast, the constitution-painters among us create diagrams and models of what truly is, and the Greek verbs capturing their activity are *graphein kai plattein*, "to write and to model." Such artists do not "imitate" (*mimeisthai*); instead they "visualize." The word for "model" or "mold," *plattein*, becomes associated with Plato. No other fifth- or fourth-century Greek author uses *plattein* with this meaning anywhere nearly as frequently as he.[16] Indeed, it is fair to say that he discovers the distinction between depicting a particular object and modeling a general idea, and therefore also the distinction between representation and visualization.

Plato goes to town with his new discovery in Books 6 through 9 of the *Republic*. They focus intently on this newly visible model-making activity: the cave image, for instance, advances and affirms the distinctions between types of image laid out through the line analogy; and Socrates carries out a lot of modeling in these books, particularly when he creates the images of the different types of man typifying each city. The focus of these books on modeling explains why there is a need to return, in Book 10, to the topic of the competing, and inferior, art of *mimêsis* or imitation. Socrates wants to ensure that the distinction between the two kinds of activity is fully and finally clarified. He does not want his interlocutors to perceive model-making simply as a new form of *mimêsis* and so he needs to nail down the distinction for them. By having Socrates clarify this distinction for his own interlocutors, Plato clarifies it for us too.

Here is how the mimetic artist is described:

> "Now tell me something about the painter. Do you think in each case he is trying to imitate [*mimeisthai*] the thing itself, the one which exists in the natural order of things? Or is he trying to imitate the work of the craftsmen?"
>
> "He is trying to imitate the work of the craftsmen," Glaucon said.
>
> "As it is? Or as it appears to be?[17] Can you make your definition a little more precise?"
>
> "What do you mean?"
>
> "I mean this. When you look at a couch from the side or from the front, or from anywhere else, does the couch itself change? Or does it stay the same and merely look different? And the same with other things."
>
> "Yes, that's how it is," he said. "It looks different, but it's really the same."
>
> "Well, that's the point of my question. In each individual case, what is the object of painting? Does it aim to imitate what is, as it is? Or imitate what appears, as it appears? Is it imitation of appearance or of truth?"
>
> "Of appearance," he said. (598ab)

This domain of appearances is where the "mimetic artist" works; again, the emphasis is on merely representing what our senses grasp. In this Book 10 discussion of poetry, Socrates relegates Homer and the tragic and comic poets to this realm of conjecture; their images are no more useful than shadows or reflections in a mirror. They fail to relate perceptible material realia to imperceptible truths, but such a cognitive shift would be necessary to salvage their image-making, according to the argument made with the line analogy.

The artists who do make that cognitive shift and provide models of true concepts are allowed in the ideal city. We met them originally in Book 3 as the "craftsmen of what is fine in nature," who make healthy images for the symbol garden that constitutes the city's culture. These craftsmen must produce the kinds of images that reside in the domain of thought: images and models that can be "used" by listeners and readers to gain concepts that help them toward cognitive access to what really is. The constitution-painter, recall, will "work away with frequent glances first toward what is in its nature just, noble, self-disciplined, everything of that sort, and then again towards what [he is] putting into mankind" (501b). The original definition of the constitution-painter turns out to have captured just the task of cognitive shift recommended by the line analogy, where the artist pivots between imperceptible and perceptible domains, and finds a way of linking them through symbols that convey true concepts.

In contrast to the tragic poet, then, the constitution-painter is a committed metaphysician. When looking at material realia, he shifts cognitive registers, considering people and things in relation to "what really is" in the domain of the Forms. By virtue of these cognitive shifts, the constitution-painter is able to bring metaphysically sound conceptions of justice, virtue, and self-discipline to bear in his model-making activity.[18] He never becomes an imitator, he does not represent, but only "uses" images to "visualize" and provide access to conceptual truths that he admits are in themselves susceptible neither to perception nor, consequently, imitation.

But if the respective arts of the tragic poet and the constitution-painter both produce images, how are we to tell one kind of image from the other? How can one tell a shadow from a model? At the start of Book 10, just after proscribing imitative poetry, Socrates proposes a medicine to protect against the misuse of images: "Mimetic poetry seems to me to be a destructive influence on the thought [*dianoia*] of those who hear it. Unless of course they have the antidote [*pharmakon*], the knowledge of what *mimêsis* really is [*hosoi mê echousi to eidenai auta hoia tungchanei onta*]" (595a–b).[19] Because both the shadowy images of the realm of conjecture (the *eidôla*) and the models of the realm of thought (the *paradeigmata*) are images or *eikones*, the tragedians' shadows may confuse audiences; they may seem to be worth more than they are and cause harm by means of their aesthetic proximity to the more valuable models.[20]

And the antidote is simple: nothing more than knowledge of what *mimêsis* is. Socrates has already supplied us with this knowledge in Book 6 with the line analogy; but Book 10 amplifies the analysis initiated there. As Myles Burnyeat points out, Book 10 focuses precisely on the problem of cognitive conflict, "in which the reasoning part of the soul appears to be at variance with itself."[21] To explain this, Burnyeat (like Socrates) asks us to consider an oar that is half in the water; it looks bent, but we know it is not. Our perception tells us one thing; our reason another. Or consider an airplane seen from a distance that, in passing to the north of a city, looks, from your southern vantage point, as if it is about to fly into a skyscraper. One's eyes communicate one thing, and one's body responds with fear, while reason conveys another. The line analogy has already prepared us to see such cognitive conflict as both a possibility and a problem. *Mimêsis* produces images that trigger cognitive conflict; its images do not capture reality, but only misleading appearances; yet they work on us with the force of reality. The images resulting from model-making, in contrast, do capture reality and therefore introduce no cognitive conflict. Only with this knowledge of what *mimêsis* is, and of what model-making is in contrast, can the philosophers and constitution-painters produce their models and paradigms, instead of shadows. The relative proximity of their symbols to metaphysical truth and the fact that their symbols are crafted as vehicles to provide access to the imperceptible, and so inimitable, truth distinguishes their art from that of conventional poets.

On the basis of a sociological and psychological argument, then, Socrates had established that the production of durable symbols, including written ones, is important to human life, and that philosophers should attend, like watchdogs, to their production for the sake of protecting people from unhealthy images, whether visual, verbal or material. At the end of Book 10, he reveals that his ideal city will include symbol-makers, but only those who produce hymns to the gods and encomia to good men (607a). Indeed, the original rustic utopia, the city of pigs rejected by Glaucon, had also included symbol-makers, who also would focus entirely on hymns to the gods (372b). Socrates apparently thinks that symbol-making is not merely an important but even an inevitable part of human life.

Now, thanks to the epistemological argument, we also know what art will be permitted to produce those necessary hymns and encomia: not poetry any longer but model-making. Model-making, like poetry, works with images or symbols, but its symbols are different in kind. Most importantly, they are non-mimetic and therefore metaphysically sound. Nor do they trigger cognitive conflict: in them image and reality match. Models, in contrast to the shadows of the poets, convey abstract concepts in order to help those who assimilate them access the truth. And who are the model-makers among us? Only philosophers are in a position to produce such symbols.

This brings us to the second step in Socrates' argument in favor of philosophical writing. The image-making art that survives Socrates' critique of poetry turns out to be philosophy itself, though it will be kept company by mathematics. It is philosophically acceptable for philosophers to write, provided that they use their writing to make models instead of imitations. They have only to hew to a simple rule: that their symbols be non-mimetic, which is also to say, that they be metaphysically sound.

3.4 The Necessary and Sufficient Criterion of Philosophical Writing

If only things were as simple as it sounds to say that philosophers have only to follow one simple rule in turning out their symbols. In fact, metaphysical soundness is not the only rule that Socrates lays down for the symbols produced by philosophers. In addition to being metaphysically accurate, the constitution-painter's symbols must also be pragmatically efficacious. But what exactly does that mean? Getting clear on Socrates' requirement for pragmatic efficacy will complete our account of the kind of writing that is philosophically allowable.

The contrast between the work of the traditional poets and the work of the new "craftsmen of the fine" does not end with the question of whether a given symbol-maker has the necessary metaphysical commitments. The final section of the Book 10 argument against poetry is wholly pragmatist, and on the terms of pragmatism, too, the traditional poets fail.

Socrates makes the point, essentially, that if someone sent you a single photograph of a table he had recently bought, you would be unlikely to be able to make a duplicate table. Even a skilled craftsman would probably want multiple photos taken from different perspectives before attempting a replica. This need to supplement the single image in order to have access to the truth of the table's construction points to the inadequacy of ordinary images. Images in the realm of conjecture do not enable action.

Socrates ultimately condemns Homer and the tragedians in just such pragmatist terms:

> "When it comes to the greatest and finest of the things Homer tries to tell us about – war, military command, the founding of cities, a man's education – then I think we are entitled to be curious, 'My dear Homer,' we can say to him, 'if you are not two removes from truth in this matter of goodness – not a maker of images, what we defined as an imitator – if you are even at one remove from the truth, and if you were capable of distinguishing the behaviour which makes men better or worse in private life or in public life, then tell us which city has ever been better governed because of you. Sparta is better governed because of Lycurgus, and so are many other cities, great and small, because of many other individuals. What about you? Which city says that *you* are its great lawgiver, or attributes its success to you? Italy and Sicily say it is Charondas. We say it is Solon. Which city says it is you?' Will he be able to name a city?"[22]
> "No, I don't think so," said Glaucon. "Even Homer's most devoted supporters don't make that claim."
> "Is any war in Homer's day recorded as having been won by his leadership or strategy?
> "No." (599d–e).

Beliefs are rules of action, as William James wrote, and can and should be tested as such. Socrates is applying just such a test to Homer. The beliefs he propounds, argues Socrates, do not usefully govern action. In contrast, the symbols produced by philosopher-modelers must make a difference for action in the direction of the good. Even mimetic artists will be allowed back into the city, Socrates says, if they also can prove that they produce not only pleasure but also practical goods (*ôphelimê*, 607e).

But what exactly does it mean for a philosopher-modeler or a constitution-painter to be a pragmatist? After all, "pragmatic efficacy" has two different meanings. Concepts that are fully assimilated by their audience will produce reactions, actions, and outcomes in those people; a "pragmatically efficacious" concept will have come to govern action for those who hold it as a belief. Its meaning can be known or recognized by its outcome. But the phrase "pragmatic efficacy" also captures powers of language that can make concepts assimilable in the first place so that they are internalized and can begin to govern action.

The symbols of the constitution-painter will not merely convey truths but will also, in so doing, govern action and, therefore, mold souls. In order to understand how the models of a constitution-painter can be pragmatically efficacious, we would do well to take apart the images produced by Socrates over the course of the dialogue. As we have seen, Socrates' images are typically designated as paradigms, types, images, paintings, and diagrams.[23] He never calls his images "imitations" or *mimêseis*, nor does he use the verb *mimeomai* (imitate) to describe his image-making practice; indeed, he uses the word *eidóla* or "shadow-images" for his own images only in two important cases to which we will return. The words used to describe the mathematician's diagramming were *graphein* and *plattein*, and Socrates accepts these verbs to designate his own image-production. Thus, when Socrates proposes to develop an image of the soul, Glaucon says to him that such would be the work of a "formidable molder of models" – or in Greek, the work of a *deinos plastês* (540c).

Socrates is that *deinos plastês* or formidable modeler. His images are good examples of the sorts of symbols that philosophers might produce to aid thinking. In what sense, though, do they achieve the pragmatic effects that Socrates demands from philosophically acceptable symbols? Through what resources of language do his symbols make concepts so immediately assimilable as beliefs that they can directly govern action?

Socrates most dramatically exposes his image-making art when he introduces the exercise of designing a utopian city. After Thrasymachus challenges Socrates to prove that justice is not the advantage of the stronger, and Adeimantus and Glaucon extend the challenge, Socrates commits to a full investigation (*diereunesasthai*) into justice and injustice and describes himself as needing a method whereby those with weak eyesight (*mê panu oxu blepousin*) may nonetheless see justice:[24]

> I think we should conduct our search in the same sort of way as we would if our eyesight were not very good, and we were told to read some small writing from a bit of a distance away, and then one of us realized that a larger copy of the same writing, apparently, was to be found somewhere else, on some larger surface. We should regard it as a stroke of luck, I think, to be able to read the large letters first, and then turn our attention to the small ones, to see if they really did say the same thing. (368d)

Socrates considers justice in the city and in an individual to be equivalent, and suggests that it is more easily identified at the level of the city.[25] The interlocutors will therefore draw the "big picture," an ecphrastic description of a just city, in order to discern justice in the "small picture," the individual soul.

Since Socrates and his colleagues have "weak eyesight," they need props to see what really is. Their image of the city will serve as such a prop. Instead of suggesting, as he eventually will, that true understanding requires abandoning visualization, Socrates here describes their intellectual challenge as equivalent to seeking visual understanding of objects that are beyond view. Images built to convey the meaning of justice will serve in the same fashion as mathematical diagrams. And here, as in the image of the symbol garden, discussed in chapter 2, reading serves as a metaphor for the process of seeing and assimilating the essential content of the virtues (or vices) as diverse concrete particulars participate in them.[26] Without directly saying so, Socrates has begun to introduce his companions to the idea that they seek truths that are finally imperceptible, despite their reliance on their senses to gain access to them through concept-conveying images.

But the idea of "learning to read" functions here as a metaphor for the processes not only of coming to see abstract truths through diverse concrete particulars but also of learning to enact those newly cognized virtues (or vices). When Socrates describes the constitution-painter, he says that this artist sketches an outline of the constitution (to schêmatês politeias). The Greek for "sketch" is hupograpsasthai, a word that has several concrete meanings. First, it designates addenda to stone inscriptions. Second, it designates writing done on command, as in the taking of dictation. But third, and most important, and as Plato uses the term in the Protagoras, hupograpsasthai indicates the practice of writing out letters for children to trace over as they learn how to write and read; what's more, Plato analogizes the children's process to how citizens learn to live by modeling their own behavior on the pattern of the laws.[27] As children trace over the tops of letters, learning to produce their own, they convert a principle into a basis for an action that they can repeat throughout their lives. Similarly, Socrates and his friends will sketch out the symbolic pattern of a constitution that they (and all other readers) may then repeatedly trace over in action in the future. As in the example of the child tracing letters, learning to read turns out to be more than a metaphor; it is also literally a means of assimilating beliefs that can govern action.[28] By conveying concepts, the symbols of the constitution-painter will mold souls.

How, then, should we read the images that Socrates makes for us? First, we should do so warily, knowing that Plato expects us to assimilate their ideas, and consequently to change our souls, simply in the reading of them.[29] Second, we might attend to the reading instructions that Socrates himself provides. After the interlocutors conclude the work of designing Kallipolis, Socrates gives his interlocutors, and us, an explicit reading lesson. Notice once more, in the following passage, Socrates' use of the metaphors of sight and light to describe the process of cognition and coming to know.[30] Socrates says:

> "Son of Ariston, your city can now be regarded as founded. The next step is to look inside it, and for that you are going to need a pretty powerful light. You

can provide your own, or get your brother and Polemarchus and the others to help you. Then perhaps we shall find some way of seeing just where in the city justice is and where injustice is, what the difference is between the two, and which of them people who are going to be happy must possess, whether all the gods and all mankind realize they possess it or not."

"O no you don't," said Glaucon. "You told us *you* were going to look for justice. You said it was impious not to do everything you possibly could to support justice." ...

"I take it our city, if it has been correctly founded, is wholly good ... Clearly, then, it is wise, courageous, self-disciplined, and just ... With any four things, if we are looking for one of them in some place or other, and it was the first thing we caught sight of, that would be enough for us. But if we identified the other three first, then the one we were looking for would *ipso facto* have been identified as well, since clearly it could then only be whatever was left ... Well, I think the first one to catch the eye is wisdom." (427d–428b)

The process of reading to which we are being introduced is cast as an experience of discovery. We will have to bring a light to bear on the image and find something in it that is not immediately apparent. Socrates is teaching his interlocutors to make the cognitive shift from cognizing what is immediately before their eyes to grasping, instead, something that is beyond the reach of sense perception. The fact that the city is described as being Glaucon's own will be important. Glaucon will be personally responsible for whatever conceptual truth is discovered to reside in the image he has just helped to create.

Then, in one of the dialogue's most famously bizarre passages, Socrates amplifies the representation of reading as discovery by comparing the process to hunting:

"Now, Glaucon, this is the moment for us to position ourselves like huntsmen, in a ring round the thicket. We must concentrate and make sure justice does not escape. We don't want it to vanish and disappear from view. It's obviously here somewhere, so keep your eyes open and try your hardest to see where it is. If you see it first, give me a shout."

"Some hope," he said. "No I'm afraid the only help I'm going to be to you is if you want a follower, someone who can see things when they are pointed out to him."

"Say a prayer, then, and follow me."

"I will. Just you lead the way," he said.

"'The place is impenetrable," I said, "and full of shadows [*episkios*]. And it's certainly dark. Not an easy place to dislodge our quarry from. Still we must go on." ... And then I caught sight of it. "Aha! Over here, Glaucon," I cried. "This looks like the trail. I think our quarry is not going to escape us, after all." ...

"We've been complete idiots ... It's been lying under our noses all this time. Right from the start, though we couldn't see it. We've been making fools of ourselves. You know how sometimes you look for a thing when you're holding it in your hand. Well, that's what we've been doing. We haven't been looking in the right direction. We've been looking miles away in the opposite direction, and that's probably why we haven't seen it." (432b–e)

What is the quarry of this epistemological hunt? Justice, it turns out, consists of the complementary principles, first, that each part in any given organism – city or man – should do to the best of its ability the one job for which it is best suited, and second, that relations among these diverse parts should be coordinated so that the whole harmonizes. Once the principle of justice with which Socrates has been working is made explicit, we immediately recognize that the two images of the just city had, of course, been built around these principles. Both are allegories where every detail in them aligns with conceptual axes established by the principles they are built to convey. The language of discovery, the elaborate hunting metaphor is, in other words, a cheat. One has to have known the truth to have built the model in the first place. If that is so, in what sense can one claim to use the model to cognize some new, heretofore inaccessible truth? But mathematical diagrams function no differently, after all. Images such as this – models and diagrams – are techniques for conveying, not finding, abstract concepts.

But Socrates wants to make the experience of learning feel like discovery. Why should he want to do this and how does he achieve it? Socrates' sleight of hand lies not in the fact that he has constructed an allegory but in *how* he has constructed it. As each detail was added to the city, it was tested against the intuitions of Glaucon and the others for reasonableness; some details were even added against Socrates' suggestion because the young men had demanded them. This test against their intuitions might not seem like much of a trick since Plato has, after all, crafted these characters and can give them whatever sort of expectations he chooses. But Plato is testing the details of the construction of Kallipolis against our intuitions too.

On a first reading of the dialogue, well before we have any idea of the principle generating the utopia, we are expected to find each detail plausible:

> "And the first and most important of those needs, if we are to exist and stay alive, is the provision of food."
> "Unquestionably." (369d)

This seems like a non-controversial step, and our basis for considering it reasonable has nothing to do with the final abstract principles of justice that will eventually be revealed to be entailed by the city, which we have helped to found. These allegories are constructed not only around a guiding conceptual principle but also out of expectations about social order that Plato takes his readers to have.[31] Thus, when the abstract truth contained in the allegory stands revealed, we have been implicated in its appearance. Because we had already agreed to individual pieces as seeming intuitively reasonable, we may be inclined to feel that the allegory expresses something natural. This gives these allegories a special power and a commanding moral authority. Plato, or Socrates, wants to tap into the psychological feeling of discovery in order to create just this moral authority derived from "naturalness."

In fact, Socrates explicitly acknowledges and explains his trick when he helps Glaucon and the others to read the word-picture they have created together. He says:

> So this principle, Glaucon – that if you are a shoe-maker by nature, you should confine yourself to making shoes, if you are a carpenter, you should confine yourself to carpentry, and so on – really was a kind of image or *eidôlon* of justice. Which is why it was so useful to us ... But the truth is that, although justice *appeared to be* something of this kind, it was not concerned with external performance of a man's own function, but with the internal performance of it, with his true self and his own true function, forbidding each of the elements within him to perform tasks other than his own. (443c–d)[32]

Here is the first of our two exceptions, where Socrates uses the term *eidôlon*, or "shadow-image," for an image of his own.

Socrates' theoretical model, constructed to engage the cognitive capacity of thought or *dianoia*, has been built out of shadowy images from the realm of conjecture. Socrates provided images of the sort of concrete phenomena – for instance, a self-disciplined shoe-maker – that would emerge should any given shoe-maker in fact live in accord with justice. The descriptive detail is not a visualization of justice itself but only an imitation, or representation, of one of justice's concrete consequences. This detail is therefore merely an *eidôlon*. By using *eidôla* such as this, Socrates can organize an ecphrastic model around his abstract conception of justice without Glaucon and the others immediately perceiving that central, organizing abstraction; he distracts them with shadows that keep their attention on material phenomena. Then at the last minute, suddenly, he commands them to direct their attention toward the abstract principles ordering the image. This cognitive trick makes it possible for Glaucon and other readers of these Socratic images to "learn" something that was under their noses all the time. Socrates produces the feeling of discovery by playing on the several cognitive registers.

And this sense of discovery, which brings with it an intuition of naturalness, gives force to the concepts so conveyed. They are memorable; the psychological charge that occurs with their emergence into visibility ensures that. And because concepts so conveyed are memorable, they are more likely to be activated as rules of action; that is, psychologically, they are more likely to become full-fledged beliefs, internalized so as to govern action, for Socrates' interlocutors. We have therefore discerned at least one element of the pragmatic efficacy that inheres in Socrates' models: his models use the diverse cognitive registers to generate the experience of discovery and thereby trigger for the concepts so conveyed the moral authority of nature. This increases the likelihood that the concepts will be internalized and so govern action. It is through language powerful enough to effect internalization that a constitution-painter can deploy symbols but make real constitutions in the actual souls of citizens.

Now the fact that Socrates, in achieving pragmatic efficacy for his images, has slipped back into the domain of shadows, deploying *eidôla*, in order to make his models efficacious, should set off alarm bells. How can that be justified, given what we have learned about the metaphysically problematic status of images so classified?

We will have to scrutinize the concept of pragmatic efficacy more closely, for, indeed, it does let shadows back in. Remember that at the end of Book 10, Socrates gave the poets an escape clause: they can return to the city if they can prove that their shadows are pragmatically efficacious in the direction of the good.

Before we take up this issue, though, let's pause to summarize the arguments laid out so far in favor of philosophical writing. They are, first, that symbols, including written ones, are both important to and inevitable in human life, – they mold souls – and, second, that only philosophers know how to make epistemologically valuable symbols. While these arguments support the conclusion that philosophers may write, they do not yet support the argument that philosophers *should* or *must* write.

To find this argument, we must turn next to a fuller consideration of pragmatic efficacy – and to the problem of Socrates' reintroduction of shadows. This will bring us finally to the third and final stage of Socrates' argument in defense of philosophical writing: he identifies powers inherent in language itself that make written discourse no less effective than oral dialectic at sowing conceptual seeds in individual students; he also identifies powers inherent in language itself that make non-dialectical discourse more effective than dialectic at sowing conceptual seeds broadly among the unlearned. And this will provide a basis for the conclusion that philosophers not only may but even should write.

We will pursue this topic in the next chapter, as we dig more deeply into the concept of pragmatic efficacy, as Socrates develops it in both the *Phaedrus* and the *Republic*.

The Philosopher as Shadow-Maker

4.1 Introduction

Plato's famous critique of poetry is subtler than is usually seen. In the
Republic Socrates does not wholly reject symbol-making but introduces a
new kind: model-making. Philosophers are expert modelers; model-making
can and should be the basis of any writing they do. As modelers, they should
produce symbols that are metaphysically sound and pragmatically efficacious. By conveying true concepts with rhetorical force, their models will
mold souls.

In order to understand this art of making metaphysically sound and
pragmatically efficacious models, we have to be clear about what the art
is *not*, namely, *mimêsis* or imitation. But we are more familiar with imitation;
we had gotten used to it when we fell in love with Homer and the tragedians.
Socrates asks us to lift our sights. Yet as we began to explore Socrates' own
modeling practice, we soon noticed that he too seems occasionally to have
indulged in imitation. After all, in his picture of justice, the just shoe-maker
was, he says, only an *eidôlon* or shadow-image. Is the philosopher *cum*
constitution-painter *cum* modeler permitted also to be a shadow-maker?

When, where, and how do shadows have a role in the constitution-
painter's art? How should the philosopher's use of shadows be evaluated
within a framework requiring metaphysically sound and pragmatically
efficacious symbols? Determining when, where, and how the constitution-
painter may deploy shadows will in fact clarify Socrates' requirement that
philosophically acceptable symbols be pragmatically efficacious.

At the end of Book 10, Socrates gives poets an escape clause: they can
return to the city if they can prove that their shadows are pragmatically
valuable. The philosopher-modeler gets the same escape clause. He too can

Why Plato Wrote   Danielle S. Allen. © 2010 Danielle S. Allen

use shadows, if they can be salvaged by pragmatic efficacy. A close look, therefore, at when and how the philosopher-modeler may use shadows, taking Socrates as our prime example, will reveal a category of images that are valued *only* for their pragmatic efficacy. Looking at these images will bring into clearer view just what Socrates means by that idea. Once we have a clear view of Socrates' account of pragmatic efficacy, the third and final step in the argument in favor of philosophical writing will be within reach.

4.2 Salvaging Shadows

Socrates' confession that his theoretical model makes use of *eidôla* or shadows indicates that mimetic images, typically the province of the poets, are not entirely bad. They can be salvaged. Although the principle that the shoe-maker would care only about shoe-making turned out *not* to be a *paradeigma* or pattern of justice but only an *eidôlon*, this shadow was not damaging, because it had the effect of causing its hearers, Glaucon and the others, to make the kinds of commitments that would result if they were in fact to assimilate the core principle of justice, namely that each person should keep all the parts of his psyche in the appropriate place and relation to one another. These shadows can be pragmatically correct even if they are metaphysically inaccurate; they can generate the hoped for principles and rules of action without themselves being metaphysically sound. There is, in other words, a crucial exception to the Socratic critique of shadows.

Indeed, *eidôla* such as this can be pragmatically correct even when their problem is not metaphysical inaccuracy but, worse, moral danger. Let's take another example of Socrates' use of problematic images: the episode in Book 4 when Socrates, in his effort to convince Glaucon about the existence of the tri-partite soul, imitates a particular man named Leontius.

Socrates' imitation of Leontius is surprising because Socrates has already, by this point in the dialogue, vigorously criticized dramatic *mimêsis*. Dramatic *mimêsis* is problematic, he argues, because it is habit-forming. Whenever we carry out an action, even play-acting, our body and spirit develop a familiarity with that action, which becomes the basis of habit. This is why we tell young boys to "act like men," just as Socrates tells Theaetetus in the dialogue of that name (151d). We know that, by acting a part, they will acquire the habits of that part as their own.[1] Socrates argues that writers should directly imitate only good characters, whereas bad characters, if they must be presented, are better depicted only through narrative discourse (392d, 395d, cf. 398a). But at the end of Book 4, in depicting Leontius, Socrates directly imitates a particular man in the midst of a vicious action.

On a journey back from the Peiraeus, Athens' main harbor, to the city-center, the Athenian Leontius encounters corpses of executed criminals and wants to look at them but reason restrains him. After a struggle, or a civil war in his soul, he rushes up to the corpses to glut his eyes, but curses himself at the same time, saying: "Have your fill of this fine spectacle, you evil spirits!" (440a).[2] Socrates does not describe Leontius in this action but directly quotes him; he plays the part of Leontius cursing his own eyes. What are we to make of Socrates' direct imitation of a bad action?

Two details save this vignette from condemnation. First, Socrates conducts some metaphysical clean-up work on it. He does not actually imitate Leontius, the whole man; he does not, for instance, ventriloquize the desires driving Leontius to ogle the corpses. Socrates enacts only the spirited element of the soul, which first tries to hold Leontius back from vice and then expresses anger at his failure to resist. Socrates thus imitates a bad man, but only his good element. This characterization of Socrates reveals the precision with which Plato divides material phenomena into elements patterned after the good and those patterned after the bad, coloring each pattern differently, to draw attention to the good.[3] He has thus connected his dramatic rendering of this particular incident to the knowledge of what is and provided Socrates with a script that will do him no moral harm. By shading his image this carefully, Plato has turned the story of Leontius from a shadow or *eidôlon* into a model. Plato thereby proves that he too knows what *mimêsis* is, what its stakes are, and how to convert even dangerous dramatic imitations into valuable models.

The second saving grace for the narrative of Leontius is that, as in the case of the *eidôlon* of the shoe-maker, the image achieves valuable pragmatic effects. Immediately before the story, Glaucon expresses doubt that the soul can be tri-partite; Socrates is trying to convince him that the soul consists of reason, spirit, and desire – and not of two parts – reason and desire (*erôs*) – as in the conventional Athenian understanding. When Socrates concludes the story and says, "This story [*logos*] signifies [*sêmainei*] that anger can sometimes be at war with the desires, which implies that they are two distinct and separate things," Glaucon responds: "Yes, it does signify [*sêmainei*] that" (440a). Only the story, an *eidôlon*, has intervened to change Glaucon's mind.[4] What exactly has happened to Glaucon, on account of hearing the story, that brings about this change?

With his imitation of Leontius, Socrates has made an invisible phenomenon, the tri-partite soul, visible to Glaucon. Socrates has used a concrete particular, a specific man acting, to identify a moment when the soul acts but where neither reason nor desire can be said to guide the action. There is nothing for it but to accept that there must be a third part of the soul; the young man is utterly persuaded. The direct imitation of the soul speaking in anger to itself did the trick of making the invisible visible.

By making a new concept visible to Glaucon, Socrates shifts the landscape of Glaucon's imagination. Such a shift, Socrates clearly hopes, will manifest itself in a change in Glaucon's beliefs and so in his rules for action. In particular, knowledge of the spirited part of the soul should help Glaucon improve his own efforts at self-control. The pragmatic efficacy that Socrates hopes for from his symbols lies in just this capacity to shift the landscape of someone's imagination, whose contours define what that person takes to be real, possible, and valuable; such shifts are accomplished by making the previously invisible visible. The metaphysical and pragmatic tasks of symbols turn out to be closely allied to each other, since each brings into visibility some fragment of truth linked to the realm of the Forms. But those symbols that depend for their validity entirely on pragmatic efficacy bring those truths into visibility by cloaking them in concrete actions that may be adopted. In giving readers and listeners actions to imitate, they also convey to them, albeit only implicitly, such beliefs as make those actions meaningful.

Socrates thus salvages his shadows by ensuring that they are vehicles for metaphysical beliefs that they do not directly articulate; they directly express instead only the principles of action that flow from those beliefs. The pragmatic efficacy, which saves them, lies, however, in this capacity to convey principles and rules for action that are connected to the metaphysical principles of which Socrates approves.

4.3 The Meaning of Pragmatic Efficacy

Significantly, Socrates' aspiration for all his images – whether they are models or shadows – is just this goal of making the invisible visible; he aspires to make imperceptible truths cognizable either as concepts conveyed through symbols or through the representation of concrete actions and realia that flow from them. At the conclusion of the lesson in how to read his image of the utopian city, he says:

> If we look at the two [the good city and the good individual] side by side, perhaps we can get a spark from them. Like rubbing dry sticks together. If that makes justice appear, we shall have confirmed it to our satisfaction. (435a)

His goal is to make the invisible flash like a spark into visibility.

I have already introduced the technical term that Socrates' uses to designate this production of a sudden and vivid clarity; images that achieve this have *enargeia*. Socrates had used this term in the *Phaedrus* to describe words that are capable of implanting themselves and, like healthy seeds, coming to life in students' minds. He also uses this word in the *Republic* to explain the positive value of the models of the mathematician and philosopher. And as I indicated, the word boasts a Homeric pedigree; in epic it is used to describe the sudden appearance in the flesh on the battlefield of the usually invisible gods. It captures, in other words, exactly what Socrates hopes the philosopher's images will achieve: the sudden emergence into perceptibility, of some being, or idea, or phenomenon that properly dwells only in an invisible realm that usually eludes our sensory grasp.

This conviction that the goal not only of oral dialectic, as in the *Phaedrus*, but also of philosophical modeling is to achieve *enargeia* also shapes Socrates' basic description of the constitution-painter. As we have seen, this artist "works away with frequent glances back and forth" between abstract truths and real people, aiming "to produce the true human likeness based on that model which Homer called, when it appeared among mankind, a 'godlike form and likeness [*theoeides te kai theoeikelon*].'" (501b). The relevant model guiding the work of the constitution-painter is that provided by the hero. Socrates follows Homer in crediting heroes with "a godlike form and likeness" because they convey the content of divine virtues with a clarity as vivid as an appearance by the gods themselves, suddenly, in the fray. As heroes link the world of invisible gods to the mortal realm, so vivid concepts (packed in symbols) link the realm of the Forms to material reality.[5]

Although the Socrates of the *Phaedrus* agrees with the Socrates of the *Republic* that *enargeia* or "vivid clarity" is a central goal of philosophical discourse, he argues that only oral dialectic can achieve it. Yet his argument on the point helpfully expands his definition of the concept. At the end of the *Phaedrus*, when he asks whether it is noble or shameful to be a writer (*to logous legein te kai graphein*), he describes the man worth emulating as:

(A) the man who first of all thinks (1) that in the written word there is necessarily much that is playful; (2) that no written discourse, whether in metre or in prose, deserves to be treated seriously (and this applies also to the recitations of the rhapsodes, delivered to sway people's minds without opportunity for questions and teaching); (3) that the best of them [written discourses] really serve only to remind us of what we know; and (4) that *only in words about justice and beauty and goodness spoken by teachers for the sake of instruction and really written in a soul* [tois tôi onti graphomenois en psuchêi] *is there clearness* [to enargês] *and perfection and serious value* [axion spoudês]; (5) that such words should be considered the speaker's own legitimate offspring, first the word within himself, if it be found there, and secondly its descendants or brothers which may have sprung up in worthy manner in the souls of others, and (B) the man who secondly pays no attention to other words. (277d–278b; my emphasis)

There is a paradox here since writing now serves as a metaphor for the full assimilation of concepts by a student; they are to be "really written in a soul." The term *enargeia* turns out to indicate an aspiration to permanence, as well as vividness. And the goal of oral teaching is the durability achieved by writing! Moreover, we now also see that words that are *enargeis* or "clear" lead to growth in the student's mind until he too can sow further ideas. Concepts are assimilated by a listener and transform a way of life; like seeds, concepts have a principle of life in them. The notion of concepts that are *enargeis* implicitly conveys the pragmatist's idea that beliefs are fully realized (and fully recognizable) only once, internalized, they govern action.

Aristotle, in a moment of subtle playfulness in his central text on political language, the *Rhetoric*, puns *enargeia* with a second word, *energeia*, to deepen this argument that vivid language possesses a principle of life capable of transforming human action. The Greek word *energeia* gives us the modern English "energy." *Energeia* more literally means "en-acted," or "that which appears in the doing of a thing." In Greek, the word *energeia* is typically contrasted with *dunamis* (think: *dynamic*), which expresses capacity or potentiality, while *energeia* captures the actuality of action. Indeed, *energeia* is no ordinary word for Aristotle but a fundamental term of his metaphysics, and the contrast between potentiality and actuality is for him a critical distinction.[6]

And in the *Rhetoric*, in a discussion of what it means for language to set something before a listener's or a reader's eyes, he slyly substitutes *energeia* where *enargeia* would have been expected as the name for the capacity of language to achieve vividness. He says that the writer who generates *energeia* "gives movement and life to all things, for *energeia* is action [*kinoumena gar kai zônta poiei panta, hê d'energeia kinêsis*]" (1412a10). When a speaker expresses an idea with *energeia*, a listener or reader will not merely comprehend but also begin to act on that idea.

With this lovely slide from vividness as *enargeia*, a visual and mystical vividness, to vividness as *energeia*, the vividness of action and work, Aristotle makes explicit what is at stake in the Platonic concept of vividness: a principle of life attaches to the emergence of a concept in the mind of a reader or listener; the result of effective teaching will be enactment, and not merely comprehension. This is why Socrates is so interested in dramatic *mimêsis*; this technique most directly takes listeners, viewers, and readers (for instance, of the dialogues themselves) from comprehension to enactment.[7] Perhaps we should translate *enargeia* as not merely a "vivid" but even a "life-giving" clarity. Importantly, this idea that fully vivid, fully assimilable concepts are by definition life-giving and so life-changing provides the bridge between metaphysical and pragmatic approaches to philosophical discourse that underlie Socrates' account of symbol-making in the *Republic*.

4.4 The Sources of Pragmatic Efficacy

What gives concepts the clarity or vividness, the *enargeia*, that makes them immediately assimilable as principles and rules for action? For all that the

Socrates of the *Phaedrus* and of the *Republic* agree on the value of *enargeia* or "life-giving clarity" as the object of philosophical discourse, they offer radically different accounts of how to achieve it. According to the *Phaedrus*, only oral dialectic can generate *enargeia*, whereas in the *Republic*, model-making is first and foremost credited with the capacity to achieve *enargeia*.[8]

But the Socrates of the *Republic* also concedes, as we have seen, that the poets' shadowy images have a closely related power. They function in the cognitive space where human psychology and epistemology combine to generate metaphysical concepts of imperceptible things; these concepts have authority over ordinary human life. Stories about the after-life were the key example. The Greek poets had, for instance, made Hades, the underworld home of the dead, brilliantly visible. And the Leontius story too suggests that shadowy symbols can sometimes achieve *enargeia* or life-giving clarity. Although Socrates did not use the words *enargês* or *enargeia* to describe his tale, the story of Leontius brought the tri-partite soul to life for Glaucon. Why does the Socrates of the *Republic* think that discourse this far from dialectic can still achieve *enargeia*? What are the linguistic bases of poetic power that can give word-pictures force enough to be *enargês*, to irradiate like a god on a battlefield?[9] This is also to ask why poetry and its materials – image-making, narrative, and dramatic *mimêsis* – should have a particularly powerful hold on the human imagination. Here we come to the greatest point of disagreement between the Socrates of the *Phaedrus* and of the *Republic*.

The Socrates of the *Phaedrus* sees pragmatic efficacy as residing in truth-fulness; the Socrates of the *Republic* sees pragmatic efficacy as residing instead in the various materials that make up language itself as an instrument of communication – meter, verbal images, psychic immediacy, and so on. This difference in their two accounts of the sources of pragmatic efficacy will lead us to the final argumentative steps involved in Socrates' defense in the *Republic* of philosophical writing.

At the end of the *Phaedrus*, Socrates argues that *logos* or discourse that achieves *enargeia* or vivid clarity will have two features. First, the seeds of discourse must have been planted in fitting ground (*to prosêkon*); that is, they must be sown in minds capable of philosophy. Second, the seeds of discourse must be conjoined with true knowledge (*met' epistêmês logous*). Socrates of the *Phaedrus* grounds language's power in truth, not linguistic structure. He has nothing to say here about how specific literary techniques succeed (or not) at generating *enargeia*. The prioritization of oral discourse has made this unnecessary.

But once again, there is a hole in Socrates' argument in the *Phaedrus*. Life itself painfully teaches us the falseness of his claim that language takes its power exclusively from the truth. As we all know too well, lies work on people's souls. But why? To inquire why even false speech can implant concepts in the soul is to identify the features intrinsic to language itself – apart from degrees of truthfulness – that endow it with communicative power. The *Republic* is fundamentally motivated by this question about the authority of falsehood.[10]

In the *Republic*, Socrates answers this question about the authority of falsehood by drawing on his accounts both of the tri-partite soul and of our several cognitive capacities. His basic explanation of the efficacy of lies is that different features of language appeal to different parts of our soul. Thus, what we learn through meter and *mimêsis*, Socrates argues, we learn through our bodies, not our minds, which is to say through desire (or *erôs*), not reason (see 400a–d).[11] Since desire (*erôs*) is incapable of discriminating true from false things, it cannot guard against falsehood.

Image-making, in contrast, is linked not to our bodies generally but to the stronger perception of sight. Images can trigger sense-perception alone or intellection, but the latter only if the spectator undertakes the sort of cognitive shift described in the passage on the line analogy. A spectator may easily consume images without shifting from perception to intellection. As with the sort of learning we do with our bodies, we are therefore as capable of assimilating images uncritically as critically.[12] In his arguments in the *Republic*, Socrates concentrates on cognitive capacities that wield great power over learning but do not depend on argument or intellection for their effect.[13]

And he is right that we learn all kinds of things without our minds being obviously engaged. A track athlete, for instance, can learn endurance simply by running during each routine work-out a bit beyond yesterday's point of easy comfort. Then, having learned that capacity through physical activity, the same runner can transfer the lesson to moral and intellectual struggles, with consequences for how she will seek solutions in disparate domains.

Similarly, the spectator of a picture assimilates features of it that are not necessarily the immediate object of his attention yet at a later point these unnoticed elements may acquire the greater salience. He will have learned something that he proceeds to use, without even having been aware of the moment of learning.

Or maybe our lover tells a story meant to hide betrayal. Our desire not to have been betrayed may lead us to turn a blind eye, as the saying goes, to obvious inconsistencies in the story; the lie will make its way into our soul thanks to our desire for the world it promises, not because our reason has fully vetted it for truth.

These are unsophisticated examples of the sorts of ideas Plato is articulating. By now psychology has generated many more powerful accounts of non-rational elements in human learning, but understanding those precisely is not our purpose.[14] Even if we doubt specific details in Plato's treatment of language's pragmatic power, we should at least recognize that in the *Republic* Plato has attempted an explanation for why lies successfully implant themselves in our souls. In particular, he presents the case that the tri-partite nature of the soul and its split cognitive structure acquit rationality of sole responsibility for the errors made when people accept lies as truths. Some falsehoods work their way into our minds without reason's being even engaged. The successful implantation of a lie in someone's soul is not necessarily a reflection of the caliber of that person's capacity to reason.

For our purpose, though, of answering the question of why Plato wrote, Plato's account of why lies work finally decides the question of whether writing can achieve the vividness, or *enargeia*, of oral discourse. Does writing have the same power to implant concepts in human souls as oral dialectic? Since, as in the case of lying, conceptual implantation can occur without the involvement of reason and argument, conceptual implantation can indeed be effected by means other than oral dialectic. Writing's resources include both dialectic and poetry; that is, its tools include argument but also all the forms of communication that may elude reason's vigilance and enter our spirits through our bodies, our eyes, or our imaginations. Socrates' account in the *Republic* of the sources of linguistic power finally requires the view that not merely false speech, but also written language generally, whether true or false, has, like oral dialectic, the power of implantation.

4.5 The Noble Lie

Writing, whether true or false, has the power of implantation: Socrates' investigation of pragmatic efficacy in the *Republic*, in contrast to the *Phaedrus*, disconnects that concept from truthfulness. This returns us to the disquieting idea, which I introduced in the first chapter, that philosopher-rulers must be expert in the production of fictions, or lies. Socrates had called these lies "some pretty strong medicine." Here, again, is the passage:

> "Help! I exclaimed. We're going to need some extremely expert rulers, my dear friend" ...
> "... But why do they have to be expert?"
> "Because they are going to have to use some pretty strong medicine," I replied ... "The probability is that our rulers will need to employ a good deal of falsehood and deception for the benefit of those they are ruling. And we said, if I remember rightly, that useful things of that kind all came in the category of medicine." (459b–d)

Although this passage comes midway through the *Republic*, it is really only by the end of the whole dialogue that we are in a position to understand the expertise in fiction that Socrates refers to here and the sense in which it qualifies as medicine, that is, as a *pharmakon* or potion that can either cure or kill.

Poetry and *mimêsis* achieve their governing authority over human souls not through concepts, propositions, or argument but from the materials out of which they are made – sound, image, control of temporality, and psychic immediacy – and from the effects of these materials on the different components of the human soul, on the different cognitive capacities, and on their interplay. Poetry's narratives, images, metaphors, analogies, music, and dramatic imitations can be used to implant either true or false concepts in the minds of audiences; this is the sense in which fictions and images are like potions, capable of either curing or killing.[15] On this analogy, fictions that implant true concepts cure; those that implant false ones, kill.

The problem that emerges from locating the pragmatic efficacy of language in the material of language itself, rather than in truthfulness, is identical to the problem resulting from the invention of guardian-rulers. Socrates had asked: What will keep the guardians, as expert soldiers, from tyrannizing their own citizens? Or, what keeps a guard-dog from turning on the sheep it guards? This question now applies also to those who wield linguistic power, about which Socrates casts an aura of danger.[16] He says:

> If lies really are useless to the gods, and useful to men only in the way medicine is useful, then clearly lying is a task to be entrusted to specialists. Ordinary people should have nothing to do with it. (389b; cf. 381d, 458c)

Once philosopher-rulers have the capacity to implant concepts in citizens' minds, what will keep them from implanting bad concepts instead of good ones? Or, what protection is there against abuse of poetic or linguistic power? Even Socrates does not limit himself to the creation of models and paradigms; he also produces, albeit rarely, shadows or *eidôla* and expects the philosopher-rulers to do so too. But what will keep them honest, so to speak, when working in the realm of illusion?

As we have seen, at the start of Book 10 of the *Republic*, Socrates proposes a medicine to help constitution-painters create models instead of shadows; they need knowledge of what imitation truly is. But the passage has a further meaning. Socrates is in fact proposing a medicine not only for the constitution-painter as distinct from the shadow-maker but also for the constitution-painter *qua* shadow-maker. The medicine is not merely a guide to the production of the better kind of images – that is, to the production of models instead of shadows; it is also an inoculation against temptations arising from involvement in producing the worse kind of images. The antidote must enable the production of shadows that will help, not hurt, those who assimilate them.

What exactly have we learned about *mimêsis* or imitation, then, that might constrain the production of *eidôla* or shadows by the philosopher-rulers?

Above all, we have learned that imitation is not merely a matter of amusement or entertainment. Because of its power to shift the landscape of an audience's imagination, imitation has life-changing force. Because it can slip round reason's guard-posts, imitation has a particularly powerful effect on those who are not able to participate in oral dialectic, as few can. Imitation can therefore change more lives than dialectic can. But because the art of imitation is not in itself bound to metaphysics (in contrast to the art of modeling), the direction of its life-changing force is unpredictable; it can either help or harm. That *mimêsis* or imitation has this power over the many is what philosophers know; their obligation to do no harm is what ensures that they will use imitation responsibly.

So what does it mean to use shadows responsibly? Since shadows simply cannot be true in an essential sense, the requirement to use shadows responsibly must be a requirement for pragmatic, not metaphysical, accuracy. Can we get to a fuller definition of such accuracy?

I said above that Socrates twice describes himself as producing an *eidôlon* or shadow. One instance was when he introduced the image of the just shoe-maker to his picture of justice in the city. The principle that the shoe-maker would care only about shoe-making turned out *not* to be a *paradeigma* or pattern of justice but only an *eidôlon* or shadow. This shadow was, however, not damaging because it had the effect of causing its hearers, Glaucon and the others, to make the kinds of commitments that would result if they were in fact to assimilate the core principle of justice.

Socrates also uses the term *eidôlon* or "shadow-image" to designate the noble lie.[17] The noble lie, once more, is the fiction that the citizens of Kallipolis, the ideal city of the *Republic*, were all born with one of four metals in their souls: gold, silver, iron or bronze. Those with gold in their souls become members of the guardian class; those with silver, merchants; and those with iron or bronze, farmers or craftsmen.

On what grounds is this fiction acceptable to Socrates? Let's recall how it was introduced. Socrates had just completed his plan for how to identify and train prospective guardians and auxiliaries. He then remarks that the more senior guardians will above all make sure that friends of the city do not want to harm it and that enemies are not able to harm it, and he charges the younger members of the guardian class, now called auxiliaries, or soldiers, with defending the rulers' beliefs (*epikourous te kai boêthous tois tôn archontôn dogmasin*) (414b). He then asks, almost in a *non sequitur*:

> What sort of device [*mêchanê*], from among those necessary lies or fictions [*tôn pseudôn tôn en deonti gignomenôn*] that we were recently discussing, might come into being to bring about some one noble or grand belief [*gennaion ti hen pseudomenous*] in those being regaled with it, hopefully even in the rulers themselves and if not them, in the rest of the city? (414bc)[18]

The point of the noble lie is to tell citizens a story that will cause them to act as they would if they were in fact able to cognize the truth of justice. The noble lie does not give citizens access to the metaphysical claim that justice lies in ensuring that each part of the soul does its job and is properly related to the other parts of the soul. But it provides a basis for the social hierarchy, harmonization of social classes, and social stability that would result from universal acceptance of Socrates' metaphysical truth. The noble lie, drawing on the resources of imitation, will be pragmatically efficacious for the whole citizenry, implanting principles and rules for action that could just as well have flowed from the metaphysical beliefs that Socrates propounds but which he is unable to bring a whole citizenry to see through dialectic.[19]

Such a tale is not only a shadow (*eidôlon*) or a noble lie (e.g. *gennaion pseudos*, 414bc), Socrates says, but also a useful falsehood (382cd). The Greek is *to pseudos chrêsimon* – we might also say it is a "useful fiction" or "serviceable falsehood." Socrates defines such serviceable falsehoods as lies that are assimilated to the truth as much as possible (*aphomoiountes tôi alêthei to pseudos hoti malista*, 382d) and, through proximity to the truth, foster in hearers and readers an assimilation of correct principles and rules for action.

On the example of Socrates' own *eidôla*, then, the requisite resemblance of a useful falsehood to the truth resides not in the meaning of the words uttered in the lie in comparison to those in the true statement, but instead in the consequences that flow from believing each. The consequences of believing the serviceable lie should look very nearly identical to the consequences of knowing the truth.

Plato's fullest presentation and analysis of pragmatism appear in the dialogue, the *Theaetetus*, where Socrates tries to put forward the strongest possible case of Protagoras' version of pragmatism, so that he and his interlocutors might debate its merits. The philosopher Myles Burnyeat summarizes and paraphrases the full Protagorean pragmatist thesis as: "that the true or truer state of mind *is* the one which has the most satisfactory consequences, the one which selects itself as the most serviceable to live with." The term that Burnyeat here translates as "serviceable" is *chrêstos*, closely related to the term *chrêsimos* that Socrates uses in the *Republic* to designate the noble lie as a useful fiction.[20]

In hoping for poets and playwrights, or better yet, poetical philosophers, who will make useful or serviceable *eidôla* or images with knowledge of what really is, Socrates joins pragmatism to metaphysics. That is, he adopts a pragmatist approach to truth that conforms with his presentation of that view in the *Theaetetus*: as long as the shadows produced by the poets lead to good outcomes in the world, he can accept them. Moreover, he admires their power to reach an entire citizenry. But as a metaphysician, he defines good outcomes as including only those that conform to actions that would result from knowledge of the good. For Socrates, the question of what counts as a good outcome is decided not on the basis of experience, as for a true pragmatist, nor on utilitarian grounds, which some forms of pragmatism eventually employ, but on metaphysical grounds. For Socrates, the pragmatist test of experience can tell us the truth of what a proposition means, but whether it is choice-worthy is a matter instead of metaphysics. In the final analysis, Socrates' useful *eidóla* should specifically lead people to act nearly as they would act if they had in fact cognized metaphysically valid truths.

There will, though, be a hair's breadth of difference. Those citizens who do not have access to the truth but who believe the noble lie will, as a consequence, act justly on Plato's definition of justice – they will do their job and obey the philosopher. They will not only obey but even revere and honor philosophers. This they will do, though, not because they understand that their rulers are philosophers but because they think that those philosophers have gold in their souls. They will have gotten right that the rulers possess something more valuable than they themselves do, but what it is they will misunderstand. Socrates seems to think that this kind of motivational structure – namely, one that gets value hierarchies right, albeit without an accompanying understanding of their true meaning – is the best that can be achieved by those without a capacity for philosophy. In contrast, the philosopher who does have access to the truth beneath the noble lie will similarly act justly, on the Platonic definition of justice, in those areas of action open to the ordinary citizen, but in addition he will also knowingly orient his soul entirely around an understanding love of philosophy.[21]

The Protagorean pragmatist had recognized that beliefs are rules for action and therefore can be assessed by the actions they generate. Socrates recognizes that more than one set of beliefs can generate the same sorts of actions. Only a metaphysician – not a pragmatist – is in a position to distinguish between true and false beliefs. But a metaphysician can draw on the pragmatist's insight to find and disseminate false beliefs that complement the truth by having very nearly the same effect as truth. So Socrates' argument runs. Shadowy images must be allied with knowledge in order to avoid causing harm; but, conversely, the truth can use appearances to further its own cause because of the relation between belief and action.[22] This is the argument of the noble lie.

In an important sense, then, the argument of the *Republic* is directed toward explaining why the noble lie should work and also toward justifying its use. Strangely enough, the justification of the noble lie and the argument in favor of philosophical writing are roughly the same, and this brings us to the third and final step of the argument for philosophical writing laid out in the *Republic*: since one doesn't need strict adherence to the truth in order to convey pragmatically valid concepts, tied to sound metaphysical goals, one can proceed to convey important concepts without oral dialectic. Through writing, and other forms of discourse beyond the reach of oral dialectic, philosophers can, as in the noble lie, reach "the whole citizenry." Since philosophers have the power to convey concepts broadly through writing, their obligation to do no harm requires them to do so,[23] in addition to whatever work they may do through dialectic. And in their role as symbol-makers, they may make use of shadows because these are so stunningly efficacious, so long again as philosophers tie their shadows to sound metaphysical goals.[24]

Efficaciousness, finally, is the real ground for Socrates' defense of philosophical writing as an art distinct from dialectic: written texts can change more minds than dialectic and, as long as they are produced by a philosopher whose eye is on the realm of the Forms, they will, at worst, be closely assimilated to the truth and, at best, sometimes even make the truth itself spark forth.

We are at last at a point where we can answer the question of why Plato wrote.

4.6 Why Plato Wrote

Remember that in the *Phaedrus* Socrates treated writing and painting as direct parallels: "Writing, Phaedrus, has a marvelous and strange [*deinon*] quality that is altogether like painting [*zôgraphiai*]" (275d). A "constitution-painter" is therefore also a "writer of constitutions." The Greek title of the *Republic* is, of course, *politeia* or "constitution." As the author of the *Republic*, Plato seems to have designated himself as a constitution-painter. Socrates' defense of such artists must therefore have been Plato's self-defense.

As a "constitution-painter," Plato would have "worked away with frequent glances back and forth – first toward what is in its nature just, noble, self-disciplined, everything of that sort, and then again toward what [he was] trying to implant in mankind." He sought to be a "craftsman of the fine," producing metaphysically accurate and pragmatically efficacious images and models, among which masses of democratic citizens, whether intelligent or not, might graze and thereby assimilate new rules for action in line with the principles of justice he had developed. As these citizens would internalize new principles and rules for action, a new constitution would also come into being. On this account, Plato's dialogues were so many seeds sown broadly under the hot Athenian sun to implant culturally and politically salient changes in the democracy's system of value, that is, its constitution.[25] Plato wrote to re-order the symbol garden of Athenian culture.

* * *

Is this in fact why and what Plato wrote? Before we can embrace this conclusion finally, we will have to evaluate Plato's dialogues in light of the literary criteria articulated by Socrates in the *Republic* to see whether there is a match between Plato's art and that of the constitution-painter as described by Socrates. This is the project of chapter 5.

5

What Plato Wrote

5.1 Introduction

One of the basic, orienting questions students ask year in, year out is: Why does Plato write dialogues rather than essays? Why doesn't he just say directly what he thinks?[1]

Taken together, the *Phaedrus* and the *Republic* discuss four ways that a philosopher might write without shame. First, she might accept the priority of oral to written discourse and write texts that are primarily reminders of the practice of dialectic itself. Second, again accepting the priority of oral discourse, the philosopher might write poems, speeches, and laws but convey that those texts are necessarily tied to practices of conversation and oral defense; we can imagine a poet who produces critical scholia to her own poems. In contrast, with the third type of writing, a philosopher might embrace the distinctive value of written texts and produce theoretical models and diagrams of what truly is in order to help those who are not yet philosophically mature gain access to metaphysical truths. Or, finally, in the fourth case, again harnessing the power of writing, she might write noble lies: shadowy tales easily assimilated by the general population whose consequence would be that readers who believe them would act more or less as they would if they had in fact assimilated the truth itself.

5.2 Plato's Choice

In choosing to live a writer's life, Plato made an important choice. Since he wrote consistently and extensively, he must have accepted the arguments of

Socrates in the *Republic* about language's inherent power even apart from oral argumentation. But since he wrote dialogues primarily, he must also have accepted Socrates' arguments in the *Phaedrus* that a responsible philosopher-writer should consistently indicate oral dialectic's superiority. But of the four genres of philosophical writing, which did Plato practice?

We can rule out the second: he wrote few poems and no speeches or laws even if he included examples of all of these in his dialogues.[2] As to the other three, in my view, he did not choose among them. His dialogues are reminders, theoretical models, *and* noble lies.[3] Sometimes they are all this simultaneously, as in the *Republic*. At other times one or another genre is prioritized, as in the *Theaetetus*, where the dialogue is launched, as we have seen, when one character produces a written text of a conversation with Socrates precisely because he cannot repeat it from memory and needs a reminder (142d–143a).[4]

But there is a further complication. When in the *Phaedrus* Socrates describes the main value of writing as the provision of reminders for oral dialectic, he describes the written text as "at best only a 'shadow-image' (*eidôlon*) of the living and breathing word of him who knows" (*ton tou eidotos logon legeis zônta kai empsuchon, hou ho gegrammenos eidôlon an ti legoito dikaiôs*) (276a). In other words, reminders, too, are shadow-pictures; they themselves are therefore already noble lies. Remember that Socrates was, after all, said to exclaim upon hearing a reading of Plato's *Lysis*: "O Hercules! what a number of lies the young man has told about me!" Since reminders collapse into noble lies, there are not three genres at stake here, but only two. To understand what Plato wrote, then, we have mainly to focus on how his dialogues function either as shadow-pictures or as theoretical models or as both simultaneously.

The view that some of Plato's dialogues might function as reminders *cum* noble lies and some as theoretical models, and that some might even function in both ways simultaneously depends on applying Plato's theory of cognition to his own writing.

Remember that, as we saw in chapter 3, the theory emphatically developed a distinction between two types of image: shadows, on the one hand, and models on the other. Each image results from a different image-making practice – the shadows flow from the mimetic and representational work of traditional poets; the models emerge from the visualizing work of metaphysical modelers, for instance, mathematicians, philosophers, and constitution-painters. Importantly, however, both the traditional imitators – whether poets or painters – and the new, metaphysical modelers begin their image-making practice through acquaintance with the same set of concrete, material objects in the "real" world. The traditional artist imitates the table immediately here before us to produce a painting or photo of it or a poem about it. The metaphysical artist looks back and forth between the table immediately before us and the Form, or abstract idea, of "tableness" in order to produce a theoretical model conveying the concept of "tableness."

Now Socrates, no less than a table, couch or house, was a perceptible object in Plato's world. As a consequence, he too could be the object of representation in himself as a historically specific man or he could be used as visualization for an abstract concept. He could be represented, for instance, *qua* particular, historical Athenian citizen; or he could be made vivid *qua* just man. In the former case, such a representation would be a reminder. In the latter, when Socrates is considered in relation to what really is, a vivid presentation of Socrates would provide a model of the nature of justice, wisdom, courage, moderation, and virtue themselves. In this sense, a dialogue about Socrates might be either a reminder or a model.

But where does the reminder *qua* noble lie fit in? Happily, Socrates' analysis of shadows in the *Republic* has shown us that there are two kinds: those that cure and those that kill. On the terms of the argument of the *Republic*, if a philosopher were to undertake to imitate the historical Socrates, he would need to ensure that the reminders or shadows that he produced would function as noble, not damnable, lies. A philosophically acceptable mimetic representation of Socrates – a reminder – would need to be pragmatically efficacious.

Plato had a choice, therefore, not among three genres – reminder, theoretical paradigm, and noble lie – but only between two. For Plato, to write reminders about Socrates was necessarily also to produce a kind of noble lie. A rendering of Socrates, in a written dialogue, might therefore be either a noble lie about the historical Socrates or a life-giving theoretical model of Socrates *qua* just man. Or a dialogue representing Socrates might just be both.[5] But we will have to elaborate how the dialogues function as noble lies/reminders, on the one hand, and as theoretical models, on the other, before we can return to an explanation of how a dialogue could be both simultaneously.

5.3 Platonic Dialogues: A Multipurpose Genre

Let me explain, first, how the dialogues are shadow-pictures. In the *Republic* Socrates regularly expresses a desire to convert the many from hatred of to respect for philosophy. The dialogues are whopping great lies about Socrates that attempt just such a conversion. Scholars have often pointed this out, most frequently with reference to the *Phaedo* where the dialogue fully obscures the nasty physical symptoms that accompany death by hemlock in the service of a picture of a dying philosopher capable of self-mastery until the last.[6] When we believe that the historical Socrates and his practice of dialectic were such as Plato represents, we will be likely to treat philosophy in such a way as we would if we knew its true essence and worth.

But how do we know the dialogues (or at least those that feature Socrates as the main character) also deserve to be read as theoretical paradigms? This requires a longer account. If Plato is indeed writing about Socrates not merely to provide himself and others with a reminder of his mentor that serves to shore up the cause of philosophy but also to transform Socrates into a model or diagram of the just man, then we should expect two things: (1) that Plato would use the literary techniques that Socrates endorses for the production of models; and (2) that the dialogues themselves would, in literary terms, generate sparks where justice (on the Platonic definition) seems to appear.

In fact, Plato does use the literary techniques that Socrates endorses precisely to cause justice to seem to appear. Some of the especially notable literary details in the *Republic* are best explained this way. For instance, late in the dialogue, Socrates explains how to cultivate a crop of legitimate philosophers in a city. He says:

> "This is an area where we have to proceed with extreme caution . . . If the people we introduce to an education in such an important branch of knowledge and such an important discipline are sound of limb and sound of mind, then justice herself will have no fault to find with us, and we shall be the saviors of our city and its regime. But if we introduce people of a quite different character, we shall achieve entirely the opposite result, and expose philosophy to a further flood of ridicule."
> "That would certainly be something to be ashamed of," Glaucon said.
> "It would indeed. Meanwhile *I* seem to be making a bit of a fool of myself, here and now . . . I forgot this is just a game we are playing and I got rather carried away. My eye fell on philosophy as I was speaking, and I think I got annoyed when I saw her undeservedly covered in filth. I spoke with too much heat, as if I were angry with those responsible."
> "You didn't speak with too much heat. Not for this hearer's taste anyhow."
> "Well, it was too much for the speaker's taste." (536a–c)

Socrates manages his own psyche so expertly that he represses his anger before anyone even sees it. He masters the invisible. While this vignette might possibly be an accurate representation of the man himself, within the dialogue it more plainly serves as a model of the principle of justice as psychic self-control for which Socrates has been arguing. Plato renders the invisible tri-partite soul visible, dramatizing the non-event of reason's control over the spirited part of the soul. He does for us, via Socrates, what Socrates had done for Glaucon, via Leontius. In Socrates' behavior, as represented by Plato, justice sparks.

A comparison of this mimetic representation of Socrates here late in the dialogue to the earlier portrayals of Thrasymachus will help underscore the point that Plato is controlling his dramatic representations this minutely. First, Plato notably uses narrative in place of *mimêsis* more frequently in representing Thrasymachus, clearly the worst character in the dialogue, than he does with other characters. So, for instance, when Thrasymachus has his moment of heat, as Socrates will have his, Plato describes but does not imitate it. He has Socrates offer this narrative description:

> Thrasymachus conceded all these points, but not in the easygoing way I have just described. He had to be dragged every step of the way, sweating profusely, as you might expect in summer. This was the occasion when I saw something I had never seen before – Thrasymachus blushing. (350d)

Plato is adhering strictly to his own requirement not to imitate, but only to describe, men when they are bad.

Moreover, the specific choice in the *Republic* to imitate even the invisible movements of Socrates' soul but only to describe the most easily perceptible elements of Thrasymachus', imitating him as little as possible, points toward Plato's self-consciousness about molding his own life and character around the pattern of the good, not the bad.[7] The *Republic*'s development of allegories extends to its use of literary style to convey the same principles that it conveyed through the argument and action.[8]

Now what about the idea that a single dialogue might function simultaneously as both a noble lie *qua* reminder and a theoretical model? Am I not erasing the distinction between two kinds of symbolic communication with that claim?

To the contrary, the claim reinforces Plato's core point about cognition, which undergirds the distinction in the first place. Theoretical models are to be used for thinking; shadowy images, to engage the imagination. The distinction between these two kinds of symbolic communication depends, finally, on which cognitive faculty is brought to bear in cognizing a particular object. Do we read the dialogue for a depiction of a man named Socrates or in order to see what abstract concepts might be conveyed to us by means of such a depiction? Plato has prepared his text to meet the demands of both kinds of reading.

If we read in the first way, and come away with a strange attachment to Socrates (as so many do despite protestations to irritation over his various frustrating conversational habits), then, like the citizens who assimilate the noble lie, we come to value something represented by Socrates (dialogic exchange, for instance), without knowing why we should value it. But if we read the dialogue as a theoretical model of a just man, and also unpack all the other models fashioned by that just man, we get an answer to the question (among others) of why we should value philosophy.

As noble lies, the dialogues should give us the correct (on Plato's view) hierarchy of values; as theoretical models, they give us the grounds to embrace that hierarchy with knowledge, should we choose to do so. The distinction between the dialogue as noble lie and as theoretical model captures at least some of the very different sorts of effects that a single dialogue can have on readers.

5.4 The *Republic* as Theoretical Model

For all, though, that the dialogues can be simultaneously reminders/noble lies, on the one hand, and theoretical models, on the other, Plato does seem to highlight one or another approach in different texts. The *Phaedo*, with its blatantly false depiction of death by hemlock, plainly exposes itself as a noble lie. The *Theaetetus*, as we have seen, begins by foregrounding the concept of reminder. Dialogues like the *Parmenides* seem also to serve primarily as reminders of philosophical discourse. The *Republic*, fuller of models and theoretical images than any other dialogue, concludes with the symphonically rich allegory of the Myth of Er. This conclusion drives home the point that the dialogue should be taken as an example of the new kind of symbol-making. It both is itself and also conveys theoretical models.

By concluding his argument with the remarkable Myth of Er, Socrates drives home the point that his new and superior practice of model-making should displace the poets' mimetic craft and their shadowy tales of the underworld, with which the dialogue began. The final model, the Myth of Er in fact encapsulates the core argument of the dialogue. I cannot here offer a full reading of the Myth but will sketch a few basic points.[9]

Er was a hero killed in battle (or so people thought) who comes back to life twelve days later to report on what happens in the afterworld. He recounts that we are reincarnated and that the life we have led in the here and now determines the sort of life we are likely to choose when the time comes for us to re-enter life in a new form. After narrating Er's report, Socrates interprets it by saying: (618c)

> The greatest care, [my dear Glaucon], must be directed towards having each and every one of us ... be a follower and a student of this branch of study of ours, in the hope that he can learn and discover who it is who will give him the ability and knowledge to distinguish the good life from the bad [*bion chrêston kai ponêron diagignôskonta*], and to choose always and everywhere, out of all those possible, the life which is better.[10]

The core activity of Socratic study is thus defined as discernment between the good and the base, and the central point of the Myth is that whatever happens to us next – whether in this life or in some after-life is irrelevant – is the result of our success or failure at identifying and molding ourselves after the good. What follows from this? As I indicated in chapter 2, this new story of the after-life displaces standard Athenian accounts of the gods. It replaces them, in fact, with the core principle of the *Republic* and of Platonic philosophy. As Socrates says, "The choice makes you responsible. God is not responsible" (617e).

When Socrates and his colleagues were developing rules for the kinds of stories that might be told to the children in Kallipolis, one core principle was just this, that the gods are perfect and unchanging, responsible only for good, never for evil. Here in the Myth of Er Socrates and Plato produce the necessary mythical ground for a thorough rejection of moral luck.[11] This stringent view of personal responsibility is one of the culturally revisionist outcomes of the dialogue. It is among the concepts conveyed by the dense network of symbols developed over the course of the dialogue's extensive engagement in model-making.

The story of Er, with a lesson this serious, is clearly not meant for children only. What we suspected all along turns out to be true: namely that Socrates (and Plato) do not think that children are the sole constituency for education through models, stories, and shadowy images that make the invisible visible. All the while, when Socrates discussed the poetic education of children, he was actually describing how ideas and images affect everyone. This myth of Er, the myths of the *Republic*, should work on Glaucon and also, dear reader, on you.

Plato invests so much energy in exploring how philosophic concepts can be conveyed to the unlearned – ranging from children to Glaucon and all prospective readers of the text – that we can reasonably infer that his own writing, which follows the rules and methods for communication that Socrates outlines, is designed to sow in the minds of adult readers concepts that might bring psychological, cultural, and, consequently, political change.

5.5 Plato Politikos

We at last have in view a fourth account of how Plato participated in politics. In chapter 1, we explored the three accounts offered to date; these were the views: (1) that Plato did wish to realize the actual plan of the *Republic*; (2) that Plato hoped mainly to educate elites into forms of conservative rule that would protect space for philosophy; and (3) that Plato had used his dialogues to provide Athens with sustained critique.

But Diogenes Laertius may have gotten it right long ago, when he wrote that "*in his own city . . .* Plato was a politician or political leader, a *politikos*, *to judge from his writings*" (Diog. Laert. 3.23; my emphasis).

Plato thought written texts could drive cultural change, and as a *politikos* Plato used text to produce durable symbols that revised the conceptual foundations of Athenian culture. (Among the core concepts that he revises, as I have argued elsewhere, are *orgê* or anger, *dikê* or justice, *timôria* or retributive punishment, and *psychê* or soul.)[12] He accepted the pragmatist thesis that beliefs are principles and rules for action and so are fully recognizable in their consequences; this widened for him, beyond the Socratic view, the range of discourse that might legitimately be used for conveying and securing the internalization of beliefs. In this regard, and in his decision to write, Plato unified metaphysics and pragmatism.

Every culture, every community, has always developed some group of people who claim to understand well enough how their language is built to contribute intentionally to the revision of its architecture, and so to the evolution of their culture. In an essay called "The Defence of Poetry," the nineteenth-century English poet Percy Bysshe Shelley made what remains the strongest claim on this point when he wrote that poets are the "unacknowledged legislators of the world." This is precisely how Plato saw the poets, Homer and the others, whom he criticizes so relentlessly in the *Republic*. They had given his fellow Greeks their basic moral vocabulary and filled the landscapes of their imagination – but not, in Plato's view, to good effect.[13] Plato sought to arrogate to philosophy a comprehensive power to construct culture, a power that the poets had accidentally, each working individually and haphazardly, managed to accrue to themselves.

Plato wrote, I would argue, not just the *Republic*, but all his dialogues, to displace the poets.[14] And he expected this displacement to have cultural effects and, because cultural effects, political effects.

This fourth approach to answering the question of how Plato related to real Athenian politics unifies the three pervious alternatives. On this fourth view, Plato did seek wholesale transformation of Athenian life in the direction of the ideals outlined in the *Republic*. He sought to effect such transformation, however, through education, not revolution. Yet he did not restrict himself to educating the elite, and instead sought to implant his conception of justice as widely as possible, through pragmatically efficacious and metaphysically accurate symbols, anchored by and disseminated in his texts.[15] Insofar as he sought to replace Athenian values with new ones, he was constantly critically engaged in Athenian life. But his engagement was also consistently positive as he sought implantation both of new meanings for old virtues and also of some new values to replace those he simply critiqued. Plato's hypothesis was that the assimilation of symbols such as his own would change Athenian politics by reshaping the citizenry's orienting ideals.[16] Plato wrote, in short, as a constitution-painter, not an artist who describes constitutions but one who attempts to bring them into being by dominating the symbol-world of a citizenry's imagination.

So what did Plato write? We can finally answer that question. Plato wrote unacknowledged legislation.

* * *

Yet there is still one more barrier to overcome before we can rest easy with this conclusion that, as Diogenes Laertius put it, Plato wrote as a *politikos*, as a politician or political leader. Is Plato not famous for having drawn a strict distinction between the lives of philosophy and politics? Did he not celebrate the superiority of the former? How can he have written as a politician if he pursued a life of philosophy as an activity distinct from politics? To answer this, we must turn in chapter 6 to the question of the philosophical significance of the kind of life that Plato chose.

How Plato Lived

6.1 Introduction

Throughout many of his dialogues Plato seems to draw a distinction between philosophical and political lives, and to argue for the superiority of the former. There is, for instance, the remarkable digression on the two lives in the middle of the *Theaetetus* where Plato has Socrates depict the politician as a slave to necessity, not at liberty to engage in inquiry, whereas the philosopher is a free man:

> Look at the man who has been knocking about in law-courts and such places ever since he was a boy; and compare him with the man brought up in philosophy, in the life of a student. It is surely like comparing the up-bringing of a slave with that of a free man. (172d)

Yet this stark opposition of the philosopher to the politician must be a caricature.[1] If one looks more closely at the description of the philosopher, one recognizes that it does not reflect even how Socrates lived:

> The philosopher grows up without knowing the way to the market-place, or the whereabouts of the law-courts or the council-chambers or any other place of public assembly ... Whenever he is obliged, in a law-court or elsewhere, to discuss the things that lie at his feet and before his eyes, he causes entertainment not only to Thracian servant-girls but to all the common herd, by tumbling into wells and every sort of difficulty through his lack of experience ... To him it is no disgrace to appear simple and good-for-nothing, when he is confronted with menial tasks, when, for instance, he doesn't know how to make a bed. (174c–175e).[2]

Why Plato Wrote   Danielle S. Allen. © 2010 Danielle S. Allen

Socrates clearly knew where the market-place was and, while he wasn't prepared for success in the law court, the dialogues do not suggest that his practical incompetence reached the heights mocked here.

If these two pictures of the politician and philosopher are caricatures, then the right relationship between philosophy and politics must, on Plato's view, be more subtle than this. As a final step in ascertaining who Plato was, and what his relationship to Athenian politics was, we will have to ask the following questions: What did it mean for Plato to choose the life of a writer? What kind of life choice was that? The *Seventh Letter* will be helpful here. As we delve into it for clarification of the right relation between philosophy and politics, as Plato saw it, we will also find support for the argument that Plato saw writing as an instrument of political work. By the end of this chapter we should at last be able to say who Plato was and to confirm the nature of his relationship to Athenian politics.

6.2 The *Seventh Letter* on Writing

As we have seen, the *Seventh Letter* claims that Plato had gone to Sicily to "attempt to realize theories concerning laws and government [*ei pote tis ta dianoêthenta peri nomôn te kai politeias apotelein engcheirêsoi*]" (328bc). That effort largely entailed educating in philosophy two of Syracuse's leaders, Dion and Dionysius II, the brother-in-law and son respectively of Dionysius I, Syracuse's archetypal tyrant. Plato was more successful with Dion. Dionysius II seems sometimes to have desired a philosophic life, only to reject it violently at other times; worse still, he began to make claims to have become a philosopher, despite his paltry intellectual development (339c–341a). According to the *Seventh Letter*, Plato found one of Dionysius' claims particularly obnoxious: namely, that the young man had written metaphysical treatises (341b). The *Letter* casts Plato as responding to this claim of Dionysius II with an extraordinary disquisition on who should write, and for what purposes.

The disquisition begins with what initially seem to be contradictory claims. First, Plato is depicted as arguing that language is so inherently weak, as a medium for the expression of truths, that metaphysical truths simply cannot be recorded in written form. Yet then he is made to argue that written texts have a special power because they can reach all mankind; consequently, if it were possible to record metaphysical truths in written form, doing so would be a service to humankind.[3] Here is the statement:

> There does not exist, nor will there ever exist, any treatise of mine [Plato's] dealing therewith [i.e. with metaphysical truths]. For it [metaphysical truth] does not at all admit of verbal expressions like other studies [*rhêton gar*

oudamôs estin], but, as a result of continued application to the subject itself and communion therewith, it is brought to birth in the soul on a sudden, as light that is kindled by a leaping spark, and thereafter it nourishes itself. Notwithstanding, of this much I am certain, that the best statement of these doctrines, in writing or in speech would be my own statement; and further that if they should be badly stated in writing, it is I who would be the person most deeply pained. And if I had thought that these subjects ought to be fully stated in writing or in speech to the public, what nobler action could I have performed in my life than that of writing what is of great benefit to mankind and bringing forth to the light for all men the nature of reality? But were I to undertake this task it would not, as I think, prove a good thing for men, save for some few who are able to discover the truth themselves with but little instruction. (341c–341e)

This passage has often been taken by scholars to indicate that Plato taught two sets of doctrines, exoteric teachings that existed "outside" of his texts and esoteric doctrines that existed within them.[4] This distinction is sometimes also taken to mean that Plato orally taught "secret truths" to elite students while using his written texts to generate a protective smokescreen for those truths. But this interpretation gets Plato wrong.

The clue to understanding the argument about writing made in this passage of the *Letter* inheres in the remark that metaphysical truth is "brought to birth in the soul on a sudden, as light that is kindled by a leaping spark, and thereafter it [truth] nourishes itself." This, of course, recalls the language of the *Republic* when Socrates describes the project of comparing the image of the good city and of the good individual to the act of rubbing dry sticks together in order to make a spark appear.

In that particular case, Socrates and his interlocutors hope to make a spark of justice appear. But it is by working with appropriately designed models and symbols – and not through dialectic – that Socrates there hopes to help make sparks of truth appear for his interlocutors.[5] As we have seen, language that can generate such sparks is *enargês* or vivid. And it is the goal of Plato's written language, too, to achieve the *enargeia* or vivid, life-giving clarity that generates the sparks described here. If written texts can help generate the relevant sorts of sparks, then they can directly aid students in the pursuit of metaphysical truths; they can make concepts visible that both allow students to participate in the truth and facilitate their move forward toward dialectical engagement with the Forms themselves. Written texts that aim to provide such aid straightforwardly align with those truths. They neither contradict nor hide them.[6]

In fact, the *Seventh Letter* repeats the arguments about cognition made in the *Republic* to defend philosophical writing as a method for training cognition. In a remarkable passage, the *Letter* combines the arguments made in the line analogy with those made about names in another dialogue, the *Cratylus*:[7]

> Every existing object has three things which are the necessary means by which knowledge of the object is acquired; and the knowledge itself is a fourth thing; and as a fifth one must postulate the object itself which is cognizable and true. First of these comes the name; secondly the definition; thirdly the image [*eidólon*], fourthly the knowledge [*epistémé*]. (342a–b)

In other words, every existing object has five epistemological modes. First, it is apprehended by its name. Second, it is apprehended by a definition. Third, it is apprehended through images, representations, and models. Each of these first three means of apprehending something is problematic. Names – as we ordinarily use them – are too often arbitrary. Definitions are inherently unstable; they always introduce the contraries of the object being described and other forms of particularity that deflect us from true knowledge of the thing itself.[8] Images are defective in the ways that the *Republic* painstakingly lays out. Nonetheless we use these tools – for they are all we have – to pursue knowledge, imperfect and incomplete though it may be, of each thing. Such imperfect knowledge, since it is the best we can achieve with these tools, is here called right opinion, which constitutes the fourth epistemological mode (although this use of "opinion" conflicts with treatments of that topic in the dialogues). And then, fifth, there is the thing itself which exists with the capacity to be known; its knowability in itself is the fifth epistemological mode and the only one that belongs firmly and completely to the realm of truth.

How exactly does this argument about five epistemological modes relate to the line analogy, which uses the four sections of the line to describe four different cognitive registers? The line image turns out not to describe the whole of human cognition but only that half that depends on images.[9] It is in the *Cratylus* that Socrates anatomizes the registers of human cognition that depend on categorization (through names and definitions). In the *Republic* the bottom three sections of the line represented as the objects of cognition, respectively, shadows, material objects in the world, and graphs and models. They are here, in the *Seventh Letter*, collapsed as the objects of the single epistemological mode of apprehending things through their images (called *eidóla* here, instead of *eikones*, but still capturing the entire category of images). Thus, the *Letter* describes the third epistemological mode as follows: it cognizes "that object which is in the course of being painted and erased [*zógraphoumenon te kai exaleiphomenon*], or of being shaped with a lathe and falling into decay" (342bc). Here the category of images explicitly includes both the graphic representations of circles produced by a painter (*zógraphoumenon*) and material objects made by a lathe. The argument in chapter 2 that, in the line image, the concrete objects of the third section of the line and the graphs and models of the second section overlap, is here confirmed.

The next step in the argument in the *Letter* is very important. Having laid out the five epistemological modes, and having made clear that the third – images and the apprehension of things through images – envelopes all three categories of image that were held apart from each other in the *Republic*, the *Letter* then goes on to argue that names, definitions, and images "form a single whole [*hen touto au pan*] which does not exist in vocal utterance [e.g. in names or definitions] or in bodily forms [e.g. in pictures, objects, and models] but in souls" (342c). That single whole is "knowledge" or "true opinion." Human knowledge, Plato is interpreted as arguing, is formed out of whatever we do, on a regular basis, with our names, definitions, and images. But precisely because even "knowledge" or "true opinion" is built out of names, definitions, and images, our attempts to achieve "knowledge" or "true opinion" have all the weaknesses and defects of human cognition (as the *Theaetetus* repeatedly and emphatically demonstrates).

At this point in the argument, the *Letter* restates the idea that metaphysical truths can be acquired by philosophers only through processes that generate sparks that bring the truth to light for them:

> It is by means of the examination of each of these objects – names and definitions, visions and sense-perceptions – comparing one with another, proving them by kindly proofs and employing questionings and answerings that are void of envy – it is by such means, and hardly so, that there bursts out the light of intelligence and reason regarding each object [*exelampse phronêsis peri hekaston kai nous*] in the mind of him who uses every effort of which mankind is capable. (344b)

Again, we are reminded of the passage in the *Republic* when Socrates said that he and his interlocutors might hope to see a spark of justice jump forth by comparing justice in the paired images of the ideal city and the ideal man. Here in this passage too sparks are ignited through comparison. The relevant concept – say, justice, beauty, or the good – is to be considered in several of its imperfect epistemological modes – through names, definitions, images, and true opinions – and by comparing one imperfect representation of the concept at issue with another, the philosophically inclined can make sparks burst forth.

But what exactly are these sparks and what is their role in the project of philosophy? Whoever wrote the *Seventh Letter* picked up something in Plato, since the *Republic* uses the same image to describe philosophical progress. When the neo-Platonist, Plotinus, wrote in the third century CE, he would use this image to argue that "our highest task as knowers" is to achieve non-discursive insight.[10] On his argument, which he attributed to Plato, metaphysical truths are simply inarticulable. But that does not seem to be the point of the image of the spark in the *Republic*. If we follow the use of the spark image there, we notice that the sparks arise before people have begun to engage in dialectic. In the case of Glaucon's hunt for justice, the spark captures the moment when the concept of justice, conveyed by a model, suddenly becomes visible to him.[11] On the argument of the line analogy, the use of such conceptual visualization would simply be preparatory to the harder work of engaging in dialectic to cognize the Forms themselves and to articulate metaphysical truth. Dionyius II's mistake is to claim to do more with the tools of writing than this preparatory work. No serious philosopher, Plato is represented as saying, should make that mistake.

But as to the preparatory work itself – developing names, definitions, images, and "right opinions" that might give readers a shot at seeing true concepts spark out before their eyes – what did Plato think of that? This project Plato surely adopted. After all the *Letter* attributes to him the view: "What nobler action could I have performed in my life than that of writing what is of great benefit to mankind and bringing forth to the light for all men the nature of reality?" The key is to understand that, for Plato, bringing reality to light through writing is preparatory only; it is the practice of using highly refined literary techniques to train the cognition of his readers such that "sparks" will perhaps appear for them, enabling them to pursue further investigation through dialectic. The latter occurs, of course, by the light of the sun, not sparks. Yet the image of the sparks indicates that the goal of the dialogues might be said to be the generation of "ontological confrontations" for readers.[12] Since oral dialectic has the very same goal, there is no cause to think that the different modes of discourse present different doctrines.

Whereas in his education of Dionysius II, Plato clearly sought to sow in the minds of a ruler concepts that might bring political changes, the theory of language that he articulates in the *Republic*, that is captured again, albeit imperfectly, in the *Seventh Letter*, and which his texts are constructed to embody, stakes a claim for the view that it is also possible for a philosopher to sow the seeds of his concepts far more broadly than simply in the minds of a single ruler or handful of aristocratic leaders.[13] Plato's life project was fundamentally political simply by virtue of depending on the written word, with its capacity to reach all humankind, as the *Letter* puts it. When the *Letter* represents Plato's main ally in Syracuse, Dion, the uncle of Dionysius II, as turning to Plato for political help, it is very particular about the kind of political help Plato can offer. Dion turns to him not for "foot-soldiers and horse-soldiers but for arguments and persuasions [*logous kai peithous*]" (328d). Like foot- and horse-soldiers, Plato's forms of discourse have power and will travel.

Yet there are no indications that Plato considered his interest in politics to compromise his status as a philosopher. (Indeed, in the *Republic*, although philosophers must be forced to return to the cave, their status as philosophers is not compromised by that return.) Thus, a final step in establishing the case that Plato did indeed write as a politician entails clarifying exactly what he meant by his distinctions between the philosophical and the political life.

6.3 The *Seventh Letter* on Ways of Life

The *Seventh Letter*'s expression of what Plato hoped to achieve through the education of Dionysius II is enlightening. The *Letter* repeatedly invokes the idea that Plato's project was to teach a way of life. The Greek for "way of life" is *bios* (327b, 327e, 328a); its sense is something like our "lifestyle" or "life project." In particular, Plato hopes that Dionysius II will "gain a desire for the philosophic life" (*hê philosophou zôê*, 330b) and a love of the best life (*hôs beltistos bios*, 339e); this entails lessons about how Dionysius II should order his daily life (*zên to kath' hêmeran*) (331d). And when the *Letter* gets specific, we learn something very important: living the philosophical life does not in fact require that one spend all one's time doing philosophy.
Instead:

> It is as one fully committed to philosophy that such a student lives, *occupied indeed in whatever occupations* [praxesi] *he may find himself*, but always beyond all else cleaving fast to philosophy and to that mode of daily life which will best make him apt to learn and of retentive mind and able to reason within himself soberly; these are the truly philosophic. (340d; my emphasis)

One can live a philosophic life regardless of the occupations in which one finds oneself. The competing occupations envisaged in this passage are specifically political.

According to the *Letter*, then, the famous distinction Plato draws between the philosophical and the political life does not mainly mark out the kinds of activities (*praxeis*) in which an individual will spend the majority of her time. Rather, it distinguishes two possible sets of orienting ideals – the sorts of goals, values, and priorities used by an individual to organize her life.[14] Someone who chooses a philosophical life maximizes personal moderation for the sake of bringing the maximal degree of calm and order to her life, conditions necessary for the pursuit of wisdom, but making this choice is compatible with a range of daily occupations.[15] Someone who chooses a political life maximizes, presumably, opportunities for accumulating honor.

Plato himself chose the philosophical life, understood this way, but devoted a considerable amount of his time to the political project of writing his dialogues. To live philosophically did not require him to spend all of his time in dialogic inquiry; the philosophical life had room for political engagement.

We are at last in a position to say who Plato was.

A student of Socrates, Plato chose the philosophical life. At the Academy and in his private teaching of Dion and Dionysius II he continued a tradition of dialogic engagement initiated by his teacher. Yet he also routinely occupied himself with writerly projects, which were fundamentally, but not exclusively, a method of political engagement. As Diogenes Laertius would put it, Plato wrote as a *politikos*, or as a political leader.

We can presume, however, based on the recommendations of the *Seventh Letter* to Dionysius II, that whatever occupations engaged Plato, he always beyond all else sought "to cleave fast to philosophy and to that mode of daily life which would best make him apt to learn, of retentive mind, and able to reason within himself soberly" (340d). Thus, living philosophically, he nonetheless participated in politics. And participating in politics, he nonetheless lived philosophically. Such was the life of Plato Politikos.

* * *

Plato Politikos, I have argued, developed his writerly style based on a theory about the kind of language that is most likely to function successfully as unacknowledged legislation. How reasonable was his hypothesis that writerly projects like his would have political effects? We can test his theory about the role of language in politics and about what is political in philosophy by looking to Athenian politics. Did Plato's dialogues have any influence on Athenian politics? If so, did they have the sort of influence that he thought writing like his should have? We will go on in chapters 7, 8, and 9 to consider that question. If Plato was right, that writing like his should function as unacknowledged legislation, we should be able to find its trace in the lives of Athenians.

Part II

What Plato Did

The Case for Influence

7.1 Philosophy in Politics

In Athens, during the fourth century, after the death of Socrates, the philosophers lived lives apart, neither seeking nor effecting any influence on Athenian politics. Such is the picture conventionally presented of the relationship between philosophy and politics in classical Greece. The burden of the last six chapters has been to argue the opposite: that Plato in fact considered his philosophical project to entail engagement with Athenian politics.

Plato functioned as a critic of the democracy from within, but my argument has gone beyond that claim to this one: Plato established theoretical grounds for thinking that philosophy can and should positively impact politics and, by writing his dialogues, he even acted on that theory. In particular, Plato developed a comprehensive theory of the role of language and of philosophy in politics with the following hypotheses:

1 Philosophy is not an activity apart from politics; its core work – of understanding and/or fashioning concepts that have their full life only as principles and rules for action – directly engages the formation of values, norms, and interests, and so touches the heart of politics.
2 The concepts of philosophy come to be implanted in students through language that is *enargês* or vivid; this includes both dialogic language and language that is full of metaphors, ecphrastic images, allegories, and other techniques that engage cognition in all its registers, the sort of language Plato used in writing the *Republic*; language that is *enargês* generates a surplus of linguistic power, which can be deployed in politics alongside other forms of power.

Why Plato Wrote   Danielle S. Allen. © 2010 Danielle S. Allen

3 Not only oral discourse but also written texts, which can reach broad audiences, can be vivid or have *enargeia* (or *energeia* on Aristotle's terms).
4 If the concepts of philosophy are broadly disseminated, they will affect contests over values, norms, and interests for the mass of citizens, and not merely the elites.
5 Philosophers can therefore affect politics by means other than the immediate personal education of elites; in particular they can do so through vivid writing, which is to say, through the deployment of surpluses of linguistic power.

By writing his dialogues, Plato tested his own hypotheses.[1] If his theory of the role of language and philosophy in politics is right, we should expect to see traces of his influence on the politics of Athens. More specifically, we should expect to see just those of his concepts that he conveyed in his most vivid, most metaphorical language playing an especially important part in Athenian discourse. We would need to see those concepts functioning as principles and rules for action. And we would need to see uptake of his concepts not merely by elites but also by the mass of democratic citizens.

In fact, a case for the influence of Plato (and Aristotle too) on Athenian politics is easy to make – we've seen already that his ideas did reach a public well beyond his own students (see chapter 1), but there's much more to be said still. Importantly, the particular pattern of Plato's impact does unfold along lines his theory would predict.

Moreover, the fact that Aristotle seems to have communicated so differently from Plato, without Plato's techniques of vividness, gives us a chance to consider whether Plato's argument about *enargeia* in language has any merit. Aristotle can serve as a sort of "control" case. If Plato was right, his influence on Athens should have been different in kind from Aristotle's.

In fact, we will see that it was. We have to be careful, though. Since none of Aristotle's dialogues has come down to us, we don't know what the full range of his literary style might have been; we will therefore have to hold our comparative conclusions only tentatively. Nonetheless, the case for the influence of both philosophers on Athens is clear, and the differences between the traces of their influence are intriguing.

7.2 The Case for Influence

Let me begin, then, by outlining the basic case for the influence of Plato and Aristotle on Athenian politics. Although Aristotle was the younger man, his influence on the city shows up somewhat earlier, so we will start there.

The written version of Aristotle's public lectures on rhetoric, which were given in the mid-350s BCE, includes frequent use of an unusual term, *prohairesis*. We might loosely translate this as "deliberated commitment." That translation sounds technical, and the word was technical. The text of Aristotle's treatise *On Rhetoric* includes fifteen instances of the word, which is central to his ethical theory, and the extant Aristotelian corpus has 156 instances. Before Aristotle, almost no one used this word. Plato used it once. Isocrates used it six times, but only three times before Aristotle's lectures, and it is absent from early Athenian oratory, which means from Antiphon, Andocides, Isaeus, Lysias, and early Demosthenes (including both his private and public speeches). Nor does it occur at all in the two other major prose writers of the period: Thucydides and Xenophon. Then, after Aristotle's lectures, every single Athenian orator writing between 353 BCE and 322 BCE uses the term – late Demosthenes (in both private and public speeches), Aeschines, Lycurgus, Hyperides, and Dinarchus. All used the term *prohairesis* as part of a discourse of legitimating and critiquing leaders.[2]

Although Aristotle elaborates his concept in his ethical treatises and connects it to his theories of agency, responsibility, and character, the orators do not deploy that full philosophical content when they adopt the term; they do, however, consistently use its metaphorical structure. As I have argued elsewhere, that metaphorical structure focuses on trajectory.[3] In the *Eudemian Ethics*, Aristotle reminds his reader that *prohairesis* comes from *hairesis* which means "choice" (1226b). But this comes from the verb *haireô*, which means "to take with the hand." Something inside people makes them reach out and "take" parts of the world. This is the notion of trajectory. An actor starts "here" and then, through processes of choice, extends herself in space to "there" in order to take something, thus affecting the surrounding environment.

The orators' particularly used the concept of *prohairesis* (deliberated commitment) to connect what happened "here" – in a person's soul or behind closed doors – to what happened "there" on the outside, in the visible events of the world. The Demosthenic *Erotic Essay*, for instance, argues that a perfectly virtuous *prohairesis* ought to shine from a man's eyes ([Dem.] 61.13), and Aeschines, in his prosecution of Timarchus for male prostitution, relies literally on the idea of *prohairesis* to see the essences behind facades:

Consider, he says, [Timarchus'] case with the help of illustrations. Naturally the illustrations will have to be like the pursuits of Timarchus. You see the men over there who sit in the houses of ill repute ... Now if, as you are passing along the street, any one should ask you, "Pray what is that fellow doing at this moment?" You would instantly name the act, though you do not see it done, and do not know who it was that entered the house; knowing the choice [*prohairesis*] of career of the man, you know his deed too. In the same way, therefore, you ought to judge the case of Timarchus and not ask whether anyone saw but whether he has done the deed. (1.74–75)[4]

Examples such as these highlight the fact that the orators have taken the same metaphorical structure from Aristotle: *prohairesis* entails the observable, external manifestation of something internal. But they do not connect that metaphorical structure to any sophisticated account of character or agency.

Plato too was said to have given at least one public lecture, but his influence on Athenian political discourse does not show up until after his death, which occurred in 348/7 BCE.[5] His texts must have been his more significant medium of dissemination.

Fourteen speeches given between 345 BCE and 307 BCE adopt identifiably Platonic vocabulary, recognizably Platonic forms of argumentation, and Platonic symbols. They are Lycurgus' *Against Leocrates*; Aeschines' three extant speeches; Dinarchus' *Against Demosthenes*; Demades' *On the Twelve Years*; Hyperides' six extant speeches, including his *Against Demosthenes* also; and two speeches prosecuting the orator Aristogeiton, both by an unknown politician who was an ally of Lycurgus.[6] How can we establish the case for influence? And what was the nature of that influence?

Most dramatically, all these speeches adopt the vocabulary for discussing punishment that Plato crafted in the *Gorgias*, *Republic*, and *Laws*. As I argued at length in *The World of Prometheus*, the standard approach to punishment in Athens was retributive and deterrent, and the vocabulary most commonly used by the city's orators reflected this. The Athenians expected that prosecutors would be motivated by personal anger toward the defendant and a desire to restore their own honor. The prosecutor had the job of "taking justice" from the defendant and of requiring the defendant to "give or pay justice." The Greek phrases were *lambanein* (take) and *dounai* (give) *dikên* (justice). The Athenians expected such an approach to punishment to minimize the number of trials by restricting legitimate prosecution to those who had been directly wronged.[7]

In contrast, the Platonic approach to psychology and politics rejected anger as a justification for action.[8] Playing with words, Plato also argued that one should never "take justice" from anyone for that would only harm him; throughout his corpus he never once used the phrase *lambanein dikên* (take justice).[9] Instead, he argued for reformative punishment that cultivates souls in the direction of straight, healthy growth. He used the verb *kolazein* (to reform) to designate reformative and educative forms of punishment and emphasized the previously rare substantive *kolasis* (reformative punishment), as well as the word *akolasia*, which describes the state of souls that have been neither properly cultivated nor corrected.[10]

Other important political ideas are connected to the switch from retributive to reformative commitments. The retributive approach reflects the Protagorean dictum that "man is the measure"; the angry person is himself the judge of whether undertaking punishment is appropriate, and the political arena becomes a domain for negotiating, through competition, the many, diverse judgments about the world that have been proffered by different, essentially equal people.

In contrast, the reformative view requires that punishment be designed by experts in education and human psychology. In Plato's argument this expert design requires an analysis of virtue (*aretê*) and what is fine (*to kalon*). Plato did not think, however, that every wrong-doer could be reformed; he designated some as "incurable" with the uncommon word *aniatos*. He tended also to refer to such incurable wrong-doers as "wild beasts" (*thêria*). Plato's *Republic* and *Laws* use this term in this metaphorical sense more than does any other fifth- or fourth-century prose text.[11] The only orators to use the words *thêrion* or *aniatos* to describe the wrong-doer or his acts were Aeschines, Dinarchus, Demades, the author of *Against Aristogeiton I*, and Demosthenes. The first four of these orators were all authors of the speeches I listed above as showing a Platonic influence, while Demosthenes uses both terms mainly in response to Aeschines' own usages of them in *Against Ctesiphon*.[12] Similarly, while eight of the ten Attic orators preferred the standard, retributive vocabulary for punishment, only Hyperides and Lycurgus preferred the verb *kolazein*.[13] They are both reliably reported by biographers to have studied with Plato.[14]

Importantly, these orators did not always use this new penal vocabulary just as Plato had employed it. Lycurgus, for instance, whose prosecution of Leocrates, the owner of a blacksmith's shop, on a treason charge is famously aggressive, calls for Leocrates' execution. And yet he uses the word *kolazein* (to reform) to describe the punishment that should be meted out to Leocrates. Clearly, killing Leocrates would in no way reform him. Yet Lycurgus has understood the reformative elements of Plato's arguments about punishment; his whole speech is organized around the idea that the trial and the punishment should provide an education, if not for Leocrates, then at least for the citizenry. While many Attic orators supplemented their retributive view with the argument that punishments should also deter, they made the case for deterrence by arguing that the wrongdoer should be used as an example (*paradeigma*) to teach other citizens to be more self-disciplined (*sôphronesteroi*). Lycurgus, in contrast makes a case for educating people toward virtue (*aretê*) and what is noblest (*to kalliston*).[15]

But Lycurgus' use of the term *kolazein* (to reform), and allied portions of Plato's penal vocabulary, is by no means the only Platonic feature of his speech. Of the fourteen speeches that adopt distinctively Platonic vocabulary, his is the most deeply so marked.[16] Like Plato, Lycurgus rejects the idea that an angry, personally wronged, and self-interested victim is the most legitimate prosecutor. He was in no way personally involved with Leocrates and presents his prosecution as entirely a matter of the public interest.

Highly anomalous in this regard, his prosecution deploys rhetoric that is equally anomalous. In particular, more than a third of his speech is given over to quotations of monuments, traditional oaths, and even poets. But when he introduces the poets, he does so in terms Plato would have approved, presenting the quotations from Tyrtaeus, for instance, with the remark that the Spartans consider Tyrtaeus to be the exception to their general rule that poets are bad (Lyc. 1.106). And Lycurgus uses the Platonic superlative *to kalliston* (the most beautiful or the most noble) six times in his speech, as when he argues that: "Laws, because of their brevity, do not teach but determine what must be done; but the poets, who imitate the [properly] human way of life [*hoi de poiêtai mimoumenoi ton anthrôpinon bion*], by selecting the noblest of actions [*ta kallista tôn ergôn*] convert people with argument and demonstration" (102).[17] Only three other Athenian forensic speeches use the superlative *kalliston* (the noblest) so frequently and two of these were given in the months following Lycurgus' speech. And Lycurgus' use of the verb *mimeomai* for "imitate" is another Platonic touch.[18]

These examples from Aeschines and Lycurgus of the use of Aristotelian vocabulary on the one hand and Platonic vocabulary on the other are representative. A major difference distinguishes how the Athenian politicians drew on each philosopher. The orators adopted the term *prohairesis* (deliberated commitment) without adopting its accompanying conceptual apparatus, while the opposite was true for the term *kolazein* (to reform). Plato had found ways of elaborating his concepts through sets of connected metaphors. As the orators adopted his concepts and vocabulary, they adopted a system. They don't get the Platonic system exactly right, but they do try to redeploy his concepts systematically. Aristotle, in contrast, did not, as far as the extant record allows us to judge, actively seek to build a coherent metaphorical system through which to convey his concepts. In his case the orators took only those elements of his ideas which were encapsulated, albeit accidentally, in metaphors, leaving behind the rest.[19]

In other words, the Aristotelian concept is plucked from its context, adopted by the orators, and used idiosyncratically by each as a useful *idea*. In contrast, those orators who used Platonic concepts adopted and deployed a metaphorically linked system of concepts; they had adopted an *ideology*.

And, indeed, in the case of *prohairesis* (deliberated commitment) all the orators used this new word, regardless of the position they took on any given political issue or even on the most controversial matter of the day: how to handle the rise of Macedonian power in the north, where Philip, King of Macedon, had begun building up a substantial empire. In contrast, only some orators used a Platonic conceptual apparatus, and those who did, with one exception, shared a recognizable policy outlook on Macedon. What was that shared policy outlook?

A century ago scholars were prone to distinguish between pro- and anti-Macedonian parties in Athens, that is, between parties that wanted to make peace with or to fight Philip, King of Macedon. But as many scholars have more recently pointed out neither the language of "parties," which brings with it the connotations of modern forms of political organization, nor the stark contrast between "pro-" and "anti-" Macedonian views can do justice to Athenian politics in the later fourth century.[20]

Since all major Athenian politicians defended Athens' freedom from Macedon and asserted Athens' equality to this rival power, all were in effect "anti-Macedonian."[21] Recognition of this fact has more recently led scholars to argue that personal networks, instead of policy or ideological differences, were the main driver of Athenian politics.[22] But this also overstates the case. While politicians did work with political allies to advance distinct policy positions, and while there was consistency over time in some of these alliances, there was also a fair amount of fluidity in the relations among Athenian politicians. A particularly dramatic example of this is the 323 BCE prosecution of Demosthenes for bribery by his former ally Hyperides.

Pragmatic policy differences, ideological differences, and social networks were all important to Athenian politics in the later fourth century; the difficulty of tracking camps of opinion in Athens flows from the fact that different issues could prompt different sorts of alignments and antagonisms at different points in time. At crisis moments, particularly, one can identify distinct political camps, but between one crisis and the next there was likely to be some evolution in political affiliations.[23] How then should we talk about the diverse policy camps that arose in response to rising Macedonian power?

At the end of the fifth century, Athens had been brought to its knees by defeat in the Peloponnesian War, but after the restoration of the democracy in 403 BCE, the city managed an impressive recovery, rebuilding its wealth and dominance in the Greek world. From 403 to the mid-350s, Athens struggled variously with Thebes and Sparta (despite being allied with each at different times) for the hegemonic position in Greece. But from 357 to 355 BCE, the Athenians also found themselves fighting their own allies in the Second Naval League, who had begun to chafe under the city's leadership and launched the "Social War" against them.[24] While Athens was fighting the Social War, Philip II (382–336 BCE), who had acceded to the Macedonian throne upon his brother's death in 359 BCE, was building up his own power in the north.[25] He moved quickly and aggressively to consolidate a regional power base, and soon enough Athenian interests, which extended to Byzantium and the Black Sea region, were affected by the growth of his kingdom. By 357 BCE Athens found itself at war with Philip over Amphipolis, a city in the north Aegean that was critical to protecting Athenian grain trade routes from the Black Sea region.

Macedonia and its dependent territories at the death of Philip II

150 miles

150 km

The Athenians were slow to recognize Philip fully as the threat that he was.[26] But by the 340s Athenian politics turned fundamentally around the questions, initially, of whether to make peace with Philip (and on what terms) and then, later, on whether to maintain peace or vary the terms or to return to war to resist the further growth of his power. All Athenian politicians sought to defend Athens against Macedonian aggression and also to maintain Athenian pre-eminence among the Greek city-states, but they differed at key junctures over whether this could be done with Philip or only by standing against him.[27]

In 346 BCE, the Athenians signed a treaty with Philip, the Peace of Philocrates. This proved dissatisfactory in various ways, and in 343 BCE, Philip sent an ambassador to Athens to propose amending the treaty. This amendment would have entailed converting the treaty between Athens and

Macedon into a collective security pact incorporating a multitude of Greek city states. The Athenians sent back a strange response. They were interested but only if Philip would return Amphipolis, the city that he had taken in 357 BCE and which he had made abundantly clear he would not be returning to its independent status.

Scholars have often viewed this Athenian response as a deliberate provocation intended to lead to the dissolution of the treaty and a return to warfare.[28] This seems right, but another point should be made too. The response was also a way of testing a very specific policy question: with the proposal for a collective security agreement, did Philip seek to be the hegemonic power within the group, or did he imagine that Athens would be sharing in leadership with him on equal terms? His unwillingness to cede Amphipolis was evidence that his view of the collective security pact entailed the maintenance of a position for himself as hegemon within the group. In this episode one can see the shape of the political debate running in Athens.

The question was mainly this: was it possible to cooperate with Philip on equal terms or did any cooperation necessarily entail, if not explicit then at least implicit, subordination? Those who believed the former sought to preserve Athens' pre-eminence within Greece through cooperation and collective security structures that included Philip; those who believed the latter sought to preserve Athens' pre-eminence through alliances that excluded Philip and were formed for the purpose of fighting him. We might therefore say that there was a group that pursued an Atheno-Macedonian collective security agreement and another group which, thinking such an agreement impossible, pursued various multilateral alliances and, ultimately, war against Macedon. Both groups were anti-Macedonian in the sense that each intended to defend Athens from Macedon. Neither group was pro-Macedonian insofar as both groups understood themselves to be pursuing Athenian pre-eminence within the Greek world.

Now, as I mentioned above, all but one of the orators who drew on Platonic vocabulary shared a particular policy outlook on Macedon. The list of orators who used Platonic vocabulary includes the orator who was the strongest advocate of an Atheno-Macedonian collective security agreement in the 340s, namely, Aeschines, and also those who were the strongest advocates of that position after the devastating military loss to Philip at the Battle of Chaeronea in 338 BCE, Lycurgus and Demades. In contrast, the fiercest advocate of independent multilateralism and war, Demosthenes, is not on the list.

Did the adoption of Platonic ideas bring with it, then, a preference for greater cooperation with Philip, a desire to be more rather than less trusting of him? It seems to have done so – for the most part. But there is an exception. Like Demosthenes, Hyperides consistently advocated direct offensive resistance of Philip, but his speeches betray Platonic lessons. The ideological framework adopted by those orators who worked through Platonic concepts did not in itself strictly determine their foreign policy orientation. The choice to use Platonic vocabulary must have represented a position taken on a cluster of issues independent of the Macedonian question. But what were they? We will have to broaden our understanding of fourth-century Athenian politics beyond the Macedonian question in order to understand Plato's influence. While the speeches that show traces of Platonic influence track the cleavages in the foreign policy debate to some extent, they more directly offer a fascinating glimpse of an intense culture war on the home front. At the same time that the Athenians were hotly debating whether to pursue an Atheno-Macedonian collective security pact or independent multilateralism aimed at war, they were also debating fundamental questions about their domestic political culture. And one side was fighting on Platonic turf.

Scholars have long seen in fourth-century Athens a battle over the meaning of *paideia*, a word typically translated as "culture" but also meaning "education" and "human development."[29] The protagonists were the city's leading intellectuals, the teachers of rhetoric and philosophy, and, in particular, Plato, Isocrates, and Aristotle.[30] Ordinary Athenians called all these men "sophists." But the argument among these "sophists" over how best to teach virtue, rhetoric, and political leadership was largely conducted on a plane that did not engage ordinary Athenians. The opposite was true for the oratorical debates and controversies that made use of Platonic and Aristotelian vocabulary, as in the examples above.

In the battles among Lycurgus, Aeschines, Demosthenes, and others, the orators crafted public accounts of civic virtues, intended for adoption by the mass of citizens, and the citizens, in voting for one or another orator's position, ratified, for the moment at least, that man's view of how best to describe Athenian ideals, institutions, and practices. When votes were close, as in the case of Lycurgus' *Against Leocrates* where the vote tied, the argument between the orators was equally an argument among citizens. The battles among "the sophists" as to whose school was most worth attending could run on indefinitely without impacting Athenian politics. But when the city's leading orators drew on philosophy to formulate novel accounts of Athenian cultural ideals, offered these as arguments to frame judicial deliberation and policy-making, and (as we shall see) met resistance from other orators on just the points of their innovations in cultural ideals, then battle was joined over intellectual matters on the very ground where the city's culture was formed. At moments such as this, questions of academic philosophy became also the basis of "culture war."

In identifying a "culture war," then, in later fourth-century Athens, I am pinpointing a moment in Athenian history when coherent alternative conceptual visions gained argumentative traction at the core of Athenian politics. In the case of the particular "culture war" that I have identified, those coherent alternative conceptual visions derived from philosophy, and particularly from Plato along with some significant contributions from Aristotle. As for Isocrates, although his writings plainly indicate a desire to inspire cultural change in Athens, his vocabulary and conceptual schema do not seem to have gained traction within oratorical discourse to the same degree as those of Plato and Aristotle.[31] The culture war I identify here was, in short, inflected mainly in a Platonic direction. To understand, in full, the case for his influence on Athenian politics, we need to turn to the content of this war.

7.3 A Culture War

This Platonically inflected culture war bursts forth most visibly in 330 BCE.

That is the year in which Lycurgus gave his major speech, *Against Leocrates*, which as we have seen is the extant Athenian speech most deeply marked by Platonic vocabulary. Two other great speeches were also given later that same year: Aeschines' *Against Ctesiphon* and Demosthenes' *On the Crown*. In *Against Ctesiphon* Aeschines prosecutes the citizen who in 336 had successfully moved a decree in the Athenian Assembly that the politician Demosthenes be awarded with a crown to honor him for his service to the city. *On the Crown* is Demosthenes' response to Aeschines' prosecution of Ctesiphon; he defends Ctesiphon by offering a comprehensive justification of his own role as a political leader in Athens in order to prove that he deserved the crown. These three speeches constitute a rhetorical group. Not only were they given in the same year; they also share some important stylistic anomalies.[32]

First, all three speeches give a central place to philosophical vocabulary. We have seen how that is so with Lycurgus. As to the other two, Demosthenes, for instance, defends his policy of resistance toward Philip II of Macedon in the following terms:

> My *prohairesis* [or "deliberated commitment"] not only saved the Chersonese and Byzantium in preventing the subjugation of the Hellespont to Philip and in bringing distinction to the city, but exhibited to all mankind [*pasin edeixen anthrôpois*] the noble goodness [*kalokagathia*] of Athens and the baseness [*kakia*] of Philip ... You [Athenians] appeared as the deliverers [e.g. of the Chersonese] from which you took renown, and the goodwill of the whole world [*ex hôn doxan, eunoian para pantôn ektasthe*]. Moreover, all know that you have awarded crowns to many politicians; but no one can name any man – I mean any statesman or orator – except me, by whose exertions the city itself has been crowned. (18.93)[33]

And from Aeschines we hear that, as regards the good politician, "it is well that his intelligence orients his *prohairesis* towards the best course" (*tên men dianoian proaireisthai ta beltista*) (3.170), and he accuses one of Demosthenes' allies of orienting his *prohairesis* toward the establishment of tyranny (*exaireton d' hautôi turannida peripoioumenos... kai toutôn tôn proaireseôn oudemias apetuche Kallias*: 3.89–92). Simultaneously he accuses Demosthenes of being himself only a fake tyrant-hater (*misoturannos*) (3.92).

In passages such as these, Demosthenes and Aeschines use the term *prohairesis* (deliberated commitment) to present incompatible, alternative political frameworks. The term *prohairesis* has come to provide the Athenians with a framework for talking about ideology. But what is the content of the alternative frameworks under debate? As we shall see, the Athenians are using this Aristotelian term to try to come to grips with the influence of Plato.

In describing Lycurgus' Platonism above, I mentioned his frequent use of the Platonic superlative *to kalliston* (noblest, or most beautiful). Only three other speeches use this term as frequently, and two were precisely the two speeches that followed Lycurgus' later in 330 BCE: *Against Ctesiphon* and *On the Crown*. Similarly, just as Lycurgus' speech spends more time quoting other texts than any other speech in the corpus, again, the runners-up on this count are *Against Ctesiphon* and *On the Crown*.[34] In 330 BCE, these three orators were fighting over the basic content and style of Athenian politics. These stylistic details are our first clue that these speeches represent a battle within a culture war.

The fight was, of course, not over style merely; more broadly, it concerned *paideia*, or how to define the appropriate cultural education for an Athenian citizen. Although that fight directly concerned philosophy, the argument about philosophy is conducted in terms so exaggerated that scholars have wrongly ignored it as mere rhetoric. Consider the conclusion of Aeschines' speech:

> Be my witnesses, O Earth and Sun and Virtue [*aretê*] and Intelligence [*sunesis*] and *Paideia* [education], by which we distinguish the noble and the shameful, I have offered my assistance and have spoken! [*egô men oun, ô gê kai hêlie kai aretê kai sunesis kai paideia, hêi diagignôskomen ta kala kai ta aischra, beboêthêka kai eirêka*] ... It remains for you yourselves [jurors] in view both of what has been spoken and of what has been left unsaid to vote on behalf of the city for what is just and beneficial. (3.260)[35]

Other than Lycurgus' own peroration, this is the most flamboyant extant conclusion to a courtroom speech. Where is the collective invocation of the gods, *ô theoi!*, which a speaker usually uses in closing? No other orator invokes the "sun" as a god.[36] As we read this passage, we can't help but think of the controversy surrounding Socrates' religious beliefs. In the *Apology* he affirms his piety by asserting his worship of the sun and moon (26b–d), but these were relatively minor gods within Athenian cult practice.[37] And, when Aeschines argues in this closing that *paideia* (education) teaches us to "diagnose" or "distinguish" the noble and the shameful (*diagignôskomen ta kala kai ta aischra*), we cannot avoid hearing the lesson of the *Republic*'s Myth of Er that philosophy teaches students to "diagnose" or "distinguish" the good life from the bad (*bion chrêston kai ponêron diagignôskonta*) (618c).

In an indication that Aeschines' rhetoric is unusual, Demosthenes in his responding speech calls out precisely this language for special attack: "It's as if he's shouting out in a tragedy, responding: 'Oh, Earth! Oh Sun! O Virtue!' and those sorts of things, and again there is his appeal to 'Intelligence and Education' [*sunesis* and *paideia*] by which we distinguish between the noble and the shameful." And then Demosthenes continues:

> Virtue! You piece of rubbish [*katharma*], what part of that belongs to you or your family? How do you distinguish between the noble and the shameful [*hêi ta kala kai ta aischra diagignôsketai*]? Where and how did you qualify to talk about this? Where did you get the right to talk about education [*paideia*]? No really educated man would use such language about himself, but would rather blush to hear it from others; but people like you, who make stupid pretensions to a culture of which they are utterly destitute, succeed in disgusting everybody whenever they open their lips, but never in making the impressions they desire. (18.127–128)[38]

This *ad hominem* attack actually has a deep point and is part of an extended argument about the role of culture and education in Athenian life. What case is each politician making?

Demosthenes, Aeschines says, has no proper education. He has no hunting comrades, for instance, and none from the gymnasium. He has been too busy chasing down men of property as targets of his prosecutions (3.255). The implication is that, lacking proper education, Demosthenes cannot possibly distinguish the noble from the shameful and therefore will fail to develop effective and morally correct policy.[39]

Against such an approach, Aeschines seeks to establish an ideal of a city led by highly educated elite politicians who lead quiet and cultured lives of leisure and who intervene in politics at key moments but do not undertake a professional political career, as Demosthenes has done. At two separate points in his speech, Aeschines describes the founder of Athenian democracy, Solon, as a philosopher and law-giver: *ho philosophos kai nomothetês*; he says he is an expert at philosophy (*philosophia*).[40] But the words *philosophos* (philosopher) and *philosophia* (philosophy) did not exist in Solon's day. For that matter, Herodotus called Solon a *sophistês* or "wise man," and Plato was the first writer to use the term *philosophia* extensively.[41] Aeschines therefore anachronistically retrojects these novel terms to a period when they did not apply.

Moreover, Aeschines' unusual emphasis on the term *nomothetês* (lawgiver) to identify a single and original founding legislator for Athens is another Platonism.[42] At the end of the fifth century, the Athenians had established a board of 500 *nomothetai* who were responsible for reviewing Athenian laws for consistency.[43] They are always referred to in the plural and their task was to review the acts of the assembly; they were not conceived by the Athenians as an original source of political authority.[44]

By turning Solon into a *philosophos kai nomothetês*, Aeschines turns him into a Platonic philosopher-legislator. Similarly, Aeschines repeatedly uses the phrase "political virtue" (*politikê aretê*) (e.g. 3.232) and calls the citizens guardians of democracy (*phulakes tês dêmokratias* e.g. 3.7, 3.250); such formulations are uncommon in Athenian rhetoric but plainly Platonic.[45] Aeschines' picture of Athenian political history thus receives a patina of Platonism, but the Platonic influence goes deeper too.

As Aeschines offers a defense of the quietness (*hêsuchia*) of his own life, he redefines the key Athenian figure, *ho boulomenos*, a phrase which means "whoever wishes to," and was used by the Athenians to designate private citizens who took it upon themselves to prosecute legal cases of public significance or to speak in the assembly:

> As to my silence, Demosthenes, it has been caused by the moderation of my life [*hê tou biou metriotês*]. And you blame me if I come before the people not constantly but only at intervals. And you imagine that your hearers fail to detect you in thus making a demand which is no outgrowth of democracy, but borrowed from another form of government. For in oligarchies, it is not he who wishes, but he who is in authority, that addresses the people; while in democracies he speaks who chooses, and whenever it seems to him good. And the fact that a man speaks only at intervals marks him as a man who takes part in politics because of the call of the hour [*kairoi*] and for the common good; whereas to leave no day without its speech, is the mark of a man who is making a trade of it and talking for pay. (3.218–220)[46]

Aeschines further desires a return to the day when citizens in the assembly were invited to speak by age-cohort, with the eldest speaking first; this is the Solonian law he particularly admires.

And what would make it possible for the city to operate on the basis of the model of aristocratically well-educated but part-time leadership? Above all, it would require a commitment to the idea that the laws take precedence above the judgment of citizens so that distinguished magistrates might establish a stable basis for public action, which they would then continue to supervise after they had retired from their magistracies to a supervisory council.

Athens had such a council of distinguished retired magistrates, called the Areopagus. Aeschylus provides a mythological account of the origins of this court in his *Eumenides* when Athena establishes it to vote on whether Orestes is guilty of murder for killing his mother. The court seems to have maintained its aristocratic ethos even after Athens began, in 487 BCE, to choose its top magistrates (the Archons) by lot.[47] By the mid-fifth century, however, it had been stripped of whatever supervisory role it may have had. But during Aeschines' day, its powers were once again expanding, and he endorsed this expansion (Aes. 3.252–253). He also makes the fullest argument extant in oratory on behalf of a rule of law-based approach to politics (1.4–10, 1.178–181, 3.6–7). By arguing against the traditional Athenian approach that prioritized judgment above the law, Aeschines set elite magistrates above the mass of citizen jurors.[48] These elements form the core of his political philosophy.

Although Aeschines does not introduce the figure of Solon as a philosopher and lawgiver (*ho philosophos kai nomothetês*) until the end of his speech, Demosthenes starts his own speech right there, by immediately contesting Aeschines' tendentious picture of the democracy's founding father. In his introduction, Demosthenes says:

> I implore you all alike to listen to my defense against the accusations laid, in a spirit of justice. So the laws enjoin – the laws which Solon, who first framed them, a democratic man and well-disposed to you, the people [*eunous ôn humin kai dêmotikos*] thought it right to validate not only by their enactment [*grapsai*] but by jurors' oath. (18.6)

The opposition is as bald as can be. Aeschines had used new-fangled jargon to talk about a founding father. Demosthenes uses the traditional terms of Athenian democratic practice. In his formulation, Solon, the leading politician, is simply one citizen among many, bound to the others by *eunoia* or good-will, who as a leader employs the traditional institutional tools of written law – where the word is the older *graphein* instead of the falsely archaizing *nomothetein* – and accepts juries and popular judgment, as the city's definitive authority.[49]

That Aeschines' unconventional views are theorized, not facile, is clear from his own presentation. In his speech, he produces mini-lectures after the style of Plato and Aristotle. For instance, right at the start of his speech, he says: "There are, as you know, fellow-citizens, three forms of government in the world: tyranny, oligarchy, and democracy. Tyrannies and oligarchies are administered according to the tempers of their lords but democratic states according to their own established laws" (3.6).[50]

And he attacks the idea that Demosthenes is a "democratic man" or "friend of the people," that is, a *dêmotikos*, using methods that recall the technique of comparative modeling that Socrates advocates in the *Republic* and which the *Seventh Letter* also recommends. Aeschines argues:

> If you look to nature and the truth [*eis tên phusin kai tên alêtheian*], you will not be deceived. Call him to account in this way: with your help, I will reckon up [*logioumai*] what ought in nature [*en têi phusei*] to inhere in the demo-cratic man and the moderate man [*tôi dêmotikôi andri kai sôphroni*], and against them I will set down what sort of person you would expect the oligarchic and base man to be. And you, setting each of these against each other [*antithentes hekatera toutôn*], reflect upon [*theôrêsat'*] Demosthenes, whether he is one or the other not in speech [*logos*] but in his way of life [*tou biou*]. (3.168)

In the Platonic style, Aeschines presents types or *tupoi* and asks that his audience set those theoretical images against each other in order that the truth might emerge from the oppositional process.

In response to Aeschines' studied performance, Demosthenes asks: "Why do you draw word-pictures?" The Greek is: *ti logous platteis?* (18.121). This jibe tips us off that Demosthenes' target is Platonic rhetoric, specifically, and not philosophy generally. As we saw (chapters 2–4) the verb *plattein* is central to the *Republic*'s arguments about good philosophical writing. Plato used the verb *plattein* far more frequently than any other Greek writer; and the word had come to be associated with him.[51] As one comic poet joked: *hôs aneplatte Platôn peplasmena thaumata eidôs.*[52] This Greek joke turns on twice punning the verb *plattein* with Plato's name (*aneplatte, peplasmena*); the comic line also draws in two other Platonic terms (*thauma, eidôs*). We could approximate the puns and meaning of this joke with the translation: "Plato perceived marvelous models (or fabulous Forms) and plastered them on paper." The Athenians knew that the word *plattein* went with the name Plato, so Demosthenes' question – *Ti logous platteis?* – might equally well mean, "Why do you talk like Plato?"

Immediately after having connected Aeschines' and Plato's rhetorical styles with his joke "*ti logous platteis?*" Demosthenes wonders out loud: "Why don't you [Aeschines] give yourself hellebore for your complaints?" (18.121). Since Aeschines is the only Attic orator ever to mention Socrates and his death (in *Against Timarchus*, 1.173, though to remind the jury that Socrates had schooled Critias), it seems just possible that Demosthenes, in recommending that Aeschines try hellebore, a drug which was used both medicinally for headaches but also for suicide, is either mocking his intellec-tualism or meanly recommending philosophical suicide to him. Whatever the case, the important point is that Demosthenes is throughout this passage clearly drawing from a cultural well of jokes about philosophers generally and, better, about Plato specifically; this is a good indication that knowledge about Plato's philosophy had spread well beyond a narrow elite.

But Demosthenes' argument is not just crude irony; there is philosophical specificity to his barbs. Take this further example of his criticism of Aeschines' style:

> Behaving in this fashion, you tell us how many features it is necessary to see inhere in the "democratic man" [ho dêmotikos] as if you had ordered a statue according to specification [hôsper andriant' ekdedôkôs kata suggraphên] and then you had received it and it did not have all the features belonging as per the order. As though men were judged "democratic men" in logos but not in deeds and policy! (18.122)[53]

Demosthenes is pointedly mocking just the techniques of enargeia, the methods for producing images, symbols, models, and allegories, that Plato elaborates in the Republic. Plutarch is the Platonist who will eventually make the most of Plato's recommendation of comparative modeling as a method of political thinking, but Aeschines, in drawing up "types" of man is grasping toward that too.[54] Demosthenes can see what Aeschines is doing; his remarks reveal that he too has a sophisticated understanding of Plato's philosophy of rhetoric and its relation to politics, and that he presumes that the Athenian audience does as well. Or at least that they understand well enough to get his jokes.

We can, in other words, see the distinct outlines of an ideological struggle in these speeches where one side of the struggle clearly drew on Platonic philosophy. This is to say neither that Aeschines was a Platonist nor that his own politics straightforwardly mirror Plato's arguments, but only that we can see Platonic traces on both his ideals and his rhetorical style.[55]

How politically important were those traces? The pitch of the rivalry between Aeschines and Demosthenes in itself tells us how great were the stakes of the fight over whether Platonically influenced politicians would succeed in securing leadership of the city. But Aeschines and Demosthenes also self-consciously assessed the seriousness of their dispute. In referring back during the debate to their previous judicial battle of 345–343 BCE (represented by the speeches Against Timarchus, On the Embassy, and On the False Embassy),[56] Aeschines says that in that earlier conflict, Demosthenes had accused him of working with others to seek a revolution. The Greek is: epi aitiais agenêtois, hôs emou meta tinôn neôterizein boulomenou (3.225). The word for "revolution" is neôterizein, to make things new; it's Thucydides' basic word for describing revolutions brought about through violent civil war.[57] The point of using such a word against a politician is to indicate that he seeks internal change. To accuse Aeschines of seeking revolution is not to say only that he is a Philippizer nor merely that he advocates an Atheno-Macedonian security pact. It is to say that his domestic agenda is revolutionary. There were issues in Athenian politics between 346 and 330 BCE that were separable (though, as we shall see, not always separated) from the question of Macedon.

Aeschines must here be repeating Demosthenes' actual charge; it is difficult to believe that he would introduce such a loaded word, directed against himself, into his own speech, unless he faced precisely the rhetorical challenge of defusing a word known to be in use about him. The use of the term *neôterizein* by Aeschines and also, we can presume, by Demosthenes therefore allows us to see how great was the impact of Platonic philosophy on Athenian politics. Demosthenes, at least, experienced the role of philosophy in politics as revolutionary and he acted on his subjective experience to resist this potentially revolutionary force as a matter of policy. But others must have agreed. Demosthenes won the case against Aeschines resoundingly, and Aeschines afterward left the city for exile. He went to Rhodes where he lived for the rest of his life as a teacher of rhetoric, which is to say, as a sophist.[58]

* * *

Given why and what Plato wrote, what effect did he have on Athenian politics? What, in short, did he do? Now we can see: he helped launch a culture war. The identification of Lycurgus' *Against Leocrates*, Aeschines' *Against Ctesiphon*, and Demosthenes' *On the Crown* – each a major speech, all given in 330 BCE – as major moves in that war goes a long way to explaining the rhetorically distinctive features of these three speeches: for instance, the Platonic vocabulary and forms of argumentation in Lycurgus' and Aeschines' speeches; the arguments about what is *to kalliston*; the unusual amount of quotation; and Demosthenes' mockery of philosophically influenced rhetorical styles.

In short, the effects of Plato's rhetorical methods were like those he predicts for the noble lie, which should be constructed so as to implant a whole set of related concepts and cultural meanings in those who come to believe it. Where his influence shows up, it shows up in sets of concepts. This difference, then, between Plato's and Aristotle's influence provides at least initial support for Plato's claim about the surplus linguistic power and pragmatic efficacy of language with *enargeia* or vividness. At the very least, the difference in the uptake of the two vocabularies does not falsify Plato's hypotheses.

But how much impact did the uptake of these Platonic concepts have on Athenian politics? As I said above, the sorts of issues that were introduced to Athenian political discourse in Platonic vocabulary by speakers like

Aeschines were separable from what scholars have always taken to be the defining issue of the period: the Macedonian question. Yet separable as these issues were, they were not always separated from one another. To understand their intersection, we will need a clearer account of the domestic debates in Athens. This is the project of the next chapter.

8

Culture War Emergent

8.1 Introduction

Plato wrote to affect politics, and Athenian politics specifically. His dialogues function as, and are full of, "paradigms," or conceptually rigorous symbols meant to help readers to right opinions that will affect their actions and so the politics that flows from them. His dialogues also function as "noble lies." They are meant to populate citizens' imaginations with pragmatically efficacious conceptual icons.

As we have seen in the last chapter, several of his core concepts – for instance, "reformative punishment" and the founding "philosopher-legislator" – were adopted by Athenian orators, as were key elements of his symbol-making methodology, particularly the comparison of "types of man." Unsurprisingly, these adoptions of Platonic concepts, symbols, and rhetorical techniques were controversial; this is indicated at least by the agonistic intensity of the three major speeches of 330 BCE – *Against Leocrates*, *Against Ctesiphon*, and *On the Crown*.

Yet despite the prominence of the cultural issue in these three speeches, the Macedonian issue is in fact no less salient. In these speeches, the debate about policy toward Macedon merges with disputes over the value of Platonic philosophy and *paideia*. To see why this is so we must, in this chapter and the next, address three questions: (1) When and how did the culture war emerge? (2) Why does the culture war reach its highest pitch in 330 BCE? (3) When and how does the culture war end?

We will see that the culture war and the Macedonian question were entangled from the start. This entanglement was not a philosophical necessity but the product of politics.

Why Plato Wrote   Danielle S. Allen. © 2010 Danielle S. Allen

8.2 The Politics of the 350s and 340s

The story of the emergence of the culture war has its origins in the politics of the 350s and 340s. After the conclusion of the very draining Social War in 355 BCE, the landscape of Athenian politics began to shift. In the 350s and early 340s it came to settle around three major issues: in addition to the question of what to make of Philip of Macedon, who was building a new power base to the north, there were the questions of how to reform Athenian institutions to reverse perceived cultural degeneration, and what to think of the conversion of democracies to oligarchies in the broader Hellenic world.

By the 350s politicians from different camps were united in the views that the Athenian citizenry had become corrupt and that re-establishing the Athenian spirit of an earlier day was imperative.[1] The effort to do so led to severe battles over Athenian political institutions, which would characterize Athenian politics for the next two decades. The battles concerned public finance, military organization, the nature of the Court of the Areopagus, and regulation of the speaker's platform in the assembly.

In the middle of the fifth century, Pericles had established pay for jury service and may also have established funds to provide poor citizens with admission fees for public festivals, for instance the annual productions of the tragedies. If the fund supporting attendance at public festivals was not initiated in the fifth century, then it was established in the mid-350s by Eubulus, a leading politician, then in his fifties. Even if Eubulus did not in fact establish this fund, he at least gets credit for having named it the "Theoric" or "Spectatorship" Fund.[2] Eubulus also proposed and secured passage of a law directing that the city's annual budget surplus flow into the Theoric Fund.[3] As Athens rebuilt its economy after the Social War, the Theoric Fund controlled increasingly significant resources. Some of these funds was directed to pay-outs to the citizens, but the greater portion was used for public works projects: dockyards, arsenals, roads, and waterworks.

As part of Eubulus' legislation, the city also established a new office, the Theoric commissioner, who oversaw the fund's use. This was an elected office, like the generalship, and so a meaningful move away from the democratic procedure of allotment.[4] There may have been only a single Theoric commissioner each year or a board of ten may have served. Whatever the case, those who served as Theoric commissioners had significant power. As Aeschines put it, "they carried out almost the whole financial administration of the city" (3.25). Eubulus' pre-eminence derived from his financial management, and he is generally presumed to have been the first Theoric commissioner. His goal in directing the annual surplus to this fund seems to have been to ensure the prioritization of public works projects over frivolous military expeditions. Five years later, a thirty-something Demosthenes sought to undo his elder's law precisely in order to direct more resources to military action.[5] He wanted budget surpluses directed to the Stratiotic or Military Fund. Demosthenes failed but his effort indicates the alternative policy position.

Although Demosthenes supported increased military funding, he did not think that business should simply continue as usual for Athens' military. In his view, the Athenians now relied too much on mercenaries. He sought funding for a military in which every citizen would serve. He argued that the Athenians needed to "make up their minds to embark and sail themselves"; that at least a quarter of every fighting force should consist of citizens; that all commanders should be citizens; and that even old men should be sent to war as citizen-overseers of mercenary troops.[6] All citizens should be paid for such service, and then the surplus funds could simultaneously support both the military and the city's lower socio-economic orders. A further advantage of sending everyone to war, Demosthenes argued, would be that, when Athenian generals were put on trial in Athenian courts, the juries would include citizens who had served in the relevant campaign; they would therefore be eye-witnesses to the events under dispute. Moreover, if the city's surplus were used to support the military more systematically, then the whole city would bear the burden of funding Athens' military might; the duty would not fall solely on a class of wealthy citizens funding this or that particular expedition.[7]

In 354 BCE, making his first speech to the Athenian assembly at the age of roughly thirty, Demosthenes proposed reform to the naval organization; in 351 BCE, he proposed reform to the infantry and cavalry. He continued through the 340s to reiterate these proposals and his ideals were consistent.[8] He sought, he said, to overturn Athenian sluggishness and idleness (bradutês kai rhaithumia) (4.8), arguing, as for instance in 349 BCE, that "all should contribute equitably, each according to his means, all should serve in turn until all have taken part in the campaign" (2.31).[9] There was resistance to Demosthenes' ideas; his naval reforms, for instance, were adopted only fourteen years later.[10] But he developed a recognizable policy position in opposition to Eubulus (under whose wing he had begun his public career).

The two men, in some sense, represented the poles of opinion within the Athenian political landscape, and each man had allies in pursuing these policies, even if these alliances shifted over time.[11] Eubulus spearheaded a policy position that focused on rebuilding Athens' strength internally, on increasing trade, on beautifying the city, and on boosting employment through public works. Demosthenes mocked Eubulus' building program (13.30; 3.21–9) and, in contrast, seems to have argued that all available funds should be directed toward military action and particularly the effort to secure or reclaim Athens' traditional and far-flung imperial assets.[12]

The third area of institutional reform relevant to understanding mid-century Athenian politics involved the Court of the Areopagus. We caught a glimpse of this issue already in chapter 7 in Aeschines' endorsement of that court's expanded authority. In the mid-fourth century, as Athenian politicians sought to reverse Athenian corruption, they all looked to the Areopagus for help. Not only Eubulus, and his allies Aeschines and Lycurgus, but Demosthenes too, argued for enhanced powers for the Areopagus. They differed, though, on the question of how far those powers should go.

Sometime between the mid-350s and mid-340s, Demosthenes proposed and secured passage of a law that renewed the powers of the Areopagus to investigate wrong-doing. They were not authorized to go beyond investigation other than to impose minor fines (below the level of 50 drachmae); instead, they were charged with handing wrong-doers over to the democratic assembly or to the Council (the agenda-setting body for the assembly) for prosecution and punishment. Demosthenes' reform was significant: it established the previously non-existent role of a standing public investigator within the Athenian judicial system.[13]

For Lycurgus and Aeschines, however, he had not gone far enough. In the years that followed Demosthenes' reforms, the Areopagus periodically exceeded the Demosthenic limits on its powers, even punishing some of the targets of its investigations with death on its own authority, without turning the defendants over to the courts.[14] Another law (the Law of Eucrates on tyranny) was passed in 336 BCE that was specifically directed against the possibility that Areopagites might overreach their authority.[15] The worry was that the Areopagites might in fact concert to overthrow the democracy. Notably, even after the Athenians specifically sought to control the Areopagus with this law, both Lycurgus and Aeschines continued to defend the Areopagus' development of power not only to investigate and indict but also to judge and execute (Lyc. 1.52., cf. 1.12; Aes. 3.252–253). Lycurgus' endorsement of the Areopagus' extended authority, made in a courtroom speech, provoked a dissenting outcry from his audience (Lyc. 1.52).

All the city's leading politicians, even Demosthenes, were, in other words, willing to develop some element of elite or expert power in the city (since Areopagites served for life), but they diverged on how much power should be transferred into expert hands and how much retained for popular institutions. On this issue, we can see clearly that Demosthenes, who defended limits on the power of the Areopagus, sought the more egalitarian of the two policy alternatives. In contrast, by endorsing the role of the Areopagus as a court of no appeal, empowered to execute, Lycurgus and Aeschines were nudging the Athenian constitution in a managerial direction.[16]

A similar difference of opinion emerged regarding the issue of regulating the speaker's platform in the democratic assembly. In 347 or 346 BCE an ally of Aeschines passed a law establishing that whichever of the city's ten tribes was responsible for chairing the Council at the time of an assembly meeting would also be charged with presiding over the speaker's platform (1.33–34). This entailed regulating who spoke and in what order as well as monitoring speakers' decorum. Aeschines says that the Athenians came to see the need for this law when one of Demosthenes' allies, a man named Timarchus, put in a particularly outrageous performance on the speaker's platform sometime in 347 or 346 BCE.

The law seems to have been the culmination of a long controversy. In earlier times, the Athenians had had a tradition that in the assembly the herald invited speakers to the stage by age cohort, calling first for any of the oldest men who wished to speak. This ideal of generational order seems still to have had some sway. In 351 BCE, in his *First Philippic*, Demosthenes did not wait for older men to speak but himself opened the debate in the Assembly. His introductory remarks indicate self-consciousness about his controversial step:

> If the question before us were a new one, men of Athens, I should have waited until most of the regular speakers had delivered their opinions, and if satisfied with any of their proposals, I should have remained silent, but if not satisfied I should then have tried to express my own views. Since, however, it is our fortune to be still debating a point on which they have often spoken before, I can safely claim your forgiveness, if I am the first to rise and address you. (4.1)

And in 349 BCE he explicitly argues that just as everyone should take their turn serving in the military, so too should everyone have a turn addressing the assembly (2.31). Demosthenes seems to have thought that some features of how the assembly was run excessively restricted citizens' rights of speech. The law passed by Aeschines' ally must have been a response to the efforts of politicians such as Demosthenes and his allies to introduce new voices to the speaker's platform. As we shall see, this controversy over speaking privileges would recur in domestic political debate later in the 340s.

These four areas of institutional reform – financial organization, military organization, the role of the Areopagus, and the regulation of the speaker's platform – do not exhaust the reforms of the period, but they were fundamental. By 349 BCE Demosthenes clearly sees these four areas of institutional reform as coalescing into alternative visions for Athens' political culture. He enjoins the Athenians:

> You must once more be your own masters and you must give to all alike the same chance to speak, to counsel, to act. But if you authorize one class of men to issue orders like absolute monarchs [the Theoric commissioners?], and force another class [wealthy elites] to equip the galleys and pay the war-tax and serve in the field, while yet a third class [the poor] has no other public duty than to [serve on juries and] vote the condemnation of the latter, you will never get anything essential done at the right time ... To sum up, I propose that all should

contribute equitably, each according to his means, that all should serve in turn until all have taken part in the campaign; that all who wish to address you should have a fair hearing and you should choose [*hairesthai*] the best policy. (2.30–31)

We can grasp the conceptual significance of this Demosthenic passage by recalling the argument between Plato and Aristotle over the value of the utopian plan proposed in the *Republic*. Whereas Plato wished to see a city consisting of one class of people issuing orders, another class fighting, and a third serving only as traders, craftsmen, and farmers, Aristotle argued that all citizens should serve in the military and rule and be ruled in turn. In this passage, Demosthenes describes a similar pair of alternatives. This is not to suggest that in this passage he indicates that the philosophers have influenced politics. Not at all. His remark reveals that the orators' debates over policy were as philosophically meaningful as the philosophers' debates over the ideal polity. During the 350s and early 340s the orators understood themselves to be facing fundamental choices about what kind of city to build.

Running alongside these domestic issues was, of course, the Macedonian question. As we have seen, the Athenians were relatively slow to recognize Philip as a threat despite the fact that they had been fighting with him from 357 BCE onward. As late as 351 BCE they were still as much attuned to the threat of Persia as to that from enemies nearer home. In *On the Liberty of the Rhodians* from that year, Demosthenes chastises the Athenians for considering Philip "of no account" and "contemptible" (15.24). He tries to draw the Athenians' attention to the "barbarian culture" of Philip's court, characterized, he says, by flatterers, drunkenness, and weakness of will (*akrasia*) (2.17), and he points out that Philip seems to be developing new methods of warfare, including the use of agents as spies and rumor-mongers (*hoi de logous plattontes*) in the cities of his enemies (4.18, 4.50). Yet in 351 BCE Demosthenes, too, despite his effort to draw some attention to Philip, still considers the King of Persia an appropriate target of major foreign policy attention.[17]

Philip becomes the overriding object of that attention only in the early 340s. In 349/348 Eubulus sought to develop alliances to fight against him whereas Philocrates proposed sending a peace embassy to him. When Philocrates was prosecuted for this proposal, Demosthenes, who would later become Philip's staunchest Athenian adversary, defended him. The policy alternatives outlined in the last chapter – whether to pursue an Atheno-Macedonian collective security agreement or to fight Philip with the resources of an independent multilateralism – do not fully crystallize until after the subsequent effort to make peace, which comes in 346 BCE.

The final issue to emerge in the 350s, another foreign affairs matter, was the question of regime change. In fact, there were two policy questions here:

how to respond to a seeming pattern of democracies converting to oligarchies in notable Hellenic cities, and how Athens should generally make decisions about intervention. In the late 350s the Athenians regularly considered the question of whether to intervene when allied or friendly cities were threatened by other powers. Thus in 353 BCE Thebes threatened the city of Megalopolis. Demosthenes argued that the Athenians should support the Megalopolitans while Eubulus argued against intervention; the latter won that particular argument. In 351 BCE Philip threatened the city of Eretria on the island of Euboea; in this case Demosthenes argued against intervention and Eubulus argued for; again Eubulus won. Also in 351 BCE the King of Persia moved to assert control over the island of Rhodes, which involved transforming the Rhodian democracy into an oligarchy. In this case Demosthenes argued for intervention. Again, he lost. Eubulus and Demosthenes drew very different maps of where it made sense for Athens to intervene.

Although Demosthenes' proposals for intervention over the course of the 350s do not indicate a fully coherent policy stance, he moves toward and articulates one at the end of the decade. In his speech, *On the Liberty of the Rhodians*, he tries to convince his fellow citizens that in all the regional instability they should detect a pattern of democracies converting to oligarchies and argues that this is what they should, above all, fend off:

> Seeing that Chios and Mytilene are ruled by oligarchs and that Rhodes and I might almost say, all mankind, are now being seduced [*hupagomenón*] into this form of slavery, I am surprised that none of you conceives that our constitution too is in danger, nor draws the conclusion that if all other states are organized on oligarchical principles, it is impossible that they should leave our democracy alone. (15.19)

Was Demosthenes right about a shift from democracy to oligarchy? Most scholars think he overstated the case, but additional examples, beyond the cases he had already named, did accrue over the course of the 340s: Oreus, Eretria, Megara, Elis.[18]

In addition to calling on his fellow citizens to see what he saw – namely a shift to oligarchies in the Hellenic world, Demosthenes also argues that the Athenians should ideologize their foreign policy. The Athenians, he says, have as often fought democracies as oligarchies, but the motives for these struggles, properly understood, he argues, are altogether different.

> With democracies [your motives are] either private quarrels, or a question of territory, or boundaries or rivalry or the claim to leadership; with oligarchies you fight for none of these things but for constitutional politics [*politeia*] and freedom [*eleutheria*]; with free men you can make peace whenever you wish but with an oligarchical state I do not believe that even friendly relations could be

permanent; for the few can never be well disposed to the many nor those who covet power to those who have chosen a life of equal privileges. (15.17)

It is time, he argues, for the Athenians to cease fighting with, and to establish themselves instead as friends of, all democracies, and to concentrate their foreign policy on warding off the further emergence of oligarchical regimes.

Importantly, these debates in the 350s and early 340s – about how to reform Athenian institutions to reverse degeneration, what to make of Philip, and what to think of the conversion of democracies to oligarchies in the broader Hellenic world – were independent of one another; they ran concurrently without converging. By 345 BCE, however, they had come together, at least in Demosthenes' analysis of the political situation, and from 345 BCE onward Demosthenes consistently argued to the Athenians that the rise of oligarchy in the broader Greek world was not accidental but driven by Philip; that the sort of domestic institutional reforms that Demosthenes himself supported maintained democratic egalitarianism and power, while those of his rivals advanced the cause of oligarchy; that his opponents on matters of domestic politics were therefore best understood as agents of Philip, since the cause of oligarchy was Philip's cause; and that the preservation not only of Athens but also of democracy required resistance both to Philip himself and to his pro-oligarchical sympathizers wherever they might be, including at home in Athens.[19] Not only does Demosthenes bring about a convergence of these issues; he also ties them to the problem of Platonic influence in politics!

Whence this convergence? And what could possibly link it to Plato? The answers to these questions lie in Demosthenes' experience in 346 BCE of serving on an embassy sent by the Athenians to Philip's court in Pella to negotiate the peace treaty that resulted in the Peace of Philocrates. We come at last to the story of how the culture war emerged and came to be intertwined with questions of foreign policy.

8.3 The Emergence of the Culture War, or the Man with the Good Memory

In 346 BCE, after several years of directly engaging Philip in warfare, the Athenians learned that he was interested in peace, as were they. The Athenians sent ten Athenian ambassadors (and an eleventh non-Athenian ambassador) to Philip's court. This group included both Demosthenes and Aeschines, and these men brought back a peace proposal, which, after some complicated political shenanigans, the Athenians ratified. Athens then sent a second embassy to Philip, again including Demosthenes and Aeschines, to secure the oaths necessary for ratification.[20]

But something had gone badly wrong in the peace process. At the start of negotiations, Philip was menacing the region of Phocis, which was allied to Athens. The Athenians desired to see Philip protect the region not only for the sake of the Phocians but also for their own sake, with respect to their struggle against Thebes. Phocis was not, however, to be directly included in the treaty. Nonetheless, upon their return from their two trips to Pella, several of the ambassadors, including Aeschines, told the Athenians that Philip had promised to leave the Phocians alone and to humble Thebes. Instead, immediately after the treaties were signed, and to the great horror of the Athenians, Philip destroyed the many small village communities of Phocis (Paus. 10.3–1; Dem. 19.325). The author of the peace treaty, Philocrates, was soon accused of treason; he fled into exile and, tried *in absentia*, was sentenced to death (Aes. 2.6, 3.79). Then in 345 BCE Demosthenes similarly indicted his fellow ambassador, Aeschines, for treason on those embassies since Aeschines had been among those saying that Phocis would be safe.

What had gone wrong? We have three speeches extant from this major political battle between Demosthenes and Aeschines. In 345 BCE Aeschines prosecuted Demosthenes' ally, Timarchus, for having worked earlier as a male prostitute, a profession that should disqualify him from political participation. Since Timarchus was a co-prosecutor to Demosthenes in the prosecution of Aeschines for treason, the purpose of Aeschines' counterpunch was to remove one of his own opponents from the fray. In this Aeschines succeeded. Timarchus was convicted and stripped of his political rights, so Aeschines' own trial then took place in 343 BCE without Timarchus' involvement. From his 343 BCE trial, we have both Demosthenes' speech of prosecution (*On the False Embassy*) and Aeschines' defense (*On the Embassy*).

The central question raised by Demosthenes' prosecution was how the Athenians had come to be misled on the question of Phocis.[21] Had Aeschines and the others who had conveyed promises from Philip to protect Phocis been deluded? Were they idiots? Had they been led astray by an evil spirit? Had they been ill? Had they been lying? If so, did they lie because Philip had bribed them or because they had been ideologically seduced by him? As Demosthenes works his way through these questions, and as Aeschines responds to them, it becomes clear that something unusual happened on those journeys to Pella and back.

Indeed, it was on those embassies that Demosthenes appears to have come to see as one and the same the issues of elitist tendencies in institutional reform at home, of the increase in oligarchic regimes abroad, and of the growth in Philip's power. It was also on those embassies that he seems first to have identified a Platonic element in that alleged convergence between an elitist domestic policy and a pro-Philip foreign policy. What happened on the way to and from Pella?[22]

Demosthenes and Aeschines carried with them to Pella a rivalry that had been developing already at home. They carried, for instance, the domestic debate over the appropriate methods of organizing citizens' rights to speak at political meetings directly into arguments about the order in which the ten Athenian ambassadors would speak at Philip's court. On the first embassy, they decided, after debate, to speak in age order (Aes. 2.108), a blow to Demosthenes, the youngest ambassador. For the second embassy, at Demosthenes' instigation (according to Aeschines) the men abandoned the principle of age order, and Demosthenes led off the speech-making (2.108).[23] The appearance of the issue of speaking privileges not only in the assembly but also during an embassy indicates the permeability of a barrier that we might imagine to exist between domestic and foreign policy arenas. On these embassies, those arenas became one and the same. And the struggle was ideological: were the Athenians going to use the archaizing and aristocratic principle of age-order or a less hierarchical, more egalitarian method of assigning speaking privileges?

The issue of ideology comes out most pronouncedly, however, in an episode that Aeschines relates as occurring on the way back from the first trip to Pella. Aeschines tells the following remarkable tale, which I think of as the story of the man with the good memory. He relates:

> When we [ambassadors] set out on our return home after completing our [first] mission, suddenly Demosthenes began talking to each of us on the way in a surprisingly friendly manner ... [He said something to the effect that:] Philip was the most wonderful man under the sun. When I added my testimony, saying something like this, that Philip had shown excellent memory [*mnêmonikos*] in his reply to what we had said, and when Ctesiphon, who was the oldest of us, added that in all his many years, he had never looked upon so sweet and lovable a man, then Demosthenes, this Sisyphus, clapped his hands and said, "But Ctesiphon, it will never do for you to tell the people [the *dêmos*] that, nor would our friend here," meaning me [Aeschines], "venture to say to the Athenians that Philip is a man of good memory [*mnêmonikos*]." And we innocently not foreseeing the trick of which you shall hear presently, allowed him to bind us in a sort of agreement that we would say this to you. (2.40, 42–43)

Demosthenes, in short, dared Ctesiphon and Aeschines to repeat their praise of Philip in front of the Athenian assembly, as if there were somehow something controversial or dangerous in their doing so.

Aeschines continues his story to say that then, when they had all returned to Athens, he and the others kept their promise and repeated their praises of Philip in the assembly. As he had done on the trip, Aeschines again praised Philip as an eloquent speaker and man with a good memory (*mnêmonikos*) and the others also repeated their compliments (2.48). In Aeschines' account, Demosthenes then sprang up and criticized Aeschines and the others for wasting time on "foreign gossip [*tên huperorion lalian*]" (2.49). He had tricked them into making publicly remarks that he then proceeded to criticize, as Aeschines reports, in the following fashion:

> [Demosthenes said:] "To Aeschines Philip seemed to be eloquent, but not to me; if one should strip off his luck and clothe another with it, this other would be almost his equal. To Ctesiphon he seemed to be brilliant in person, but to me not superior to Aristodemus the actor. One man says he has a great memory [*mnêmonikos*]; so have others. 'He was a wonderful drinker'; our Philocrates could beat him." (2.52)

The story of the man with the good memory, and its repeated use of this unusual word, *mnêmonikos*, does not end here. Aeschines then claims that when the men returned to Pella for their second embassy, Demosthenes in his speech to Philip distanced himself from his colleagues – making the point that he alone was not a flatterer – by referring once more to their now formulaic praise of the king. To contrast himself to the other Athenian ambassadors, Demosthenes said to Philip (according to Aeschines):

> "I did not say that you are beautiful, for a woman is the most beautiful of all beings; nor that you are a wonderful drinker, for that is a compliment for a sponge, in my opinion; nor that you have a remarkable memory [*mnêmonikos*], for I think that that is praise for a sophist." (Aes. 2.112).

Demosthenes does not himself report this story in his prosecution of Aeschines. Instead, the structure of Aeschines' narrative suggests that he needs to protect himself from a story that is going around about him. He is the politician who called Philip "the man with the good memory." Fifteen years later in *On the Crown*, Demosthenes makes fun of Aeschines by calling him "the man with the best memory of all [*mnêmonikôtatos*]" (18.313). The mockery a decade and a half on stands out because *mnêmonikos* is a very rare word in Athenian literature. Demosthenes must be seeking to remind his jury of this remarkable story told by Aeschines about the man with the good memory. Aeschines' defense is simple: he didn't mean anything serious by the compliment; Demosthenes has trickily turned a trivial remark into a political issue.

What on earth could this story mean? What could possibly be wrong with praising someone for having a good memory? And why might Demosthenes see use of the word *mnêmonikos* as so damning?

The answer leads straight to Plato.

First, it is worth remembering that in the *Republic* Socrates praises Glaucon for having a good memory (522a–b; cf. 486c–d, 504a–505a, 520e). This seems to be one of the features that distinguishes Glaucon from the other interlocutors in the dialogue and allows him alone to hang on until the end of the conversation with Socrates. Socrates repeatedly asks him whether he remembers some earlier bit of the conversation; Glaucon's ability generally to do so allows the conversation to continue. Even more importantly, at 486d, Socrates identifies the man who has a good memory, a *mnêmonikos* man, as a *philosophos*; in other words, the man with a good memory, like Glaucon, has the potential to become a philosopher.

The word *mnêmonikos* is rare, appearing by the end of the fourth century only thirty-one times: once in Heraclitus (Fr. 16, line 22), once in Hippocrates (*De diaeta* i–iv, sec. 35, line 11), six times in Plato, four times in Xenophon, seven times in the Aristotelian corpus, of which three are from the treatise "On Memory," five times in Aeschines (in the passages quoted above), once in Demosthenes (when he uses the word to make fun of Aeschines in *On the Crown*), once in a text wrongly attributed to Demosthenes ([59].110), once in Aristophanes, once in a comic fragment (Cratinus, Kock, *CAF*, vol. 1, Fr. 154, line 1), twice in the works of the rhetorician Anaximenes who accompanied Alexander on his travels, and once in Antisthenes (*Fragmenta varia*, Fr. 107, line 37). That's it.[24]

The word is not, however, strictly Platonic. In its single fifth-century poetic instance, Aristophanes places it in Socrates' mouth. In the *Clouds*, he has Socrates interview a potential student before deciding whether to induct that student into the world of philosophy. Why does Socrates do this? Because, Socrates says, "I wish to learn briefly whether you are *mnêmonikos*" (*Clouds* 483). The word, in short, is Socratic, although Plato develops it thematically to flesh out the connection between having a good memory and being identified as a potential philosopher. Xenophon also uses the word in this way, although with less conceptual rigor than Plato. In his *Cyropaedia*, he describes how after a group of Greek soldiers have met the Persian king Cyrus in his tent, they return to their own tents, remarking as they go on what a good memory Cyrus has or on how *mnêmonikos* Cyrus was (5.3.46).

When Aeschines praised Philip for having a good memory, then, he aligned himself with a Socratic-Platonic tradition in which that word served mainly to pick out those rare natures available for development into philosophers. What's more, to identify a king as *mnêmonikos* was to credit him with the potential to be a philosopher-ruler. Demosthenes heard Aeschines mark Philip in this fashion. This is what happened on the trip to Pella, and it explains both why Demosthenes accused Aeschines of seeking revolution and the subsequent bitterness of his attacks on Aeschines.[25]

In the person of Aeschines, Demosthenes saw the convergence of a drive toward less egalitarian institutions at home, support for Philip, and a consequent support for Philip's efforts to sow oligarchies in the Greek city-states; moreover, he saw Platonism lodged at the heart of this convergence. Soon enough, of course, Philip himself would be explicitly aligned with this tradition; in 343 he recruited Plato's student, Aristotle, to teach his son, Alexander.

* * *

The funny narrative that Aeschines tells about the man with the good memory is the most striking evidence that the ten Athenian ambassadors who went to Pella in 346 found themselves at odds in ideological terms that drew Platonism into politics. It is not, however, the only evidence.

In his prosecution of Aeschines for treason, Demosthenes drew an association between Aeschines and Dionysius of Syracuse (Aes. 2.10); the latter, of course, had brought Plato to Sicily in the hope that he might guide politics there in a philosophical direction. And Demosthenes accuses Aeschines of being among those who think that democracy is like a wayward ship on the sea (19.135–136). He also accuses him of getting the lines of poetry he quotes from texts, not even from his experience as an actor (19.245–246).

And Demosthenes is right to see traces of Plato in Aeschines' politics, for Aeschines' speeches reveal it. We have already seen how in *Against Ctesiphon* of 330 BCE, Aeschines developed several Platonic ideas and deployed Platonic techniques. The same is true of *Against Timarchus* of 345 BCE and *On the Embassy* of 343 BCE. Aeschines begins *Against Timarchus* with the same passage on the three types of regime that we saw at the beginning of *Against Ctesiphon* (1.4–6); he stresses the political ideal of *eukosmia* (right order) (1.8, 1.22, 1.34, 1.189, 1.192) and the conquest of *akosmia* (disorder) (1.169, 1.189) and *akolastoi* (licentious men) (1.42, 1.194); *akosmia* and *akolastoi* are terms that are otherwise absent from oratory but appear in Plato.[26] Here too Aeschines refers to Solon as "*ho nomothêtes*" and generally affirms the acts of "the lawgiver" (1.6, 8, 9, 11, 17, 18, 24, 27, 30, 46, 51, 139, 160, 165, 183); and he offers a discourse on chaste and lawful love (*ho dikaios erôs*; *ho sôphrôn kai ennomos erôs*) that closely tracks the argument on the same subject in the *Symposium* and *Phaedrus*; other than in these Platonic dialogues only a fragment from the pre-Socratic philosopher Democritus provides the source phrase, *ho dikaios erôs*, which Aeschines uses.[27]

As for his defense speech, "On the Embassy," this speech is far less marked with Platonic vocabulary, but there are still tell-tale terms. In addition to the story of the *mnêmonikos* man, Aeschines again invokes the concept of "a just love" (*ho dikaios erôs*) (2.166). Also he argues that he is not, as Demosthenes has alleged, a *misodêmos* or "hater of the People" but only a *misoponêros* or "hater of vice" (Aes. 2.171). These compounds formed from the *miso-* prefix proliferate in Plato's dialogues, beyond the norm for their usage in Athenian prose.[28]

These speeches given by Aeschines during the controversy over the Peace of Philocrates – both *Against Timarchus* in 345 BCE and *On the Embassy* in 343 BCE – are the earliest examples of Athenian rhetoric to reveal Platonic traces. We can now see that, although the cultural issues provoked by Plato's influence were separate from the Macedonian question, they did come to the fore precisely because of Macedon, and the novel threat it posed.

Demosthenes and Aeschines had already been contending over items on the domestic policy agenda before they traveled to Pella. For that matter, Aeschines was just one of several politicians who sought reforms that Demosthenes contested. What was the direction of the reforms sought by Eubulus, Aeschines, Lycurgus, and others? And what were the fundamental political commitments of the practical Platonism that motivated at least Aeschines? These would have been necessary political questions for Demosthenes. Then, when the Platonizing Aeschines expressed admiration for Philip and did so in Platonic terms, Demosthenes had his answer. Since Philip's methods and commitments were clearly either monarchic or oligarchic and since he could be admired by a Platonist on Platonic grounds, then the orientation of Platonism must be oligarchic. Because of Aeschines' praise of Philip, Philip could be used as a symbol of what was wrong with the new ideology flowing into Athenian politics. We should therefore see Demosthenes' unrelenting critique of Philip over the years following his prosecution of Aeschines as being also a method of criticizing his political opponents' domestic agendas and the Platonic influence on them.

Before we can feel confident in this account, however, we have to turn back to 330 BCE, the moment when the culture war climaxes in the three great speeches of that year: Lycurgus' *Against Leocrates*, Aeschines' *Against Ctesiphon*, and Demosthenes' *On the Crown*. We need to know why the culture war climaxes when it does and how it is finally concluded. We must answer these questions before we will know in full what Plato did. They are the subject of the next and final chapter.

9

Culture War Concluded

9.1 Introduction

The Athenian politicians Demosthenes and Aeschines were members of
an elite who appear to have read Plato's dialogues, though without being
members of the Academy. While various disputes within the domestic policy
arena – over the appropriate justification for punishment, speaking rights in
the assembly, and the role of the Areopagus and other offices, such as that of
Theoric commissioner – could be intellectually tied to questions generated
by Platonic philosophy, Demosthenes did not consider their Platonic connections worth raising in the early 340s. But when he thought he saw a
developing connection between Philip and Athenian politicians, particularly
Aeschines, rooted in a shared engagement with philosophy, he did then
politicize Plato's influence. At his trial in 343 BCE Aeschines was acquitted
only narrowly (by thirty votes), so Demosthenes' arguments had clearly
begun to take root.

Nonetheless Demosthenes seems not to have made much of Aeschines'
Platonic connection in the years that followed. In the 343 BCE prosecution,
Demosthenes had held up the possibilities that Aeschines had been bribed
or that he had been ideologically seduced, as potential explanations for
why Aeschines had told Athens that Phocis would be safe. In the decade to
come, Demosthenes continued his vigorous attacks on Athenians whom he
saw as sympathizers of Philip, and he continued to remind the Athenians of
the wrong allegedly done to them by Aeschines and his associates. Yet he did
not explicitly draw attention to the question of Platonism or even ideology
generally; instead, he focused these later attacks almost exclusively on the
bribery charge (e.g., 8.76, 9.36–45). He does not again explicitly call out
his opponents arguments as Platonically influenced until Lycurgus and

Why Plato Wrote   Danielle S. Allen. © 2010 Danielle S. Allen.

Aeschines themselves introduce their notably Platonic vocabulary to political debate in 330 BCE.

Why did the culture war re-emerge and reach its acme in that year? And how, finally, did that war end? Knowing the answers to these questions, we will know what Plato did in Athens.

9.2 The Politics of the 330s

After his prosecution of Aeschines, Demosthenes worked relentlessly to bring the Athenians around to his way of seeing Philip. He was at his most influential during the years from 343 to 338 BCE and succeeded in putting Athens on a war-footing, effectively building alliances against Philip even with traditional enemies such as Thebes.[1] War was fully engaged in 340 BCE, but in 338 BCE, after a brief moment of success for Athens, Philip won decisively at Chaeronea, roughly sixty miles north of Athens. In the aftermath of the battle, Philip set up a league of Hellenic city-states, called the League of Corinth by moderns. He was the League's head; the other cities had to serve in any combat force he might muster.

During the period leading up to Chaeronea, the politician Lycurgus had also worked hard to defend Athens from Philip's growing power. Although almost twenty years Demosthenes' elder, Lycurgus had kept his peace through most of the 340s, remaining disengaged from politics. But the fight against Philip brought him to a prominence that he maintained until his death in 324 BCE.

Indeed both men maintained their pre-eminence in Athenian politics after Chaeronea.[2] Demosthenes was elected to give the funeral oration for the war dead; he was also elected *sitônês*, the official responsible for securing the Athenian grain supply. He seems to have been active in proposing measures in the assembly, and he also seems to have been actively opposed.

For his part, Lycurgus was elected *tamias epi têi dioikêsei* or "treasurer of management" (this may have been a position identical to the Theoric commissioner). In this position he was the chief financial officer in the city, and Lycurgus either held the position for the next twelve years, or had sufficient influence over the men who actually held the position that the period from 336 to 324 BCE is known as the Lycurgan Age (Hyp. Fr. 23; Diod. 16.88.1).[3] But although both men remained prominent after Chaeronea, their policy paths diverged.

After Chaeronea, Lycurgus renewed Eubulus' agenda. Eubulus' projects to build dockyards and an arsenal had been interrupted when the city, following Demosthenes' policy, decided to prepare for war. Lycurgus re-started these projects. He spearheaded a massive public works program and increased the city's revenues by strengthening Athens as a center of trade.

He is reported to have distributed 18,900 talents to the people, arranged loans of 650 talents for public expenses, supplied funds for Athens' cults, arms, and 400 triremes, and built the Panathenaic stadium as well as many other buildings, among them a rebuilding in stone of the Theater of Dionysus and the gymnasium at the Lyceum, where Aristotle settled in 335, perhaps at Lycurgus' invitation but certainly with his support. Like Eubulus, Lycurgus sought to rebuild Athens' prosperity through internal measures. He thought Athens could restore its pre-eminence without taking on Macedon again and without the assets of empire.[4]

Lycurgus also famously developed policies to renew the city's religious life. He was one of Athens' representatives to the sanctuaries of Amphiareion and Delphi in 332–329 BCE and may have served as a *hieropoios* (temple overseer) to the Semnai, the goddesses whose altar was connected to the Areopagus. He had official copies made of the plays of Aeschylus, Sophocles, and Euripides, revived the support of the city's wealthy elite for dramatic productions, and also had statues to the three great tragedians erected in the city center. And as we have seen, he endorsed the expansion of the Areopagus' power to include executing capital sentences on its own authority.[5]

Last and most important, the Lycurgan age included a major reform of the *ephêbeia*, the routine military training that young men undertook at age eighteen. This reorganization, credited to Epicrates, involved the introduction of two new officers to supervise the young men, the "orderers" or *kosmêtai* and "moderators" or *sôphronistai* (*Ath. Pol.* 42.2–5). Those positions have a Platonic ring to them,[6] and indeed the reorganized *ephêbeia* bears a resemblance to Plato's proposal in the *Laws* for a two-year period of military training for young men. In Lycurgan Athens, the first thing that these "orderers" and "moderators" did with the newly enrolled ephebes each year was to take them on a tour of the city's shrines; in the *Laws* they are generally charged with coming to know all parts and districts of the land.[7] In short, Lycurgus had a domestic program with recognizably Platonic elements, particularly the *ephêbeia*, a strengthened Areopagus, and the strengthening of civic religion.

We are not able to gain the same degree of clarity on Demosthenes' agenda during this period, but we can identify some of its features. In addition to his role as *sitônês* or grain-overseer, he claims himself to have manned expeditions to procure grain. But whatever policies he pursued with regard to the Athenian food supply were consistent with continued efforts to build active resistance to Macedon, for this seems to be where Demosthenes put most of his energies.[8]

After Philip was assassinated in 336 BCE and Alexander acceded to his throne, Demosthenes worked constantly to support revolt from Macedon, making efforts both personal and political; on the latter front, he tried mainly to get Athens itself to support rebellious powers. When Thebes revolted in 335 BCE, Demosthenes may personally have helped supply the Thebans with arms, and he also secured at least initial Athenian support for Thebes.[9] But Thebes was quickly destroyed by Alexander who established a pro-Macedonian, oligarchical government there. When in 333 BCE Darius III, King of Persia, decided to fight Macedon, Demosthenes again lent support and encouragement, although he seems to have wanted Athens itself to bide its time, before joining the fray, until Darius had defeated Alexander.[10] Instead Alexander defeated Darius, who was killed in 330 BCE. Finally, in 323 BCE, after Alexander's death, Athens itself revolted. Demosthenes was living in exile at the time, on account of a bribery conviction, but when his native city decided to go to war, he was recalled and, as Plutarch reports (*Dem.* 27), he was greeted in the harbor by the whole citizenry. The project of resistance was his. This is plainly what the Athenians knew about Demosthenes.[11]

In sum, Lycurgus was willing to work within the framework set by the League of Corinth, headed by Philip, to rebuild Athenian strength in the context of a collective security pact for which Athens was not the hegemon, or leading power. In contrast, Demosthenes pursued a variety of multilateral alliances in an effort to topple Macedonian power. It was not enough for him that Athens might, through wealth, achieve parity with Macedon; he sought superiority, at least within a traditional domain of Athenian influence. The policy arguments of the 330s between Demosthenes and Lycurgus therefore probably replayed the arguments of the 350s and 340s between Eubulus and Demosthenes.

But this time, as we have seen, the battle over the value of Plato emerged even more dramatically. It's time to turn back to the speeches of 330 BCE in which we first spotted the culture war. We should now be in a better position to understand that conflict.

9.3 Who Was Fighting Whom?

As classicists have long known, Athenian politicians often launched prosecutions as strategic moves in larger political battles, just as Aeschines had done when he prosecuted Timarchus for prostitution in 345 BCE as a way to disable Demosthenes' attack on him for the outcome of the embassies to Philip and the peace treaty. The prosecutions of 330 BCE, too, may well have been proxies for political maneuvers of another kind. If so, we need to know what actual political battle is represented by these speeches and who its protagonists were. These questions hold the key to understanding why the "culture war" emerged again in 330 BCE and with greater force than a decade and a half earlier.

First, let's refresh our memories of the basic details of the two prosecutions. The origins of the two cases tried in 330 BCE both lay in Athens' defeat by Philip at Chaeronea in 338 BCE and in the politics that flowed from it. Lycurgus prosecutes Leocrates for treason on the grounds that Leocrates left the city in the aftermath of the battle. The citizens had been called to come into the city center from the surrounding countryside in preparation for a last stand, should Philip march on Athens itself, but, when everyone else was transporting their movables to the city center, Leocrates allegedly packed up all his belongings and his mistress and set sail for Rhodes. As for Aeschines, he indicts Ctesiphon in 336 BCE for having proposed in that year that Demosthenes deserved a crown for his service in the two years following the 338 BCE defeat at Chaeronea. He too criticizes Demosthenes for behavior in the immediate aftermath of the battle, including a departure from the city, to which we will return shortly.

Interestingly, both prosecutions display procedural oddities that have puzzled scholars. Lycurgus prosecutes Leocrates eight years after his allegedly treasonous departure. Why raise the issue so much later? Lycurgus' prosecution is strange too as one of only two examples in extant oratory of an orator bringing a prosecution against someone with whom he was not personally involved.[12] Nor was Leocrates a notable citizen. Why should a leading politician, Lycurgus, prosecute the very ordinary owner of a blacksmith shop with no obvious political standing? Finally, within the context of the whole corpus of Athenian court cases, Leocrates' departure from the city looks like a relatively minor example of desertion.[13] Why does Lycurgus turn it into the most significant treason prosecution in all of extant Attic oratory?

In the case of Aeschines' speech, the procedural oddity there is that he did not follow through on the prosecution in 336 BCE when he first brought the indictment. He dropped the case. Why? And why is the case raised again in 330 BCE?

These two prosecutions are linked, then, in both reaching back to the defeat at Chaeronea for their substantive charges and in sharing a relatively high degree of procedural oddity. But those are superficial connections. More significantly, Lycurgus' and Aeschines' speeches are connected substantively.

First, as we've seen (chapter 7), they share stylistic anomalies: large amounts of philosophical, and particularly Platonic, vocabulary, and extensive quotation of poetry and other texts. Second, Aeschines refers approvingly to Lycurgus' prosecution of Leocrates (3.252–253), and describes his own prosecution as paralleling Lycurgus' (3.252–253). Third, as we have seen, in these two speeches Lycurgus and Aeschines both endorse the power of the Areopagus to execute Athenian citizens, a controversial topic (Lyc. 1.52; Aes. 3.25–253).

Finally, but even more importantly, both men endorse a specific kind of exercise of power on the part of the Areopagus. Lycurgus and Aeschines both praise the Areopagus for having executed citizens who left the city after the Battle of Chaeronea. The Areopagus executed at least three people at that time: the general Lysicles, Autolycus (who sent away his wife and children), and a "private citizen who sailed for Samos."[14] Lycurgus is now trying to get for Leocrates from a jury the very treatment that the Areopagus had previously meted out to these three other men. And Aeschines charges that Demosthenes is yet another traitor who, like Leocrates and the unnamed citizen who had put out for Samos, had sailed away from the city in the immediate aftermath of the defeat. Demosthenes does have a defense: he says he sailed off that day in order to secure grain for the city. But Aeschines is trying to make him out to be the same sort of traitor that Lycurgus makes Leocrates out to be.[15]

These tight substantive links between Lycurgus' and Aeschines' speeches allow us to solve a mystery that has long plagued scholars: who actually reinitiated the trial of Ctesiphon in 330 BCE? Was it Aeschines, or might Demosthenes have done it? In the 1970s Edward Burke observed that Aeschines was too politically weak in the late 330s for the renewal of his suit against Ctesiphon to be reasonably attributed to him. The outcome of the trial makes clear just how weak and politically isolated Aeschines was; he attracted fewer than 20 percent of the jurors to his side. The Athenians had a rule to reduce frivolous lawsuits – prosecutors in public cases who did not win at least 20 percent of the votes had to pay a 1,000 drachmae fine and were thereafter barred from bringing suits in the Athenian courts. Citizen prosecutors would, therefore, generally have taken up cases only if they were confident of crossing that 20 percent threshold. Aeschines' failure to do so reveals a political weakness so severe that, given the stakes of a loss, he is unlikely voluntarily to have restarted his case. Demosthenes must have forced his hand.[16]

After Burke develops this conclusion, however, he makes a mistake, which has prevented other scholars from taking his argument on board. He argues that Demosthenes forced the renewal of the suit because he was acting as an ally of Lycurgus and both men wanted to get at Aeschines. But his own argument about Aeschines' weakness invalidates this view. Weak as Aeschines was, there was no reason to go after him. Even more important, of course, is the fact that Aeschines constructs his speech rhetorically so that his account of the kind of citizen Demosthenes has been is analogous to the account that Lycurgus gives of Leocrates. Burke's critical error is to think that Demosthenes was acting as an ally of Lycurgus in the political conflict of the 330s. It is instead Lycurgus and Aeschines whose positions align.[17]

Once we recognize that Aeschines is trying to link his cause to Lycurgus', another piece falls into place: Leocrates, who is accused of having done just what Demosthenes is also accused of having done – that is, of having set sail from the city immediately after the defeat at Chaeronea – must be a proxy for Demosthenes. In prosecuting Leocrates, Lycurgus is attacking Demosthenes. Once one recognizes, first, that Lycurgus and Aeschines were on the same side of whatever political battle was raging in 330 BCE and, second, that Leocrates is a proxy for Demosthenes, the relationships among these three speeches are clear.

In *Against Leocrates*, Lycurgus attacks Demosthenes via the proxy target of Leocrates; Demosthenes retaliates by forcing the renewal of Aeschines' suit, thus attacking Aeschines, as a proxy for Lycurgus. The attack on Aeschines as a proxy for Lycurgus gives Demosthenes two important political opportunities: both to attack Lycurgan policy and also to defend his own career and policies against Lycurgus' recent onslaught. Because of Aeschines' political weakness by 330 BCE, Demosthenes also gets to do this against an easy target.

The outcomes of the trials bear out the hypotheses that the real battle in the speeches of 330 BCE was between Lycurgus and Demosthenes and that Leocrates and Aeschines were just insignificant fall-guys. As we have seen, Lycurgus won 50 percent of the vote in his case; he had enough authority in the city, in other words, to keep half of the citizenry on his side, even when using rhetoric as unorthodox, and as richly Platonic, as any juror is likely ever to have heard.[18] And Demosthenes, of course, won more than 80 percent of the vote in Ctesiphon's trial. There was no contest between Demosthenes and Aeschines. Moreover, Lycurgus did not bother to come to Aeschines' aid. It was Lycurgus and Demosthenes who in 330 BCE commanded significant constituencies on either side of whatever set of thorny political issues lay behind these speeches. These two men are our protagonists.

So what were the thorny issues that motivated this battle between the two greatest politicians of the decade? This is really a two-part question: What political conflict are these speeches a proxy for? And why do these two great politicians fight over Plato?

9.4 What Were Lycurgus and Demosthenes Fighting About?

The major political conflict in Athens during the years 331 and 330 BCE was whether to help Agis III, King of Sparta, in his revolt from Macedon.[19] As we shall see, this conflict lies behind the three speeches of 330 BCE and also gives us the clues we need to understand why these politicians thought the time had come to tackle the question of Plato head on.

As we have seen, after the death of Philip, Demosthenes worked doggedly to support revolts against Macedon. There were the cases of Thebes and

Persia, and the Athenians' own revolt in the Lamian War of 323–322 BCE. But I left the Spartan case off the list. We need to take it up now because it was the backdrop to these speeches of 330 BCE.

The Spartan uprising may have ended before Lycurgus gave his speech against Leocrates; if so, it had ended just months before. It might also have been still under way. And when Aeschines prosecutes Ctesiphon a few months later, the Spartan envoys to Alexander, who had been delegated to discuss the terms of Spartan submission, had not yet left for the Macedonian camp. The conclusion of the revolt must still be very recent when battle is engaged between Aeschines and Demosthenes.[20]

What was Demosthenes' stance on the Spartan revolt? He had been a supporter of such efforts before the Spartan king, Agis, asked for help and he would be again afterwards. But what happened when King Agis came to town? This is a complicated question.

The standard scholarly response is that Demosthenes urged the Athenians not to support Sparta's revolt, but this misses the mark. Although the sources reporting this episode are riddling in nature, as many scholars have noted, they do contain a clue that will lead us to an answer.[21] We will need to review them in full.

Here, first of all, is how Aeschines describes Demosthenes' behavior in response to Agis' appeal:

Pray set forth to us, Demosthenes, what in the world there was that you did then, or what in the world there was that you said. I will yield the platform to you, if you wish, until you have told us. You are silent. I can well understand your embarrassment. But what you said then, I myself will tell now. Do you not remember, gentlemen, his disgusting and incredible words? Ye men of iron, how had you ever the endurance to listen to them! When he came forward and said, "Certain men are pruning the city, certain men have trimmed off the tendrils of the people, the sinews of the state have been cut [*huoptetmêtai ta neura tôn pragmatôn*], we are being matted and sewed up, certain men are first drawing us like needles into tight places." What are these things, you beast? Are they words or monstrosities? And again when you whirled around in a circle on the platform and said, pretending that you were working against Alexander, "I admit that I organized the Laconian uprising, I admit that I am bringing about the revolt of the Thessalians and the Perrhaebi." You cause a revolt of the Thessalians? What! Could you cause the revolt of a village? Would you actually approach – let us talk not about a city – would you actually approach a house, where there was danger? But if money is being paid out anywhere, you will lay siege to the place; a man's deed you will never do. If any good-fortune come of itself, you will lay claim to it, and sign your name to the thing after it has been done; but if any danger approach, you will run away; and then if we regain confidence, you will call for rewards and crowns of gold. (3.165–167)

Seven years later, when a politician named Dinarchus served on a team prosecuting Demosthenes for bribery, he referred back to the moment of Agis' appeal and described Demosthenes' behavior thus:

> In that hour, – for I need not dwell on other crises, – what was the behavior of this Demosthenes who had the power to give advice and make proposals, who will shortly tell you that he hates our present circumstances? On these matters, Demosthenes, did you offer any proposal, any advice? Did you contribute money? Were you of the smallest value to the men safeguarding us all? Not the least; you went round suborning speechwriters. He wrote a letter at home, defiling the city's honor, and walked about dangling it from his fingertips, living in luxury during the city's misfortunes, traveling down the road to the Peiraeus in a litter and reproaching the needy for their poverty. Is this man then going to prove useful to you on future occasions, when he has let slip every opportunity in the past? (1.34–36)

And four and a half centuries later, relying on sources no longer available to us, Plutarch wrote (*Dem.* 24.1): "It is true that when Agis the Spartan was active in revolt Demosthenes once more made a feeble effort in his support, but then he cowered down, since the Athenians would not join in the uprising."

In short, none of these sources suggests that Demosthenes "supported the policy of keeping out," as one scholar put it.[22] At most they simply indicate that he did not encourage the Athenians to revolt. Before we can understand these descriptions of Demosthenes' behavior, however, we need to know what else was going on at the moment of Agis' appeal.

Our sources tell us that another politician, Demades, who was an ally of Lycurgus, halted the move to war by proposing that the necessary funds not be diverted from the Theoric Fund to the war effort but be distributed instead to each citizen at 50 drachmae a head.[23] This would have been a considerable payout, roughly equivalent at that time to thirty days' pay for a skilled day-laborer.[24]

Our sources also tell us that at roughly the same time, Lycurgus successfully prosecuted Diphilus for illegal mining and that the conviction brought public confiscation of the guilty party's property, which was distributed to the citizenry in the form of 50 drachmae a head.[25] It is entirely possible, as scholars have noted, that Demades' and Lycurgus' payouts, which are both attributed to the same time period, were one and the same.[26] And if these payouts were one and the same – which seems plausible given the magnitude of giving 50 drachmae to each citizen – then Demades and Lycurgus collaborated on keeping the city out of the war by directing available resources that might have funded military action into the purses of individual citizens.

Why then would we have two separate stories of payouts with roughly the same date? The procedural details of how the funds of a single payout were acquired and distributed by the city may simply have become unclear to the authors of the histories where these details were recorded, with the result that more than one version of what happened was developed. At the very least, however, these details make clear that there was some kind of move to war and that it was forestalled by the political maneuvers of the city's financiers.

Now we come to the clue that will help us pull these pieces together. We need to take seriously the remarks that Aeschines reports Demosthenes as having made: "Certain men are pruning the city, certain men have trimmed off the tendrils of the people, the sinews of the state have been cut, we are being matted and sewed up, certain men are first drawing us like needles into tight places." Scholars have generally found those remarks baffling.[27] But there is an easy answer to their meaning, for Demosthenes had said almost exactly the same thing nearly twenty years earlier when he wished then to criticize Eubulus for using the Theoric Fund to pay off the citizens instead of preparing for war. Here is what Demosthenes said in 349 BCE, responding to the claim that great value had come from Eubulus' policies:

> To what can you point in proof? To the walls we are whitewashing, the streets we are paving, the water-works, and the balderdash? Look rather at the politicians who have done this; some of them were poor and now are rich, some were obscure and now are eminent, some have reared private houses more stately than our public buildings, while the lower the fortunes of the city have sunk, the higher have their fortunes soared ... Why did things go well before and now amiss? Because then the people, having the courage [tolmôn] to act and fight, the demos was master [despotês] of the politicians and had authority [kurios] over all good things; the rest were well content to accept at the people's hand honor and authority and reward. Now on the contrary the politicians are authorities [kurioi] over all good things, while you the people, robbed of nerve and sinew [ekneneurismenoi], stripped of wealth and of allies, have sunk to the level of lackeys and hangers-on, content if the politicians gratify you with a dole from the Theoric fund or a procession at the Boedromia, and your manliness [andreiotaton] reaches its climax when you add your thanks for what is your own ... You cannot have a great and youthful spirit [mega kai neanikon phronêma] if your actions are small and paltry [phaula]; for whatever a man's actions are, such must be his spirit ... Like the diet prescribed by doctors, which neither restores the strength of the patient nor allows him to succumb, so these doles that you are now distributing neither suffice to ensure your safety nor allow you to renounce them and try something else; they only confirm each citizen in his apathy [rhaithumian]. (3.29–33)

As quoted by Aeschines, Demosthenes' remarks during the conflict over how to respond to Sparta's request make good sense if understood as yet another effort on his part to criticize policies to direct the city's financial resources to payouts to citizens instead of to military readiness and action. Just as in 349 BCE he criticized Eubulus for enervating the citizenry, so too he now criticizes Lycurgus. His seemingly strange remarks about nerves and sinews attack Lycurgus' renewal of Eubulus' policies.[28]

Once we see that, we can see that each of our sources tells part of a story that goes like this.

As Demosthenes himself claims (according to Aeschines) and as Plutarch also claims, Demosthenes did try to rally the Athenians to Sparta's side, but he was pre-empted when the city's financiers – Lycurgus and Demades – decided to disburse funds to the citizens. Knowing that he had been out-maneuvered, Demosthenes gave up making any alternative proposals and limited himself to criticizing Lycurgan policy. He was in this sense "turning about," as Aeschines says: having set off in the direction of trying to rally support from Athens, he abandoned that effort, not because he was urging the Athenians to reject Sparta's appeal but only because he acknowledged his defeat. Dinarchus' comment that Demosthenes wrote a letter defiling the city's honor and then rode around in a litter reproaching the poor captures Demosthenes' critique of the *dêmos*, the city's poor, for accepting the payouts from the Theoric fund. The idea that he rode around in a litter doing this is just a way of saying, "Who are you, rich man, to criticize the poor for wanting money?" Dinarchus' comment about Demosthenes' letter is interesting and helpful; it reveals that Demosthenes had undertaken a campaign against Lycurgan policies outside of the assembly as well as in it. Demosthenes was "defiling the city's honor" in the sense that he was arguing that Lycurgus' policies were ruining Athens; in criticizing Athens' "enervation," he was also, as he had done in 349 BCE, mocking the citizens for a failure of manliness.

Demosthenes' campaign against Lycurgus, and his bitterly mocking critique of Lycurgus' "enervating" policy, would have occurred at most a year, and possibly as little as six months, before Lycurgus gave his speech prosecuting Leocrates. Lycurgus' speech, then, is an answer to Demosthenes' critique that he had enervated the city. Indeed, his speech has been called a "sermon of patriotism," and so it is.[29] He is no "enervator"; he seeks "to implant in the hearts of the citizens a love of their country" (1.100).

With a very slight legal case against Leocrates, Lycurgus devotes the bulk of his speech to the question of how the true patriot will think and feel. Thus he concludes:

> If you acquit Leocrates, you will vote for the betrayal of the city, of its temples and its fleet. But if you kill him, you will be encouraging others to preserve your

country with its revenues and its prosperity. Imagine then, Athenians, that the country and its trees are appealing to you, that the harbors, dockyards and walls of the city are begging you for protection, yes, and the temples and sanctuaries too. Bear in mind the charges brought and make of Leocrates a proof that with you tears and compassion have not more weight than the salvation of the laws and people. (1.150)

He is proving that his approach to the life of the city is compatible with the strongest version of patriotic vigor imaginable. And, as we have seen, he paints that patriotism in Platonic colors.

This leaves us with two final questions. Lycurgus had beaten Demosthenes politically in the conflict over how to respond to Agis; he had kept the city from supporting the Spartan revolt. Why was that not enough? Why did he think he needed to land another blow against Demosthenes? Second, there is our recurring question: Why did Lycurgus make Platonism so central to his defense of the patriotic value of his policy agenda?

9.5 Why Fight over Plato?

The underlying claim of Lycurgus' speech *Against Leocrates* is that a Platonist outlook is fully compatible with an intense democratic patriotism. He is, in other words, trying to undo the convergence, which Demosthenes had argued into being in the 340s, among commitments to Platonism, oligarchy, and a certain set of domestic reforms (expanded powers for the Areopagus, the establishment of the Theoric commissioner, more hierarchical management of speaking privileges, and so on).

In the 340s, as we saw, Demosthenes had consistently argued to the Athenians that the rise of oligarchy in the broader Greek world was not accidental but driven by Philip; that his own domestic institutional reforms maintained democratic egalitarianism whereas his opponents' reforms advanced oligarchical ends; and that his opponents were soft on Philip because they shared with Philip an interest in oligarchy that Demosthenes also associated with Platonism. As with the story of the man with the good memory, the evidence of the ideological danger introduced by Demosthenes' enemies lay in their association with Plato and the Socratic tradition.

Some events in the Hellenic world lent support to Demosthenes' view. Although Alexander supported democracies in Asia Minor, he continued to undo them in Greece. Sometime between 336 and 332/1, for instance, he installed at Pellene in the Peloponnese a tyrant who had studied with Plato, and who began his rule by banishing existing elites, who would have defended the status quo, and redistributing property and wives, both moves proposed in the *Republic*.[30] The clear associations, after Alexander's accession to the

Macedonian throne, among Plato, Aristotle, philosophy, and the Macedonian regime would have seemed to confirm Demosthenes' argument about the convergence of Platonic influence with a largely oligarchic orientation. Against this backdrop the speeches of Lycurgus and Aeschines must have constituted a defense of their Platonism as democratic.

In fact, Philip's defeat of the Athenians at Chaeronea had opened up conceptual space for the argument that Platonist and oligarchical commitments were not necessarily bound to one another. Between 343 and 338 BCE the success of Demosthenes' argument that Philip was seeking to oligarchize the Greek world had led Athens to pursue the policy of direct confrontation that Demosthenes advocated. As the conflict with Philip gathered force at the end of the 340s, Demosthenes routinely predicted that if Philip defeated Athens, the king would immediately destroy the city's democracy, and replace it with an oligarchy, as he had already done in other cities and did indeed do when he defeated Thebes.[31]

And then Athens lost at Chaeronea. Philip had Athens altogether in his power. As we have seen, the citizens gathered their belongings into the city and prepared a last stand, in anticipation of Philip's imminent arrival. But he did not come. Instead he left matters with Athens there and, most importantly, left the city to continue to govern itself as a democracy (Diod. 16.87.3).[32] The Athenians were stunned and, for at least some portion of the citizenry, Philip's restraint must have seemed a direct refutation of Demosthenes' arguments about the convergence of Philip's imperialism with a necessarily oligarchic ideology.[33]

Similarly, Lycurgus, whose Platonism appears to have been the most thorough-going of any of the orators', had worked aggressively in the period leading up to Chaeronea to prepare Athens for successful self-defense. Joined to Philip's restraint, Lycurgus' example would have opened up political space for the argument that Platonically inflected ideologies were compatible with democracy after all. Those who had in the 340s argued that Philip (and by extension, politicians with Platonic sympathies) were trustworthy, would finally have found some evidence in their favor.

Yet the mere fact that, after Chaeronea, there was conceptual space for the idea that Platonism and oligarchic commitments did not necessarily go hand-in-hand did not establish consensus on the question of how to interpret the import of Platonic ideas in politics.

In the period after 336 BCE, there were clearly two sides in Athens on the question of whether Athens was threatened internally by an oligarchical revolution. As we have seen, in the post-Chaeronean moment the Areopagus, a court of elite experts, extended its power even to the point of executing citizens on its own authority. Lycurgus and Aeschines approved of this. On the other hand, significant portions of their jury audiences disapproved and enough citizens were worried about an internal oligarchical threat that the city passed the Law of Eucrates, which read:

> If any one rise up against the Demos for tyranny or join in establishing the tyranny or overthrow the Demos of the Athenians or the democracy in Athens, whoever kills him who does any of such things shall be blameless. It shall not be permitted for anyone of the Councillors of the Council from the Areopagus – if the Demos or the democracy has been overthrown – to go up to the Areopagus or sit in the Council or deliberate about anything.[34]

Some Athenians clearly thought that the city was threatened by would-be oligarchs and they associated this threat with the Areopagites, whom Lycurgus wholeheartedly supported.

For the sake of his domestic policy agenda, Lycurgus needed to undo the association Demosthenes had been drawing between Platonism and oligarchy. He took the opportunity of the fight with Demosthenes to make the case to the Athenian citizenry that the sort of domestic agenda that he advocated, and which was scaffolded by Platonic concepts, was compatible with democratic ideology.

In 345 BCE Aeschines, in his defense on the charges of having behaved treasonously on the embassy, says that, whereas Demosthenes has accused him of being a *misodêmos*, a hater of democracy, he is in fact a *misoponêros*, a hater of vice. He thus avows his Platonism under the label of "virtue politics." The necessary meaning of this label is that aggressive hatred of vice – including policies to foster moral rectitude – is fully compatible with a love of democracy.

Lycurgus, too, in *Against Leocrates*, is trying to establish a distinction between being a "hater of vice" and being a "hater of the *dêmos*." He wants the Athenians to join him in the former project:

> Remember your ancestors and the methods of punishment which they employed against them. Capable as they were of the noblest actions, they were no less ready to punish vice [*ta ponêra*]. Think of them, gentlemen; think how enraged they were with traitors and how they looked on them as common enemies of the city. (1.111, cf. 1.82, 1.92)

While Lycurgus here enjoins his jurors to be haters of vice, on the other side of the equation, he casts his opponents – Leocrates, and those who are like him, which is implicitly to say, Demosthenes – as "haters of the people" (*misodêmoi*). Lycurgus says of people like Leocrates and Demosthenes who, on his argument, had deserted after Chaeronea:

> Surely there was no one [other than Leocrates and his kind] whose hatred of the people [*misodêmos*] or of Athens [*misathênaios*] was so intense that he could have endured to see himself remain outside the army. (1.39)

Did sailing away from Chaeronea make one a hater of the people? Demosthenes claims he had sailed away from Athens after Chaeronea to procure grain. Leocrates employs the same defense (Lyc. 1.55–58), and since he was acquitted, such a defense must have been plausible. But Lycurgus' rhetoric transforms that policy into the foremost example of traitorous ideology. Leocrates, Demosthenes, and the unnamed man who sailed to Samos, had all departed the city before it had become clear that Philip was not going to take advantage of having the upper hand. This allows Lycurgus to suggest that they had left to avoid falling into Philip's hands. Lycurgus' implicit claim is that Demosthenes' "grain-procuring policy" was really a *dêmos*-hating pretext to skip town.[35]

Thus, Lycurgus makes the case that Leocrates had presumed the city's imminent annihilation; he describes Leocrates as reporting to Rhodes an outcome far worse than the reality (Lyc. 1.14, 18, 143). Because Demosthenes was the politician who had long been predicting such annihilation as the necessary outcome of a military victory by Philip over Athens, he is the implicit target of Lycurgus' criticism of Leocrates for anticipating such a thing. Had Demosthenes' thoroughly ideologized account of Hellenic politics made people too easily prepared to think the game was over and to abandon ship? By turning Leocrates' minor desertion into a paradigmatic case of treason, Lycurgus raises this question about Demosthenes' political stance.

In the mid-340s Aeschines had argued that Philip was trustworthy; then in 338 BCE Philip's restraint opened up conceptual space for this position in Athenian politics. By 335 BCE, Lycurgus, too, thought it was possible to live peaceably beside Macedon without losing Athenian autonomy or democracy. Again, the post-Chaeronean continuation of the democratic constitution in Athens would have provided evidence for the view that Platonically inflected ideologies did not demand the institution of oligarchies. From the perspective of such a policy framework, Demosthenes' thoroughly ideologized account of Hellenic politics could be viewed as a dangerous delusion that made people act rashly, first to endanger the city and then to abandon ship, at critical moments. On this view, Demosthenes' political arguments of the 340s and 330s themselves functioned to undermine democracy, not to protect it, and his specific error was to have over-interpreted the consequences that could be expected to flow from the adoption, whether by citizens themselves or even their foreign antagonists, of a Platonically inflected ideology.

The culture war emerged as it did in 330 BCE, then, because the question of how well a politician could make foreign policy judgments and of how effectively he would defend democratic commitments at home had at least in part become a matter of what he thought about the role of philosophy in politics. The core of this debate in 330 BCE between Demosthenes and

Lycurgus ultimately concerned not resistance to Macedon, but the question of how seriously to take the novel ideologies that linked Lycurgus and Aeschines to the Macedonian court. Could one adopt Platonically inflected ideologies and pursue either democratic or oligarchic politics, such that ideology was no predictor of a politician's commitment to a regime type? This was the case represented by Lycurgus. Or did Platonically inflected ideologies lead necessarily to oligarchy? This was the case represented by Demosthenes.

What did the jurors think?

Demosthenes appears to have emerged from the two major extant prosecutions of 330 BCE as the political victor. As we have seen, Lycurgus won only half the vote in his case, but Demosthenes won more than 80 percent in his. Nonetheless, the balance would soon tip. While Demosthenes won in numerical terms, Lycurgus clearly succeeded in silencing Demosthenes, for Demosthenes does appear to have given up his active efforts of resistance around this time, not to return to that role until 323 BCE after Alexander's death.[36] Ensuing events vindicated Demosthenes.

The war that followed Alexander's death, called the Lamian War, ended in 322 BCE with Macedon's total victory over Athens. Putting a final end to Athenian autonomy, Macedon quickly proceeded to restructure Athens along oligarchic lines.[37] The Macedonian regent, Antipater, began by establishing a restrictive property requirement for citizenship, which disenfranchised more than a third of the citizenry; those who were disfranchised were invited to move to Thrace.[38] In the end, then, Demosthenes was right: Macedonian domination did entail the death of Athenian democracy.

Was he also right about the consequences of Platonic influence?

9.6 The End of the Culture War

Did the new vocabularies and symbols – and the ideas and arguments they conveyed – used by orators such as Lycurgus and Aeschines and resisted by Demosthenes matter materially? Did they have a concrete effect on Athenian politics or on the lived experience of citizens, or did they merely provide a cosmetic change in the vocabulary of decision-making?

I have argued above that ideology itself became a central point of contention in determining who would have leadership in the city. This means that questions of ideology were directly tied to concrete impacts. And Lycurgus' Platonic vocabulary was tied to a practical policy agenda that itself had many Platonic features: the *ephêbeia* and endorsement of the Areopagus' power to punish with death surely affected the lived experience of citizens.

But the final outcome of the Macedonian take-over of the city brought further institutional innovations in a Platonic direction. In 317 BCE Demetrius of Phaleron was installed by Macedon as governor of Athens. He had studied under Aristotle and was said to consider Demosthenes' speeches vulgar, ignoble, and feeble.[39] In his new role, he made important institutional innovations. For instance, he introduced institutions that we see first in Plato's texts: *nomophulakes* or "guardians of law," who were elected officials instead of being chosen by lot, and also "guardians of women" (*phulakes tôn gunaikôn*).[40] The *nomophulakes* (guardians of law) took over from the citizenry the authority to judge whether laws were constitutional. When they completed their term, they joined former archons on the Council of the Areopagus, turning this important judicial body, literally, into a council of retired guardians resembling the Nocturnal Council Plato proposes in the *Laws*.[41] It turned out that it was indeed possible to build up the authority of this elite court of experts even beyond what Lycurgus and Aeschines endorsed. Their position was not the fully oligarchical one.

The emergence of Platonic institutions is not the only evidence available for an assessment of whether Plato's influence had a material impact. We can follow the judgment of the Athenians themselves on the question. They thought that Plato's hypothesis about the political power of symbolically vigorous philosophy was correct and recognized the impact of the new concepts, symbols, and institutions as real and serious. In 307 BCE, at the start of an illusory re-establishment of the democracy (Diod. 20.45.2–2), the Athenian Assembly voted for a decree mandating that proposed heads of philosophical schools, including the Academy, be reviewed for approval by the Council and Assembly before taking up their appointments. One defender of the new law, a man named Demochares, appears, in fragments of his defense speech, to have criticized by name at least Socrates, Plato, and Aristotle for their political roles (notably, Isocrates does not make the list).[42] Like Demosthenes, Demochares seems to have thought that philosophy had had revolutionary, and negative, effects in Athens. As it happens, Demochares was Demosthenes' nephew; apparently he had inherited the fight.[43]

After the passage of the decree, all the philosophers in Athens immediately left the city, in a repeat of the exodus that followed Socrates' execution.[44] But this time, the proposer of the 307 BCE decree, which brought philosophy under political control, was soon himself successfully prosecuted for having introduced an unconstitutional measure.[45] The new measure was repealed and the philosophical schools remained autonomous. Apparently, by the end of the fourth century, in contrast to the previous one, the Athenians had decided to live with philosophy as an independent political force.

Was it the general citizenry or the new guardians of law who ruled the decree unconstitutional? We cannot know. We therefore cannot know whether "the Athenians" decided to live with philosophy because the citizenry had come to accept philosophy's distinctive power or because philosophers had become more powerful, and had perhaps even acquired institutional authority. Did social acceptance or institutional control secure philosophy's authority? We simply cannot know.

9.7 Conclusion

Plato had theorized the basis of philosophy's independent power by hypothesizing that:

1 philosophy is not an activity apart from politics; its core work – of understanding and/or fashioning concepts that have their full life only as principles and rules for action – directly engages the formation of values, norms, and interests, and so touches the heart of politics;
2 the concepts of philosophy come to be implanted in students through language that is *enargês* or vivid; this includes both dialogic language and language that is full of metaphors, ecphrastic images, allegories, and other techniques that engage cognition in all its registers, the sort of language Plato used in writing the *Republic*; language that is *enargês* generates a surplus of linguistic power, which can be deployed in politics alongside other forms of power;
3 not only oral discourse but also written texts, which can reach broad audiences, can be vivid or have *enargeia* (or *energeia* on Aristotle's terms);
4 if the concepts of philosophy are broadly disseminated, they will affect contests over values, norms, and interests for the mass of citizens, and not merely the elites;
5 philosophers can therefore affect politics by means other than the immediate personal education of elites; in particular they can do so through vivid writing, which is to say, through the deployment of surpluses of linguistic power.

If Plato's theory of the role of language in politics is right, we should, as I wrote at the start of chapter 7, expect to see just those of his concepts that he conveyed in his most vivid, most metaphorical language playing an especially important part in Athenian discourse; we should expect to see them functioning as rules for action, and we would need to see uptake of his concepts not merely by elites but also by the mass of democratic citizens.

In Aeschines' effort to describe "types of man" and to draw the Athenian jurors into a comparative theoretical exercise, we see just such vivid vocabulary at work; in Demosthenes' rejoinder with the question (in effect) "Why do you talk like Plato?" (*ti logous platteis;*), we see a politician who himself put his finger on the vividness of Platonic language as one of its distinctive features. Because we also saw Demosthenes tapping into a repertoire of jokes about Plato, we can also confirm that when the elites on courtroom stages pitched out their philosophical concepts, and criticisms of them, the mass citizen juries were understood to be capable of catching them, maybe not each and every man of them, but enough of them to make the effort worthwhile for the politicians.

More still can, however, be said about the uptake of Platonic concepts by the mass of citizens. Athenian politicians routinely advanced their political agendas by proposing in the assembly that statues be erected to one or another figure they wished to have the city honor. Demosthenes, for instance, in the 340s secured the erection of statues of Bosporan kings who supplied the Athenians with significant amounts of grain. Lycurgus similarly honored foreigners for supporting the grain supply, but he also secured the erection of statues of Athens' three most esteemed tragic poets, Aeschylus, Sophocles, and Euripides.[46] Thus he followed Plato in affirming the value of canons, while differing on the content of the canon.

Populating the garden of Athenian symbols, the statues erected by Demosthenes and Lycurgus stood as two sets of *eidôla*, or shadowy images, imperfectly capturing sometimes overlapping and sometimes opposed principles for pursuing the city's well-being. These statues themselves spoke, having been given voice by the arguments of each politician in the courtroom and assembly. To the degree that these arguments concerned the value of Plato to Athenian culture, the statues that these politicians erected – and their accompanying speeches – provided for the broad dissemination of Platonic concepts – as well as of rejoinders to them – to the mass of Athenian citizens. As terms such as *prohairesis* (deliberated commitment), *kolasis* (reform), *to kalliston* (the most beautiful), *ho nomothetês* (the legislator), and *plattein* (to model) provided principles and rules for action, these concepts transformed contests over values, norms, and interests. Most significantly, they established a framework for legitimating governance by experts. Under the influence of Platonic ideas, Athenian democracy drifted toward a managerial form.

Our look at Athenian politics has, then, sustained both Plato's general hypothesis that philosophical ideas, conveyed with vivid symbols, can have significant political impacts and also, further, the more specific hypothesis that Plato himself influenced Athenian politics. Nor can his influence be explained adequately by economic, political, or institutional changes already under way. Even if sometimes working in tandem with these other sources of power, the power inherent in influential ideas has an independent capacity to shift conceptions of personal and social identity, and therewith the framework of political decision-making. Perhaps such power is most frequently deployed when shifts generated by other structural forces – economic or political – are already under way, as was the case in Athens in the middle of the fourth century, but nothing precludes the deployment of power such as this in contexts of stability. Consequently, we have reason to recognize ideas as having the potential to be independent sources of change.

What did Plato do? Through his writerly techniques, Plato cunningly launched philosophy on its political career. In addition to participating in dialectic, he analyzed the sources of power inherent in language and released that power with his dialogues. From these he crafted an instrument that changed Athenian political vocabulary and thereby stirred up the city's politics, shifting its politicians toward defenses of elite expertise and forms of managerial, instead of direct, democracy. For all, then, that Plato praised the superiority of a philosophical life, there was also a Plato whom it is reasonable to identify as a politician and to designate, therefore, as Politikos.

Epilogue
And to My Colleagues

I hope that this account of Plato's philosophy of language and its relation to his political theory has advanced our understanding of Plato as a philosopher. In particular, I hope that several elements of Platonic philosophy now make more sense: the place of pragmatism within Platonic philosophy; the line analogy in the *Republic*; the relationship between paradigms and Forms; the difference between *mimêsis* (imitation), which is disavowed in Book 10 of the *Republic,* and other forms of image-making, such as non-representative visualization and model-making; the ethical status of the noble lie; the distinction between a philosophical and a political way of life; the philosophical meaning of Plato's own writerly style; and his view of how political change can be effected.

I also hope that this account of Plato's philosophy of language and its relation to his political theory, supplemented by the consideration of the role of Platonic ideas in fourth-century Athenian politics, has advanced our understanding of Plato as *politikos*, that is, as a politician: he developed theories of human cognition and acted on them to try to change his fellow citizens; he spoke in public, both by giving one public lecture and by leaving a corpus of texts designed for broad dissemination over time; he became the butt of jokes and, obliquely, the target of prosecution. This means he succeeded at a project of influence. Nor can his influence be explained adequately by economic, political, or institutional changes already under way. He was only one among many forces for change operating within Athens during the fourth century, but he was indeed a wielder of *pharmaka*, that is, of concepts and symbols, which served as agents of change.

Finally, I hope that – by drawing attention to late fourth-century Athenian politics, to the debates over culture and politics of 330 BCE, and to the events surrounding philosophy in 307 BCE – I have made clear that the tale of the

Why Plato Wrote Danielle S. Allen. © 2010 Danielle S. Allen

relation between philosophy and politics does not end in 399 BCE: we must widen the frame. When we study Athens, we should take in the whole fourth century, if we wish to grasp the relation between institutions and ideology in Athenian history.

This book, then, has sought to make points philosophical, political-theoretical, and historical.

But I will be especially glad if this book should turn out to provide, for my fellow political theorists and historians of political thought, a new model for tracing the relations between ideas and events or among language, history, and political theory. In brief, my suggestion is that the pragmatist recognition that beliefs are rules for action may provide the key to explaining the rise and role of organized political language (in Pocock's formulation),[1] shifts in that organizing linguistic structure, and the effects of those shifts. One needs to know where, when, and for whom ideas come into play as rules for action. And one needs to ask exactly how, and with what meanings and consequences, particular ideas are converted into principles and rules for action.

Here I am asking questions like those posed by Quentin Skinner but with a critical difference. He writes (2005: 33–34):

> We [intellectual historians] are interested in the history of the moral and political concepts that are nowadays used to construct and appraise our common world ... To understand such concepts, the intellectual historians I have cited agree, what we need to find out is when, and how, and why the vocabulary in which they are expressed originally arose, what purposes this vocabulary was designed to serve, what role it played in argument. What is needed, in short, is a history of concepts. It is true that many such histories have of late been written, above all by Reinhart Koselleck and his army of associates, who have created an entire research program centered on what Koselleck likes to call *Begriffsgeschichte*. This kind of research, however, is not what I have in mind, or not exclusively what I have in mind. The program in which I am interested is concerned not so much with the history of concepts in themselves as with the history of their acquisition and deployment in argument, the history of what has been done with them, and thus with the changing roles they have played in our culture.

Instead of asking what has been done with ideas, though, I would propose that we consider the form that ideas take as principles and rules for action; this is a somewhat different problematic than Skinner's. It is to ask what practical realities emanate from the use of the concept, instead of asking how particular users of the concept adapt its semantic content. Studying that too is useful, but it is only part of the story of how ideas become rules for action.

In *Logics of History* Bill Sewell develops a theory of "events as transformations of structures," and argues (2005: 245) that "events introduce new conceptions of what really exists, of what is good, and of what is possible."

As I have tracked the influence of Platonic vocabulary in Athenian politics, I have tried to underscore how it, like Sewell's "events," introduced new conceptions of what really exists, of what is good, and of what is possible. Because new ideas can introduce changes to fundamental conceptions of reality, value, and possibility, linguistic change can in itself contain the seeds of structural change. As political actors – whether elite or common, individual or mass actors – take up new concepts, they adopt new conceptions of what really exists, of what is good, and of what is possible. These new conceptions of reality, value, and possibility structure the practical effects that will emerge from new ideas as they become principles of action.

But how does the arrival of new principles of and rules for action on the political scene begin to manifest itself in changes to material realities? One can track the material effect of new principles of action in institutional changes, as when a new rule for action becomes the basis for a law or bureaucratic procedure, and practices and protocols begin to shift around it. I gestured at tracking such institutional change when I made note, in chapter 9, of the introduction of two new legal institutions in Athens: the "law guards" and the "guardians of women." A full analysis of the effects of Plato's ideas would require ascertaining the degree to which the legal structure of the city as a whole shifted around these new authorities.

Or one can track the material effects of new ideas by paying attention to the evolution of cleavages and alliances. Individuals form their identities around, at least in part, their beliefs about reality, value, and possibility. Thus as these fundamental concepts shift – whether because of the impact of events or the acquisition of new principles and rules for action in the form of ideas – agents will also adapt their identities and identifications to conform with their new beliefs. An immediate effect of this kind of conceptual shift is therefore to enable fresh alliances and group formations and to generate new cleavages. Hattam and Lowndes rightly write:

> [N]ot all linguistic change carries with it the same order of significance; some innovations are fleeting, momentary examples of word play, while others enact more durable shifts in meaning that reverberate through political identification and alliances in the most profound fashion . . . It is to these profound discursive reconfigurations that we attend. (2007: 203)

In the context of American politics, they analyze linguistic change to identify changing cleavages and their consequences. In particular, they use such analysis to develop explanations of the rise of the modern right, the invention of ethnicity, and contemporary efforts to reconfigure Republicanism. Like Hattam and Lowndes, I have, in chapters 7, 8 and 9, sought to trace shifting political cleavages by tracking one major change in Athenian political vocabulary in the fourth century: its conversion of terms developed by philosophers into rules for action in judicial and deliberative decision-making.

These are only two of the ways in which one can track the conversion of ideas into principles and rules for action and the deployment of these to generate material and structural effects. There are surely others. The important point is simply that it is ultimately as rules for action that ideas are linked to life.

But why are some ideas taken up as principles and rules for action and others not? I hope lastly to have contributed, as part of an answer to this question, the idea of "surplus linguistic power." Each of us in our daily exchanges hopes to be convincing when we talk, and from the ebb and flow of our casual discourse, some words or phrases may emerge that we or others repeat and that slowly spread. This seems to me to be the basic level of linguistic power that inheres in all speech and to which all speakers have access. But some ideas are given by their makers, whether intentionally or accidentally, linguistic forms that more fully engage human cognitive capacities and so more deeply lodge themselves in human psyches and memories. The active pursuit by politicians of sound-bites is an indication of their intuitive recognition that such a thing as surplus linguistic power exists.

Politicians intuitively deploy a range of mnemonic techniques – for instance, alliteration and antithesis – to make compressed statements of their views memorable. A sound-bite is a suitcase, even one's single carry-on bag. A speaker packs into no more than a sentence or two some core principles as well as some instruction to listeners on how to apply those principles to real-world examples. The good news about packing everything up so tightly is that listeners can easily pick up a sound-bite and walk around with it for days, mulling it over. And if the speaker has packed it well, it will unpack well. By this I mean that from just a few words uttered by a speaker, a listener will be able to unfold the full extent of the principle being advocated as well as the implicit arguments in support of it and its practical consequences.

Because sound-bites are easily learned and long remembered, they circulate across time and space and are particularly effective in contexts of mass communication. One can consider the sound-bite successful precisely when no one can any longer claim authorship; then the sound-bite belongs to the language, to the culture. Those who aspire to surplus linguistic power want their sound-bites to become bits of commonly spoken language that circulate without attribution; they want them, in other words, to become authoritative. Sound-bites that make the rounds create, replicate, and transform culture.

As John Cooper points out (1997a: 1677), Socrates "believed that knowing correct definitions of ethical ideas would make people morally better," but it was Plato "who urged a systematic approach to definition." A little known text, called *Definitions*, attributed to him but certainly not written by him, contains a list of 185 terms and definitions "formulated and discussed in Plato's Academy in the middle years of the fourth century" (ibid.). Some of the Platonic sound-bites that I have identified as circulating in Athenian politics appear in this text. Among them are:

> *kolasis* chastisement: treatment given to a soul concerning a past mistake;
> *theos* god: immortal living being, self-sufficient for happiness; eternal being, the cause of the nature of goodness;
> *aretê* virtue: the best disposition; the state of a mortal creature which is in itself praiseworthy; the state on account of which its possessor is said to be good; the just observance of the laws; the disposition on account of which he who is so disposed is said to be perfectly excellent; the state which produces faithfulness to law;
> *dikaiosunê* justice: the unanimity of the soul with itself, and the good discipline of the parts of the soul with respect to each other and concerning each other; the state that distributes to each person according to what is deserved; the state on account of which its possessor chooses what appears to him to be just; the state underlying a law-abiding way of life; social equality; the state of obedience to the laws;
> *hairesis* selection: correct evaluation;
> *politeia* republic: community of many men, self-sufficient for living successfully; community of many under the rule of law.

The existence of such a text as the *Definitions* is another indication that Platonic vocabulary was built to travel. As I have tried to show in the preceding chapters, among his many other talents, Plato Politikos was a master of the sound-bite. It was no casual comment to call him, as I did in the Prologue, the western world's first message man.

Appendix 1
The Relationship between
Paradigms and Forms

We can better understand the relationship between "paradigms" and "Forms" if we pay close attention to how Socrates uses his technical vocabulary for different kinds of images. He builds up the concept of "paradigm" by defining it in contrast to *phantasmata* (phantasms) and *eidōla* (shadow-images) while linking it closely to *tupoi* (types). The word *eikōn* captures both the problematic images (phantasms and shadows) and the valuable images (types and paradigms), but the proximity of the terms *paradeigma* and *eikones* to one another is made clear by the fact that *tupos* can serve as a synonym for either (*Rep.* 559a, 402b–d).

Naddaff (2002: 80) correctly notices that Socrates is quite consistent in using *eidōla* and *phantasmata* only for the banned images of the mimetic artists, while using *eikones* instead for images that successfully "participate in" a true and (materially) imperceptible original or that can be "used" to gain access to concepts derived from a true and imperceptible original. There is one exception to this, when Socrates uses *eikōn* also for the images in the realm of conjecture represented by the bottom section of the line. Thus, the word *eikōn* means image generally, but mostly is used for the images he endorses.[1]

In fact, Socrates is consistent in this distinction throughout the whole of the *Republic* and not merely in Book 10. The distinction even shows up in the distribution of these terms across the dialogue. The term *eidōlon* is densely concentrated in the cave passage, the Book 9 discussion of the souls of the pleasure-lover, honor-lover, and tyrant, and in the Book 10 discussion of *mimēsis*. The traditional poets are finally condemned with the neologism *eidōlopoiounta eidōla*; this unusual cognate accusative is the final instance of the term *eidōlon* in the *Republic*. In contrast, the words that Socrates uses

Why Plato Wrote   Danielle S. Allen. © 2010 Danielle S. Allen

for his own images (*eikones, paradeigmata*) show up in Books 2–5, but are largely absent from 6 and 7 and are altogether absent from Book 9.

Extraordinarily enough, Socrates takes the idea of the *eidôlon*, which becomes the sign of a "poetic image," from Homer himself. In Book 3 of the *Republic*, he quotes the *Iliad* (23.103–104), where Achilles reports on his dream journey to the underworld: "Alas, there is then, in the house of Hades, a spirit and a phantom [*eidôlon*], but no mind within it dwells." This *Iliadic* passage is important again in Book 7 when Socrates describes the lives of those who are stuck in the cave and do not manage to escape into the realm of dialectic (534c–d):

> Anyone who cannot use reason to distinguish the Form of the good from everything else, who cannot fight his way through all attempts to disprove his theory in his eagerness to test it by the standard of being rather than the standard of opinion or appearance, who cannot make his way through all these dangers with his explanation unscathed – won't you say that a person who is in this state knows neither the good itself nor any other good? That if at any point he does lay hold of some *eidôlon* of it, he does so using opinion, not knowledge? That he is dreaming and dozing away his life on earth, and that one day he will come to Hades and go to sleep for good, without ever waking up here at all?

The term *eidôlon*, in other words, comes with a Homeric lineage already detailing the separation of images of this kind from the realm of *nous*.

Scholars have not always noticed the precision of Socrates' terminology. Thus Annas misses this distinction between *eidôlon* and *eikón* (1997: 148), as does Shorey (1930: 412) who writes on the use of *eidôlon* at 443c, referring also to 520c:

> The contemplation of the εἴδωλον, image or symbol, leads us to the reality. The reality is always the Platonic Idea. The εἴδωλον, in the case of ordinary "things," is the material copy which men mistake for the reality (516 a). In the case of spiritual things and moral ideas, there is no visible image or symbol (*Politicus* 286a), but imperfect analogies, popular definitions, suggestive phrases, as τὰ ἑαυτοῦ πράττειν, well-meant laws and institutions serve as the εἴδωλα in which the philosophic dialectician may find a reflection of the true idea. Cf. on 520c, *Sophist* 234c, *Theaetetus* 150B.

Shorey's argument would be right if he had recognized that it is the *eikón* or the *paradeigma* that serves in this way, not the *eidôlon*. *Eikones* and *paradeigmata* provide access to reality but they do this not as "material copies" but by means of "material visualization" (see chapter 3). Socrates carefully distinguishes between representational images which are intended as copies of things and visualizing images that are "used" to learn about things at 500e, 510b–e, 511a, 529d–e, and 540a.

Although many scholars have intuitively noticed the importance of the concept of "paradigm" to the argument of the *Republic*, few have taken the time to scrutinize the concept directly. That is, they note the frequency with which the word "paradigm" is used, often simply by putting their translation "pattern" in quotation marks, when discussing the relevant passages, but they do not stop to figure out what a "paradigm" actually is and how it relates to an "icon" or *eikón*, that other fundamental term of art for Plato in his discussion of images, or to Forms themselves, nor how it is contrasted with *eidólon*, as it is.[2]

Similarly, scholars who work on the *Republic* often adopt Plato's vocabulary about the "plasticity" of the human soul but without recognizing that they are thereby assimilating a core Platonic concept that carries with it substantial conceptual baggage. So, for instance, see Naddaff (2002: 25): "Rather, Socrates' censorship forges a resemblance, a similarity, between the poetic *muthos* and the philosophical *logos* so that the future guardians' education begins again (and still) with the mythopoetic, with utterances as plastic as the malleable young souls shaped and transformed by them." Or Lear 1997: 63: "For Plato, humans enter the world with a capacity to absorb cultural influences. The young human psyche is like a resin, able to receive the impress of cultural influence before it sets into a definite shape."[3] Importantly, the terms *paradeigma* and *plattein* have a relationship to one another in the *Republic* that deserves scholarly attention and which helps explain the relationship between "paradigms" and "Forms."

If the importance of the term *paradeigma* were not already clear in the *Republic*, the *Timaeus* makes it explicitly so. In that dialogue, the Forms are described *as* paradigms, "objects to which the divine craftsman looks in creating the sensible world, and to which we must look in order to acquire knowledge" (Kraut 2005 [1992]a: 19; *Timaeus* 29b, 48e–49a, 50d, 52a, 53c). In contrast, paradigms are not equated to Forms in the *Republic*. Rather, the concept of "paradigm" provides a way of linking the Forms to the "sensibles." The verb *plattein* is important for explaining that link.

Although scholars have not yet fully developed an account of the concept of "paradigm" in Plato, Devereux (2003 [1999]: 213 n. 53) addresses the concept in a lengthy and very helpful footnote. He writes:

> In the *Phaedo* in expressing his uncertainty about the nature of participation, Socrates speaks of the Form as perhaps being "present to" its participants, or being "in communion with" them but he is not yet sure how to specify the relation (100d3–8). He [Socrates] does not mention the "paradigm–copy" relation as one possible way of understanding participation. In the *Republic* and *Timaeus* Plato no longer expresses uncertainty about how to understand

"participation": the paradigm–copy relation becomes the model for under-standing how Forms are related to their participants.

This argument that the paradigm–copy relationship explains how Forms are related to their participants, that is, to sensibles, can and should be refined.

Before we try to refine the account of how paradigms relate to Forms, we should look a little more closely at the concept of "participation." Devereux (2003 [1999]: 197) asks: "What exactly is involved in this 'participation'? The *Phaedo* provides no answer: Socrates confesses that he is 'not yet' able to specify the relationship between the admittedly vague expressions 'participation in', 'being present to', or 'communion with' (100d3–8)." Devereux adds (ibid.: 200 n. 19):

> A number of commentators have noted that the expressions "participation in," "being present to," "communion with" are strongly suggestive of immanence, and that at the very least they imply that Plato took seriously the possi-bility that Forms are immanent in their participants; ... Aristotle, however, seems to have had a different understanding of Plato's attitude towards immanence and participation. Although he complains that to describe Forms as "paradigms," and to say that other things "participate in" them is simply a cover for confusion (*Metaph.* M 5, 1079b24–6; A9, 991a20–2, 992a26–9, cf. A 6, 987b11–14), he does not suggest that Plato was unsure about whether Forms are in their participants; on the contrary, his assertions that Forms were not regarded as immanent by the Platonists are never hedged or qualified. Aristotle apparently believed, on the one hand, that the separation of Forms involved the rejection of immanence and, on the other, that Plato was unable to offer any clear account of what it is for things to "participate in" separate Forms; that is, he did not take the lack of clarity about participation to extend to the question whether Forms are immanent ... Aristotle's understanding seems to fit well with our findings: beginning in the *Phaedo*, Plato separates Forms from sensible particulars and takes this separation to entail the denial of immanence.

Finally, Devereux adds (ibid.: 203): "Separate existence for Plato is not exactly the same thing as ontological independence."

Vlastos (1997: 186) helps us to refine the notion of "participation" that links Forms and sensibles. The copy is "less real" than the Form, in being less genuine or less actual; Vlastos clarifies these evaluations as entailing a difference between the "cognitive reliability" and "reliably valuable" state inhering in the Forms and the "cognitive non-reliability" and "non-reliability of value" of the participants:

> If you want to investigate the nature of gold, coffee, courage, beauty, you must look to the genuine article; the other kind will trick you sooner or later, for

along with some F-properties, it has also perhaps cunningly concealed, some not-F properties, and if you were to take the latter for the former your mistake would be disastrous.

Vlastos (1997: 1990):

> With this account before us, let us take stock of its results. It has taken the grades of reality theory as an implied analogy or, more precisely, as a bundle of implied analogies, telling us that if we think of things which are "real" because they are genuine, true, pure, in contrast with those which are not, we will have a clue to the relation of the Platonic Form to its mundane instances.

We should keep these features of the concept of "participation" in mind as we refine the account of the relationship between paradigms and forms.

Paradigms relate to Forms in two ways, one cognitive and one ethical. With respect to their cognitive role, in the *Republic* (in contrast to the *Timaeus*) paradigms (and *eikones* also) are not Forms themselves but visualizations "used" to pursue intellectual access to concepts derived from the wholly imperceptible and non-sensible Forms. (See the argument in chapter 3 and the following passages: 500e [*paradeigmata*], 510b–e [*eikones*], 511a [*eikones*], 529d–e [*paradeigmata*], 540a [*paradeigma*].) Although paradigms provide visualization of the truths embodied by the Forms, they also contain not-F properties. They participate in the F properties but not as reliably as the Forms themselves. In this sense, they both "participate" in the Forms and are "less real" than the Forms.

As to their ethical role, "paradigms" serve to direct the molding (*plattein*) of sensibles in the direction of the Forms. Thus, the philosopher has the job of looking closely at divine order with the goal of putting that order into effect in human behavior, both "molding" (*plattein*) his own personality to that order, and trying to mold the personalities of others too (500d); the result of molding one's personality is the production of paradigms (*paradeigmata*) in one's own soul (484c; see also 409b–d).

The cognitive and ethical functions thus converge. The sensibles participate in the Forms by "patterning themselves after" or "molding themselves around" or by being molded by a craftsman around the principles and concepts conveyed through our senses to our minds by means of paradigms. In describing how the philosopher relates sensibles to the Forms, Socrates first says that the philosopher "imitates" (*mimeisthai*) the divine order, but this evolves into the following activities: "being likened to" (*aphomoiousthai*) the divine order; "being with" (*homilein*) the divine order, "molding oneself" (*plattein heauton*), "establishing customs" (*tithenai ethê*), and working as a craftsman or *dêmiourgos* of justice and public virtue. The imitation (or *mimêsis*) involved, then, in developing and using paradigms of the divine order is not a matter of "representation" but of "emulation";[4] it is a matter of creating models through which those who observe those models can learn as much as possible (but not everything) about the divine order itself, and where such learning is expected to transform the individuals who acquire it and all the products of their craft.

We have therefore identified at least one sense in which paradigms and sensibles participate in the Forms: by facilitating access to the Forms for observers, paradigms (and the sensibles that embody paradigms) do the work of the Forms, which wish to be known; they therefore participate in the Forms as their co-workers.

Notably, *eikones* (for instance, the image of the sun, the line, the cave, and the soul) do not provide us with models on which to pattern ourselves but only with models that give us access to concepts derived from and participating in imperceptible truths. In other words, they play only a cognitive and not an ethical role. Since the former type of cognitive modeling (captured by the term "paradigm") includes the latter type of ethical modeling, *paradeigma* turns out to be a more inclusive term than *eikôn*. The term *tupos* slides back and forth between indicating the more inclusive and the more restrictive idea of modeling, that is, between indicating both cognitive and ethical modeling and indicating cognitive modeling only. But *eikones* and *tupoi*, just like paradigms, also participate in the Forms as their co-workers by facilitating the access of students to knowledge of concepts that participate in the Forms.

Appendix 2
A Second Tri-partite Division of the Soul?

As Burnyeat argues, the recognition that Book 10 of the *Republic* focuses on cognitive, instead of motivational, conflict helps explain what seems like a switch of focus in that book from considering the soul as tri-partite to considering it as bi-partite. Burnyeat discusses "cognitive conflict" as that phenomenon "in which the reasoning part of the soul appears to be at variance with itself" (1999: 223, 222–228). The images of the tragedians cause confusion by triggering this cognitive conflict, although they also mislead by tapping into the desires and triggering "motivational conflicts." Burnyeat's point about the centrality of cognitive conflict to Book 10 and to the *Republic* is even more important than he himself indicates and should be extended.

The relevant two parts of the soul that are at issue in Book 10 are the two domains of cognition represented by the line analogy, the domain of the visible and of opinion and the domain of rationality and the truth. Importantly, Socrates also makes this bi-partite division function as a tri-partite division. Remember that each of the two parts of the line is divided again, so that we have a line of four parts. But then the middle two sections of the line turned out to represent a single set of cognizable objects, including both the mathematician's drawings and the sorts of material artifacts made, for instance, by carpenters (see chapter 3). Thus, the line analogy represents exactly the three categories of "making" discussed in Book 10: the shadow-images made by imitators; the objects made by craftsmen and mathematicians; and the Forms (made in Book 10 by the demiurge). The line's quadri-partite division of cognition turns out itself to be a tri-partite division. Thus, the *Republic* presents us with a soul with two different kinds of tri-partite division: one between reason, spirit, and desire; and the

Why Plato Wrote   Danielle S. Allen. © 2010 Danielle S. Allen

other between the intellectual faculty that works with Forms (*nous*), the intellectual faculty that works with models (including both images and material objects) that participate in the Forms (*dianoia*), and the intellectual faculty (*pistis/eikasia*) that works with images of material objects that are shadows only and seek only to represent the material object itself.

Socrates uses Books 8 and 9 to bring these two different divisions of the soul together. Thus, the decline from the kingly man through the timocratic to the oligarchic man is a decline from those in whom reason rules to those in whom spirit rules and finally to those in whom pleasure rules. But, then, the souls ruled by pleasure are further divided. They are represented not only by the oligarchic man but also by the democratic and tyrannical men. The oligarchic man is better than both the democratic man and the tyrannical man in still having some knowledge of the "law" of the old regime; to some, if only a minimal, extent, he still adheres to the rules established by those who chose the life of reason. Thus, the descent from the oligarchic man through the democratic to the tyrannical man is a second descent, from the man whose basis for judging what counts as pleasure comes to some extent from reason to the man whose basis for judging what counts as pleasure comes only from pleasure itself. And this second descent Socrates describes as being a descent away from truth and knowledge. In other words, it is a cognitive, instead of an ethical, descent.

Thus, the first descent (from reason through spirit to desire) results in three types of man each of whom argues for a different pleasure as the greatest: learning, reputation, and profit. This provokes the questions of how they are to judge among these pleasures and of which of them has the instrument for judging pleasure correctly. This leads Socrates and Glaucon to have the following exchange at 582d:

SOCRATES: And the instrument with which judgment should be made does not belong to the lover of profit or the lover of honour, but to the lover of wisdom.
GLAUCON: What instrument is that?
SOCRATES: We said judgment should be made using reasoned arguments, didn't we?
GLAUCON: Yes.
SOCRATES: And reasoning is essentially the instrument of the philosopher, the lover of wisdom.

Socrates allows that if those with souls who love profit or victory follow knowledge and rational thought, they will gain pleasures which are the truest possible for them. But then he argues that "when one of the other parts takes control, there are two results: *it fails to discover* its own proper pleasure, and *it compels the other parts* to pursue a pleasure which is not their own, and not true" (587a). This passage expressly conjoins two psychic registers: a cognitive register and a motivational register. In the cognitive register, what is at issue is the project of discovering (or failing to discover) what true pleasure is. In the motivational register, what is at issue is which part of the soul motivates the soul as a whole (compelling the other parts to pursue a goal).

Those who pursue a life of pleasure therefore have two problems: both that the lowest part of their soul rules them (that which pursues pleasure) *and* that they do not have the instrument which could properly discover what pleasure is. Thus, "for anyone other than the wise, pleasure is not true and pure, but a kind of shadow-picture [*eskiagraphêmenê*]" (583b). Socrates proceeds from this point, 583b through 587b, by reprising the images of ascent from a "bottom" full of shadows to a top of understanding that he had developed through the images of the sun, the line, and the cave. The tyrannical man lives "among pleasures mingled with pains, shadows of the true pleasure and shadow-paintings in which both pleasure and pain take their color from their proximity to each other [*eidólois tês alêthous hêdonês kai eskiagraphêmenais*]" (586bc; cf. 584a). As do those who dwell in the cave (515c), those with souls of this sort, fight over these images (*eidóla*) (586c). Importantly, this problem is cognitive, not motivational. In other words, the figure of the tyrant represents a person who dwells in the lowest psychic register along two different axes: the motivational axis (reason, spirit, vs. desire) and the cognitive axis (*nous*, *dianoia*, and *pistis/eikasia*).

Several times in Books 8 and 9 Socrates accuses the tragedians in particular of breeding and vitalizing the sort of soul that is both ruled by desire and dwells in the domain of *eikasia*: 568a–d and also 572e–573b, and 584a where the "magicians" (*hoi deinoi magoi, goêteia*) and "tyrant-makers" (*tyranno-poioi*) who produce illusions (*phantasmata*) must be the tragic poets of 568a–d. Naddaff 2002: 22 writes:

> In fact, the power of a poetic representation was measured by the poet's success in deceiving and tricking the audience into believing that his artistic creation was the thing itself as it truly is in reality. For this reason, the best tragedy was, according to the *Dissoi Logoi*, the one that "knows how to deceive by making things for the most part resemble the truth." Deceptive verisimilitude was considered an essential attribute, not a devastating defect, of the poetic logos.

The suggestion in these books of the *Republic*, too, is that the tragic poets have some special role to play in generating the types of soul that dwell on the lowest psychic register of each tri-partite axis. And thus, indeed, when we turn to Book 10, we are given an account, as Burnyeat so ably demonstrates, of how the tragedians, and other imitators of the world's material objects, foster and develop the weakest cognitive faculty.

A common error in the scholarship (e.g. Naddaff 2002: 80) is to think that the images of the mimetic artist are "the mirror opposite" of the images of the scientist and dialectical philosopher, the former being false and the latter emanating from the truth. This view that the images of the tragedians are the opposite of those of the scientist and dialectical philosopher emerges from focusing exclusively on the motivational conflict and the effect of images on the tripartite soul, whereby mimetic images enlarge and expand the desires. But if one considers how these images function in relation to "cognitive conflict," then opposition is not the right way to capture the relationship. Socrates is very specific. As Burnyeats points out, the issue is degrees of distance from the truth and he provides a very clear account of what it means for the images produced by the "imitators" to be at the third remove from truth (1999). The line image establishes the cognitive levels that define the possible degrees of distance from the truth that characterize different human uses of images. Burnyeat's account essentially maps out this second of the tri-partite divisions of the soul, though he does not recognize the relation between Book 10, and his account of it, and the line analogy (or at least he does not explicitly draw this connection in his lectures).

Vlastos 1997 provides a very helpful account of the different degrees of "reality" that are said to characterize Forms and sensibles; the idea of degrees of reality requires understanding "reality" as conveying "genuineness" or "actuality," rather than as conveying an "existential state." Asmis (2005 [1992]: 352) also gets this right, as does Annas (1997: 150). Indeed, Naddaff herself ultimately recognizes that the problem of the relationship between the mimetic artists' *eidóla* and the *eikones* of the philosopher is not one of opposition but of awkward proximity, or false appearances of identity (Naddaff 2002: 81). Nehamas is wrong, then, to think that "particulars participate in the Forms in different respects or in different contexts but never, so far as I can tell, in different degrees" (Nehamas 2003 [1999]: 180).

The importance of the idea of distance from the truth, or participation by degrees, to Socrates' argument in the *Republic* is captured by the number 729 which calculates the degree of difference between the happiness of the philosopher and the happiness of the tyrant. This number, which is 3 to the sixth power, captures the tri-partite motivational structure of the soul as well as the tri-partite cognitive structure of the soul. It is because the tyrannical soul dwells in the third of each of these registers that it is 729 times removed in happiness from the best soul dwelling at the top of each register.

Appendix 3
Miso- Compounds in Greek Literature

This table covers Greek literature through the time of Aristotle and is presented in roughly chronological order. Here and in the footnotes, I have listed the frequency with which particular words appear in particular authors without providing the word count for the author's entire corpus. I have sought instead to provide supplemental information about exactly where the relevant terms appear and in what contexts. To provide the word count for any given author's corpus would more often than not obscure issues of survival and of genre and, in my view, provide a misleading sense of increased precision.

Author	No. of instances	Citations	Words used	Additional notes
Homer	0			
Heraclitus	1	Fr. 1, line 12	*misanthrôpêsas*	
Aeschylus	1	*Agam.* 1090	*misotheon*	
Sophocles	0			
Phrynichus	1	*Fragmenta* (Kock, *CAF*) Fr. 3, line 3	*misanthrôpon*	
Empedocles	1	Fr. 1, line 92	*misoponêrôs*	
Herodotus	2	6.121.5	*misoturannoi*	
		6.123.2	*misoturannoi*	
Hippocrates	4	*Praeceptiones* 7.11	*misoponêriêi*	
		Letter 13.25	*misoponêron*	
		Letter 17.250	*misanthrôpiês*	
		De medico 1.14	*misanthrôpos*	
Democritus	0			
Thucydides	0			
Aristophanes	7	*Wasps* 473	*misodême*	the *misodêmos* is also an *erastês monarchias* (lover of monarchy)

Author	No. of instances	Citations	Words used	Additional notes
		Fragmenta (Kock, CAF) vol. 1, Fr.108 line 3	misodêmon	
		Fragmenta (Kock, CAF) vol. 3, Fr. 676b line 2	misogelôs	
		Wasps 1165	misolakôn	a joke about the use of miso-compounds
		Peace 304	misolamachos	
		Wasps 411	misopolin	
		Peace 662	misoporpakistatê	a joke about the use of miso-compounds
[Andocides]	2	Against Alcib. 8	misodêmias	(relating to Alcibiades' membership in a political faction)
		Against Alcib. 16	misodêmous	
Lysias	2	26.21	misodêmian	(relating to the 404/3 coup)
		30.35	misoponêrein	
Plato	14	Mexeneus 245c7	misobarbaron	
		Rep. 566c3	misodêmos	
		Phaedo 89d4	misologoi	
		Phaedo 89d1	misologoi	
		Laches 18834	misologon	
		Laches 188c6	misologos	
		Rep. 411d7	misologos	
		Rep. 535d6	misoponê	
		Rep. 456a4	misosophos	
		Phaedo 89d1	misanthrôpoi	
		Protagoras 327d6	misanthrôpoi	
		Laws 791d9	misanthrôpous	
		Phaedo 89d4	misanthrôpia	
		Phaedo 89d4	misanthrôpia	
[Plato]		Definitiones 415e4	misologos	
Xenophon	5	Agesilaus	mishellêna	
		Hellenica 2.3.48	misochrêstotatos	
		Agesilaus 7.7.2	misopersên	
		Cynegeticus 3.9.2	misothêron	
		Hellenica 2.3.47	misodêmotatos	
Isocrates	4	Areopagiticus 57.5	misodêmos	
		Antidosis	misodêmos	
		Antidosis 131.2	misanthrôpos	
		Antidosis 315.2	misanthrôpian	
Antiphanes	1	Fragmenta (Kock, CAF), tit 159, line 1	misoponêros	
Anaximenes	2	Ars rhetorica 36.5	misopolin	
		Ars rhetorica 36.5	misophilon	

Author	No. of instances	Citations	Words used	Additional notes
Demosthenes	4	21.218	*misoponêroi*	
		18.112	*misanthrôpias*	
		45.68	*misanthrôpias*	
		23. 202	*misathênaiotatous*	
Aeschines	10	2.171	*misodêmos*	
		2.14	*misophilippos*	
		3.66	*misophilippos*	
		3.73	*misophilippos*	
		1.69	*misoponêros*	
		2.171	*misoponêros*	
		3.78	*misoteknos*	
		3.92	*misoturannos*	
		3.66	*misalexandros*	
		3.73	*misalexandros*	
Xenocrates	1	Fr. 35, line 9	*misagathiai*	
Aristoxenus	1	Fr. 130, line 2	*misanthrôpein*	
[Aristotle]	3	*Virtues and Vices* 1250b	*misoponêria*	
		1251b	*misanthrôpia*	
		Category 8, treatise title 45, fragment 611, line 129	*misoponêros*	
Lycurgus	2	1.39	*misodêmos*	
		1.39	*misathênaios*	
Dinarchus	1	3.22	*misodêmoi*	

Notes

Prologue

1 To take just two examples, Cartledge (2009: 21) writes about Plato: "Plato, however, had relatively little interest in practical terrestrial politics"; Wallace (1989: 179) says: "Few now accept the opinion that Plato and Isokrates themselves had a significant or direct impact on Athenian politics. They are right not to do so." The older opinion is represented by Jaeger 1986 [1944] and Laistner 1930: 129–131. Wallace himself argues (1989: 175–206) the more general case that conservative ideologies developed by historians and theorists did impact late fourth-century Athenian politics.

2 Allen 2000b provides a thorough review of all the scholars who had pointed this out.

3 See Allen 2006b.

4 Brandwood (2005 [1992]: 103 and passim) provides a helpful, parallel account of how computers have affected efforts to date Platonic dialogues through stylo-metric analyses. Rowe (2002: 156) provides another example of an effort to use this tool to clarify the relations among texts.

5 Thomas Kuhn developed the idea of a "paradigm shift" to discuss revolutions in ideas in the sciences but thought that his own arguments for the structure of scientific change did not apply to the social world; see Kuhn 2000. Michel Foucault provided a powerful account of the linguistic structure of social and political life by focusing on analysis of the knowledge–power nexus within chronologically distinct "epistemes"; but he never really succeeded at explaining how societies evolve or transform from one episteme to another nor at explaining endogenous epistemic shifts generally (see *The Order of Things* [1994 (1971)]; *Discipline and Punish* [1977a]). More recently, within the context of the empiri-cal social sciences, the debate has settled into the poles mapped out by Theda Skocpol (1994) and Bill Sewell (1994, 2005). Skocpol has argued that structural forces – economic and macropolitical – are the main explanatory variables in revolutionary contexts; ideas are relevant but only after structural forces have brought societies to a fork in the road. Sewell argues, in a Foucauldian vein, for the

fundamentally discursive nature even of structural phenomena – such as econo-mies and macropolitical balances of power – but when he provides examples of how ideas redirect politics, those examples in fact fit within the sort of framework established by Skocpol: they are of cases where ideas define a direction after other forces have brought a fork in the road into being. More recently, scholars working within the context of American political development studies have made another sally at developing a framework for analyzing the role of ideas in politics. Thus Hattam and Lowndes (2007) analyze "significant discursive change" that "rearrange[s] the social cleavages and political alliances of the day"; they proceed by "attending to issues of circulation and to the patterning of linguistic associations."

6 Keynes 2006 (1936): 351.

7 Hirschman 1977: 11.

8 Havelock (1963) bases an answer to the question of why Plato wrote on an argument about the difference between orality and literacy. In his argument, orality and literacy foster very different sorts of intellectual capacities, and cultural dependence on one or the other brings with it different ethical potentiali-ties. For instance, Havelock takes Plato's critique of dramatic imitation or *mimêsis* to arise out of an analysis of the relationship between orality and mnemonic practices. In an oral culture, Havelock argues, one can remember, say, an epic poem only by "learning the lines" as an actor does; in Havelock's view, Plato saw this feature of an oral culture as giving oral poets excessive power to shape the souls of their fellows. Consequently, he wanted to overthrow the oral culture of fifth-century Athens, with a new text-based culture of his own devising. My own argument differs from Havelock's in that I do not see Plato as criticizing orality as such, although I do see him as seeking to exploit the durability of writing and its capacity for broad dissemination. I see the target of Plato's reformist efforts as not oral culture per se but the Athenian "system of value," that is, the ethico-political nexus of concepts that organized Athenian political life. See *World of Prometheus* (Allen 2000a) for my account of that system of value.

9 I owe this phrase to Kathleen Carroll, executive editor and senior vice president at the Associated Press. Rowe (2002: 149–150) uses the phrase "think-tank" and "consulting" in a similar way to describe the activities of Plato's Academy; he also applies the term "consulting" but not "think-tank" to Isocrates' competing school.

10 In many ways and at many points, my argument tracks Ramona Naddaff's in *Exiling the Poets* (2002). She focuses on Plato's argument about poetry and aesthetics, linking his views on this subject to a project of cultural impact.

11 Diog. Laert. 3.23.

12 Ford 2002; Harris 1991, ch. 4; Havelock 1963: 37–40, 52–53 nn. 6–10; Thomas 2009: 13–45; Yunis 2003a. Athenaeus (i.3a) reports that Pisistratus, Euripides, and Aristotle had famous book collections. This helps us know by when people had begun collecting books, since Pisistratus ruled as a tyrant in Athens on and off between 561 and 528 BCE. This list also indicates how elite an activity book-collecting was but reveals that over the two centuries the circle to whom books were available for collection widened. Pisistratus would have been one of the

wealthiest men in Athens in the sixth century, if not the wealthiest. Aristotle was not in the same category for the fourth century.

13 There are, though, indications that this elite was fairly porous and could draw in people from lower-class backgrounds. Diogenes Laertius' lists of students of philosophers include: an unemployed chorus-dancer, a poor painter, a porter who invented shoulder-pads, a boxer, the "ex-slave son of a twice-enslaved salt-fish seller," a scene-painter and builder, a slave banker, and a shipwrecked trader (Rihll 2003: 182–183). Euripides, Fr. 370 describes a "soldier, returning from the wars, [who] looks forward to spending his old age, 'unfolding the voice of the tablets which wise men recite'" (Morgan 1999: 58). The soldier must be a hoplite so this is a late fifth-century representation of middle-class participation in reading.

14 Diog. Laert. 3.46, 4.2; Themistius, *Orations* 23.295C.

15 On the wage rate, Allen 2000a: 41. Our first mention of the book trade is in a comic fragment: Eupolis 304.3. The book trade is also mentioned in a comic fragment from Hermippus from the last quarter of the fifth century: Hermippus (Athenaeus, 1.27e–28a = Kassel–Austin, *PCG* Fr. 63). According to Harris (1991: 85) an inter-city book trade was common by the 370s.

16 See Harris (1991: 99 ff.) on Plato's argument for universal education; he identifies Plato's *Laws* as "perhaps the first work to bring the idea of universal education before a sizeable public."

17 On Plato's lectures, see Gaiser 1980; Rihll 2003: 172. Aristoxenus reports (*Elementa Harmonica* 39.9–40.4): "Most of those who came to listen to Plato's lecture on The Good had expected to learn how to realize one of the things customarily regarded as good, such as wealth, health, strength or some marvelous good fortune. But when it transpired that Plato's arguments were about mathematics, numbers, geometry, astronomy, and finally that one is good, I think it seemed to them utterly perverse." Cf. Amphis Frag. 6, line 3, in Kock, *CAF*. Diogenes Laertius (5.37) reports that Theophrastus, a student and successor of Aristotle, was said to have 2000 people attending his lectures.

18 Rihll (2003: 171) counts thirteen different plays by seven different authors in which Plato is mocked. "Alexis (in four plays, Meineke *CGF* iii 382, 451, 455, 468), Amphis (two plays, *CGF* iii 302, 305), Anaxilas (three plays, *CGF* iii 342–352), Anaxandrides (Fr. 19, line 1 in Kock, *CAF*), Kratinos ([Meineke] *CGF* iii 378), Theopompus (*CGF* ii 796), and Timon (*CGF* vi 25), all conveniently in Diog. Laert. 3.26–28."

19 Theopompus, Fr. 15, line 2, in Kock, *CAF*. Rihll (2003: 171) identifies this joke as mocking the *Parmenides* specifically.

20 Cf. Walzer 2002; West 1989.

21 The relevant Lakoff texts are *Metaphors We Live By* (with Mark Johnson, 1980) and *Women, Fire, and Dangerous Things: What Categories Reveal About the Mind* (1987). Drawing a comparison between Plato and Freud, Lear (1997: 86 n. 2) writes: "Freud, of course, understood that a person's ego and superego were formed around internalizations of parental figures." See Freud, "Mourning and Melancholia," and "The Ego and the Id," in Freud 1957–1981, and Lear 1990, ch. 6. Naddaff also develops the parallel, highlighting Plato's focus on mothers' and nurses'

authority over the young (Naddaff 2002: 27, citing *Republic* 377c2–4). Stories about the gods which are deployed by parents are particularly powerful: "Poetic images of gods provide children with what contemporary psychoanalytic literature refers to as an ideal ego image. The gods represent what a human ideally should be and what he, at the same time, will never succeed in being but must always aim to achieve. Children's identities are constructed through an identification with these ideal images. As such the images need [according to Plato] to be artfully devised following specific logical, epistemological, and moral guidelines in order to serve a paradigmatic function" (Naddaff 2002: 28).

For paternal charisma in the *Republic*: see 361d, 363a, 463a.

Taylor (1997: 32) rightly identifies Plato as an analyst and advocate of "ideology" where the relevant concept of ideology aligns closely with Foucault's understandings of discourse and power-knowledge: "By ideology I understand a pervasive scheme of values, intentionally promulgated by some person or persons and promoted by institutional means in order to direct all of the most significant aspects of public and private life towards the attainment of the goals dictated by those values ... Here [in the *Republic*] is a perfect example of that seamless web of aesthetics, etiquette, education, morality and politics which is typical of an ideological society." Compare Foucault 1977 and 1978 *inter alia*.

22 My idea of "surplus linguistic power" has precedents. Thus Havelock (1963: xi) notes: "Stenzel's monograph on Socrates which appeared in Pauly-Wissowa in 1927 supplemented this insight by proposing the general thesis that Socraticism was essentially an experiment in the reinforcement of language and a realization that language had a power when effectively used both to define and control action."

23 In the *Republic* when Socrates lays out how the guardians should approach war, he makes the case that Greeks must separate themselves altogether from barbarians. Socrates asserts: "I maintain that to a Greek, the whole Greek race is 'his own,' or related, whereas to the barbarian race it is alien, and 'not its own.' ... When Greeks fight barbarians, then, and barbarians Greeks, we shall say they are at war. We shall say that they are natural enemies, and that hostilities of this sort are to be called a war. But in cases where Greeks fight Greeks, we shall say they are natural friends, but that in this situation Greece is sick and divided against itself" (470c–d).

Socrates draws one lesson from this: Greeks must cease fighting with Greeks: "Won't the citizens of the city you are founding regard a dispute with Greeks as civil war, given that Greeks are their own people? Won't they refuse even to give it the name 'war'?" (471a). Glaucon, however, draws out an additional lesson: "As for the barbarians, our citizens should treat them in the way Greeks at the moment treat one another [e.g. wasting their land, burning their houses, enslaving them, taking their weapons as trophies, etc.]" (471b).

Scholars often overlook the fact that Socrates' utopia entails such a sharp distinction between Greeks and non-Greeks, but other texts confirm Plato's interest in a sort of ethno-nationalism. Kraut (2005 [1992]a: 8) usefully draws our attention to a relevant passage in the Statesman: "In the *Statesman* (a dialogue belonging to the late period) Plato makes it clear that in his opinion there are no

Forms corresponding to names that are not supported by a justified classification of reality into groups. For example, he says, it is arbitrary to divide the people of the world into two groups – Greeks and non-Greeks – because there is nothing that unifies the latter group into a genuine whole (262c–263). And so there is no Form corresponding to 'barbarian,' even though the Greek term – which simply designated anyone other than a Greek – was a name of long standing and familiarity." This passage is important because it does suggest that Plato thought there was a Form corresponding to "Greek."

The *Menexenus* repeats the injunction of the *Republic* to separate Greeks from barbarians and to treat the two groups differently. The biographical *Seventh Letter* three times describes the separation of Greek from barbarian as necessary to the construction of the true and blissful city. Thus, Plato's and Dion's political plans had phases and, according to the *Letter*: "after ordering the city, the next project [was] to drive out the barbarians" (336a). We then hear that, following that phase, the best way to write good laws for the new regime will be to: "seek out men of Greek origin, with noble and famous forefathers, and property to establish the laws" (337bc). Moreover the *Letter* diagnoses Dionysius II's political problems as emerging not only from his own character but also from his dependence on mercenaries with "barbaric war chants" (348b). Because the mercenaries are his source of protection, he must accede to their demands regardless of whether doing so is good for the city; indeed, since the mercenaries are barbarians, their interests are unlikely (on the Platonic account) to align with the good of the city. See Cartledge 2002 on the development of anti-barbarian sentiments in Athens and elsewhere over the course of the fifth and fourth centuries.

24 On the other hand, contexts of civil strife and great division also provide fertile ground for demagogues. Homogeneity is not the only source of a dangerous politics, as M. Walzer points out to me.

1. Who Was Plato?

1 These birthdates are taken from Nails 2002: 154–156, 243–250.
2 On the oligarchic coup, see Krentz 1982.
3 On the term *sophistês*, see Irwin 2005 [1992]: 64; for a general review of what Socrates was called (including *phrontistês* or "thinker"), see Edmunds 2006.
4 Xenophon (*Memorabilia* 3.6.1) reports that the conversation between Socrates and Glaucon occurred just when Glaucon was getting started in politics, so at around age twenty. This dramatic date for the dialogue accords with Nails' assignment of a dramatic date of 408/7 for Books 2 through 10 of the *Republic* based on a comment by Glaucon about military service at Megara the previous winter; this would have been the 409 battle of Megara. This dating would indeed make Glaucon twenty-one in the two dialogues (Xenophon's and Plato's). It is important to add, though, that Plato did not aspire to avoid anachronism; to the contrary, he often seems to have put people and events in ahistorical chronological relations. Thus, he represents the *Republic* as occurring during the year that a new

god, Bendis, was introduced to Athens, but the cult of Bendis arrived in the 420s. Glaucon and Adeimantus would have been only small children then.

5 Plato's *Lysis* provides a representation of how Socrates interacted with boys in advance of their reaching the age of political maturity.

6 On the amnesty, see Wolpert 2001.

7 See Cartledge (2009: ch. 7) for a good account of the relationship between the historical background and Socrates' trial.

8 Cartledge (2009: 85).

9 Pheidias, Anaxagoras (by Diopeithes), Aspasia (by Hermippus), all mentioned in Plutarch, *Pericles*. There are doubts, however, about the historicity of these prosecutions; see Cartledge 2009: 84.

10 For Theophrastus, see Diog. Laert. 5.37. In 307 BCE the Athenians passed a law requiring that the new head of a philosophical school first be approved by the council and the assembly. This led to a mass exodus of philosophers out of Athens until the law was repealed. Sources: Diog. Laert. 5.38; Pollux, *Onomastikon* 9.42 Bekker (pp. 368–369); Athenaeus 13.610–611.

11 Cooper 1997a: 1634–1635; Nails 2002: 245. Scholars have been routinely divided on the question of the authenticity of the Seventh Letter. Thus, in the same volume, Irwin (2005 [1992]: 83, n. 40) argues that the text is spurious while Penner (2005 [1992]) treats it as authentic.

12 For these biographical dates, see Nails 2002. Her account revises the traditional date of the opening of the Academy from 387 to 383 (2002: 248). See Kraut (2005 [1992]b: 31) for a brief summary of the history of the Academy, but using the traditional opening date.

13 Indeed, he is generally thought to have written, by the time of the opening of his school (if dated to 383 BCE), the following dialogues: *Apology, Crito, Euthyphro, Protagoras, Charmides, Ion,* and *Laches, Hippias Minor, Euthydemus, Gorgias, Hippias Major, Lysis, Menexenus, Meno, Cratylus, Phaedo, Symposium,* and *Republic* Book 1. Between the school's opening and his second visit to Syracuse in 367 BCE, he would have written: *Republic* 2–10, *Phaedrus, Parmenides,* and *Theaetetus.* Between his second visit and his death, he completed: *Timaeus, Critias, Sophist, Statesman, Philebus,* and *Laws.* Kraut (2005 [1992]a: 37 n. 25, 46 n. 57) provides sound chronologies for the dialogues; his chronology is very close to that of Vlastos (1991: 46–47) with the exception that Kraut moves the *Gorgias* and *Republic* Book 1 into the first group of early dialogues (from a later group of early dialogues) and he moves the *Meno* from the middle dialogues to the late group of early dialogues. This ordering is established stylometrically: see Brandwood 2005 [1992]. One can then map the dialogues onto calendar years thanks to the handful of dialogues that mention specific historical events; this sort of information gives us the following dates for the dialogues: *Gorgias* (386), *Menexenus* (386; Kraut 2005 [1992]b: 37 n. 25), *Republic* 1 (388/7–384; Brandwood 2005 [1992]: 110), *Meno* (386–382; Kraut 2005 [1992]b: 6 and 37 n. 25), *Symposium* (385), *Theaetetus* (369), *Laws* (356).

14 Popper 1945.

15 Strauss 1978 [1964]. Aristophanes died in approximately 386 BCE and is thought to have written his play, *The Assemblywomen* in approximately 392 BCE. Plato

had certainly not yet written those portions of the *Republic* that propose the equality of women. This indicates that the idea must have been a part of conversations in philosophical circles before Plato wrote his own dialogue.

16 Ibid.

17 Translation from Morrow.

18 Ober 1998, 2009; Monoson 2000. In this argument, Ober and Monoson would place Plato in "the company of critics," so eloquently described by Walzer 2002.

19 Kraut (2005 [1992]a: 29) agrees.

20 Euben 1997, Frank 2007 and 2008, Mara 1997, Rocco 1997, Saxonhouse 1995, Tarnopolsky 2010, and Wallach 2001

21 We do not need to make "hazardous assumptions about why he wrote," a mistake Kraut cautions scholars away from (2005 [1992]a: 29), because we can uncover Plato's own account of why he wrote.

22 In addition to Plato, Alexamenes of Teos, Xenophon, Simon the Shoe-maker, Eucleides of Megara, Aeschines of Sphettos, Antisthenes, Phaedo of Elis, Leon author of the *Alcyon*, Crito, Glaucon, Cimmias, Cebes, Aristotle, Aristippus, Heraclides of Pontus. See Kahn 1998 on Socratics; see Yunis 2003b: 189–212 for a review of late fifth- and early fourth-century efforts to understand the types of interpretive effort made possible through writing and reading.

23 Kraut (2005 [1992]a: 3): "Most or all of [the dialogues] were composed after the death of Socrates in 399 BC."

24 Doyle, forthcoming b.

25 The question of how to date the *Republic* and *Phaedrus* in relation to each other is controversial. See Brandwood (2005 [1992]: 97) and Kraut (2005 [1992]a: 42 n. 39) for a review. Most early stylometric accounts placed the *Phaedrus* earlier than the *Republic* but more recent work has reversed the position, based on the appearance in the *Phaedrus* of a novel stylistic interest on Plato's part in avoiding hiatus: see Brandwood 2005 [1992]: 114, 117 n. 21. As Kraut summarizes, Vlastos and Kraut place the *Phaedrus* after the *Republic*; Ritter thought the dialogues were written contemporaneously but Brandwood reassesses Ritter's data and places the *Phaedrus* after both the *Theaetetus* and *Republic*: Brandwood 2005 [1992]: 117 n. 21, 120 n. 71. Asmis (2005 [1992]: 359–360) offers a good analysis of what can be gained for our interpretation of Plato's theory of poetry by reading the *Phaedrus* as coming after the *Republic*.

My arguments here are not dependent on the chronological order of the two dialogues. Neither text presents a final word on the subject of writing; fully understanding Plato's views requires holding the two texts in relation to one another. Here I introduce the *Phaedrus* first simply because I spend less time on it and because its arguments about writing are more familiar.

26 In Book 2 (378d), Plato pairs the terms *poiêtês* (poet) and *logopoios* (story-teller); the latter term is typically used for prose narratives. This is one indication that his interest is broadly in the imaginative arts, not in poetry alone.

27 Most recently, Bobonich (2004 [2002]: 478) has argued, along a similar line, that Plato sought general cultural reform as part of a "gradualist" approach to political intervention: "The citizen's life within the city is thus only a small part of the continuing life of the soul . . . Political activity is not simply an instrumental means

to further progress in virtue, but neither is a good city the highest venue for virtuous activity ... The tight restrictions that Plato places on the citizens' lives in Magnesia can be seen to foster ultimate intellectual growth rather than to retard it. The great danger in life is that of sinking down – a failure in virtue that results in one's next reincarnation being in a worse place that reduces one's chances of further improvement. In this case, there is a great incentive to keep citizens from going astray. Small progress in this life, for example, some grasp of basic ethical principles, even if quite imperfect, will entitle one to (and enable one to make) further progress."

My own argument is somewhat stronger since I see Plato as fostering not merely intellectual growth for the individual (Bobonich's argument) but intellectual transformation for a culture as a whole. In this regard, the nearest antecedent to my argument is indeed Havelock. He writes (1963: 12): "It would thus appear that the *Republic* sets itself a problem which is not philosophical in the specialized sense of that term, but rather social and cultural. It questions the Greek tradition as such and the foundations on which it has been built. Crucial to this tradition is the condition and quality of Greek education. That process, whatever it is, by which the mind and attitude of the young are formed lies at the heart of Plato's problem. And at the heart of this process in turn somehow lies the presence of the poets. They are central to the problem. They emerge even here at the beginning of the treatise as 'the enemy,' and that is how they are made to play out their role in Book Ten. Once the *Republic* is viewed as an attack on the existing educational apparatus of Greece, the logic of its total organization becomes clear. And once it is appreciated that the poets are central to the educational apparatus, the successive critiques of poetry fall into place."

Although Havelock correctly identifies education as the totalizing thematic frame for the *Republic*, he then interprets particular moments within that frame erroneously: he needlessly separates the "utopian political theory" from the "non-utopian educational proposals" (13) and thinks that Plato's psychology of the individual soul is "obviously devised to conform to Plato's educational objectives," (13) rather than recognizing that the relationship flows the other way round, from Plato's metaphysics and ontology, to his epistemology and psychology, and from there to his ethics, politics, and educational theory.

28 See Prologue, n. 1.
29 Kraut (2005 [1992]a: 19): "In the *Republic* we see how Plato intends to solve the problems that had preoccupied Socrates ... What follows is a unified metaphysical, epistemological, ethical, political, and psychological theory that goes far beyond the doctrines of the early dialogues. The *Republic* is in one sense the centerpiece of Plato's philosophy, for no other single work of his attempts to treat all of these topics so fully."
30 James in Menand 1997: xii.
31 For helpful accounts of what "dialectic" is, in contrast to other intellectual practices such as mathematics or eristic (among other things, linguistic controversy), see Mueller 2005 [1992]; Ackrill 2003 [1999]; and Annas 1997: 150–152.

32 The point is that Plato sees metaphysics and pragmatism as providing different kinds of insights or information about concepts; in his view, this information is wholly complementary.

33 s.v. LSJ.

34 In developing into a justification for lies the pragmatist observation that we can know beliefs by their effects, Plato embraces an argument that pragmatists are often accused of embracing but routinely defend themselves against. For a criticism of pragmatism as providing insufficient protection against a morality of deception, see Smith 1990, as one example.

35 The material in this paragraph is taken from Allen 2000a: 85–86.

36 But see Derrida (1989) who defines pharmacology in a more limited fashion as a set of highly unstable techniques that involve pursuing a purportedly curative end through acts of exclusion, ritual killing, and other forms of violence.

37 Or we might use Naddaff's intuitively apt phrase; she writes (2002: 36) that Plato draws on the resources of poetry to make "philosophy as theoria [into] an agent of change."

2. The Importance of Symbols in Human Life

1 Many scholars have noted Plato's arguments against writing in the *Phaedrus* but rather than motivating pursuit of an answer to the question of why he wrote at all, this has instead inspired an effort to piece together an account of Plato's "oral teachings" (see Kraut 2005 [1992]b: 20–21 and accompanying notes on this phenomenon and this approach). On the dating of the two dialogues in relation to each other, see chapter 1, n. 25.

2 This material in the *Phaedrus* has been treated frequently and effectively. See Asmis 2005 [1992]; Derrida 1989; Ferrari 1987; Morgan 2000: 56. For other ancient criticisms of writing, see Oenopides (Diels–Kranz 1.41.4); Antisthenes (Diog. Laert. 6.5); Xenophon, *Cyropaedia* 13.11; *Cynegeticus* 13.1–3.

3 On this dialogue, see Scott 2003 [1999].

4 *Iliad* 20.110; *Odyssey* 7.198, 16.135.

5 As will be clearer in chapters 2 and 3, I am not using "concepts" as a translation for the "Forms." "Concepts" are simply the things our thoughts are made out of. They can refer either to things we can sense (fire, houses, tables) or to things beyond the reach of our senses (justice, courage, virtue). I will refer to the latter types of concepts as "abstract concepts." Concepts can be true or false. In the Platonic schema, true concepts are those that derive from or participate in the Forms. See appendix 1 for an account of this meaning of "participation."

6 The *Crito* presents the "do no harm" obligation. The arguments about punishment in the *Gorgias* make this case that leaving unhealthy souls (souls with ignorance) uncorrected is an act of injustice. The theme is touched on in other places, as at *Protagoras* 310d. There, when Socrates asks Hippocrates whether Protagoras has wronged him, Hippocrates replies: "Yes, because he keeps his wisdom to himself, and does not make me wise."

7 Thus, we end up with three metaphors for learning and education: (1) recollection; (2) sowing seeds; and (3) activating the capacity of the soul for sight by
turning it to the light. This last metaphor appears at *Republic* 518d where Socrates
distinguishes the virtues of soul and body which are "implanted" by custom and
habit from the virtue of rational thought. The former are not present at first but
are implanted (*ouk enousai proteron husteron empoieisthai*). The *Phaedrus* thus
suggests that texts can aid the implantation of virtues of soul and body; the
Republic draws this point out.

8 As Naddaff (2002) points out, Plato is conventionally recognized as the first
advocate of censorship. See also Annas 1981: 37; Cornford 1945 [1941]: 314;
Finley 1985; Halliwell 1988: 118–119; Janaway 2006: 388–402; Shorey's introduction to *The Republic* (1930: xxxi); Zuckert 2009: 374–378.

9 Havelock 1963; Naddaff 2002; Asmis 2005 [1992] all make this argument at
length.

10 Janaway (2006: 393) disagrees, writing: "We should resist an optimistic reading
that was once popular: that Plato thinks only 'bad art' is a *mimêsis* of appearances,
implicitly leaving open a space for a 'good art' that imitates the true paradigms of
the Forms." The error of Janaway's view is to think that all images are the product
of *mimêsis*. Socrates in the *Republic* does draw a distinction between bad and
good images, as we shall see in the next two chapters. The former "imitate"
perceptible things; the latter "participate in," "instantiate," or in modern par-
lance, "provide a visualization that may be used to give us access to" imperceptible things. A good example of the latter would be astronomical photographs that
use color to help us develop awareness of difference within the phenomenon being
considered, although that difference in fact may not be a matter of color at all.
These images do not "imitate" that for which they provide a visualization but only
provide us access through perception to important but imperceptible features of
the thing under consideration.

11 For *eidôlon*, see 382b–c; 386d; 443c; 516a; 520c; 532b–c; 534c–d; 586a–c;
587c; 587d; 598b; 599a–b; 599d–e; 600e; 601b; and 605b–c. LSJ provides the
following definition of *eidôlon*: "phantom, any unsubstantial form, image
reflected in mirror or water, image in the mind, idea, phantom of the mind,
likeness, later image of a god, idol." Although LSJ does not include "shadow" in
the definition, the word is closely associated with the word for shadow (*skia*) and
translators of the *Republic* have developed a convention of periodically translating *eidôlon* as "shadow." This is reasonable, both because Plato often makes
eidôla and *skiai* synonyms and also because he gives *eidôlon* itself a Homeric
genealogy, as identifying the shades who live in Hades (see 386d). See also
appendix 1.

12 *Paradeigma*: 409b–d (used for problematic *paradeigmata*); 472c–d; 484c; 500e;
529d; 540a; 557e (used for problematic *paradeigmata*); 559a; 561e (used for
problematic *paradeigmata*); 592b; 617d (in Myth of Er, for the types of life
available); 618a (in Myth of Er, for the types of life available). See also appendix 1.

13 *Tupos*: 377b–c, 379a, 380c, 383a, 383c, 387c, 396e, 397c, 398b, d, 402d (used
with *eikones*), 403e, 412b, 414a, 443c, 491c, 559a (used with *paradeigma*). See
also appendix 1.

14 *Eikón*: 375d, 401b, 402b–c, 487e, 488a, 489a, 509a (for the sun analogy), 509e, 510b (for images used by mathematicians), 511a, 515a (for the cave image), 517a (for the cave image), 517d (for the cave image), 531b (for a Socratic metaphor), 533a, 588b–d (image of the soul). See also appendix 1.

15 See appendix 1.

16 See Naddaff 2002. Fine (2003 [1999]b: 226) writes: "Much of the epistemology of 6–7 is presented in the three famous images of the Sun, Line, and Cave. Plato apologizes for this fact; he resorts to imagery, he tells us, because he lacks any knowledge about the Form of the good (506c), whose epistemological and metaphysical role he now wishes to explain. When one has the best sort of knowledge, he later claims, one can dispense with images and speak more directly and literally (501b)."

See also ibid.: 236. Annas, in contrast, criticizes Plato's use of such images (1997: 152): "The scheme of the Line breaks down … The insolubility of this problem is a good illustration of the difficulties that Plato runs into by using images to make a philosophical point. The imagery is apt to get overloaded, as happens with the Line, because Plato is trying to do two things at once with it."

17 *Eikazô*: 377e, 488a; *graphein*: 377e (linked to *eikazô*); 420c–d (also about "statues"); 472d (also about *zôgraphia*); 488a (linked to *eikazô*; also about *zôgraphia*); 501a–b (also about *zôgraphia*); 510d–e (*plattousi te kai graphousi*, used for the models of mathematicians); 529d–e (also about *diagrammata*); 598c–d (also about *zôgraphia*); 601c (also about *zôgraphia*); 602a; *plattein*: 13 instances at: 374a, 377b (twice), 377c, 414d, 415a, 420c, 466a, 500d, 510d–e, 588b, 588c, 588d.

At 487e, Glaucon teases Socrates for his frequent uses of *eikones*. Socrates responds by saying: "First you drive me to an assertion I can never prove. Then you make fun of me. Well, if you need any further proof of how firmly I cling to analogies, then listen to this one" (488a).

18 Myles Burnyeat's 1997 Tanner Lectures (Burnyeat 1999) drew my attention to this passage. Socrates repeats a version of it later in the dialogue when he is criticizing the sort of person who devotes all his energy to pleasure (586a ff.): "In which case, those who know nothing of wisdom and human excellence, who are always engaged in things like feasting, apparently go down to the region at the bottom and back again to the middle. They spend their whole lives wandering in this way. Higher than this they never go. They never look up at the true top, or go there… They are like cattle, their gaze constantly directed downwards. Eyes on the ground – or on the table – they fatten themselves at pasture, and rut … Aren't they bound to live among pleasures mingled with pains, *eidôla* of the true pleasures and shadow-paintings, in which both the pleasure and the pain take their color from their proximity to one another?"

This second use of an image of grazing in which the animals graze among symbols confirms how important the sociological point is in the first use of the image.

19 The phrase "the rise and role of organized language" is from Pocock 1989 [1971]: 104; cf. Burnyeat 1997; Taylor 1997. Pocock assigned to the "political scientist" – not to the political philosopher or historian of political thought – the task of

determining in general terms when and how ideas matter. For Pocock, the political scientist should take an interest in past political ideas in order to develop at a theoretical level "the study of the rise and the role of an organized political language in a society's political activity, or in the political activity of society in general." When Pocock describes the political philosopher, the historian of political thought, and the political scientist as each taking on a different intellectual project with respect to past political ideas, he makes an important mistake. The task that he assigns to the political scientist, of studying "the rise and the role of an organized political language," generally in fact belongs both to the historian of political thought and to the political philosopher. Indeed, it is not clear whether it can in fact belong to the political scientist.

20 Lear (1997: 63–65) writes: "For Plato, humans enter the world with a capacity to absorb cultural influences. The young human psyche is like a resin, able to receive the impress of cultural influence before it sets into a definite shape." In general, Lear here discusses the psychological process of "internalization." See also Burnyeat 1997; Habermas 2001; Lakoff 1987, 2004; Lakoff and Johnson 1980.

21 Asmis (2005 [1992]: 345), reading the *Symposium*, unpacks Diotima's argument as leading to the conclusion: "A poem is a linguistic reflection, or image, of a psychic disposition. It is essentially a moral rather than a linguistic construct; formulated in language, it is realized by being imprinted in the soul of another."

22 Cornford (1945 [1941]) agrees with this analysis and translates *poiêtês* as "writer" at *Rep.* 397c8 and *poiein* as "write" at 598e4 but Havelock (1963: 68) disagrees and thinks that all mentions of poetry in the *Republic* have oral performance in mind. It seems to me that this is not an either/or question. Poetry existed in oral and written forms by the time Plato wrote the *Republic*. Plato clearly has durable cultural products in mind, including physical artifacts, and "poetry" understood under this construction must include written as well as oral exempla. Indeed, the evidence Havelock introduces in his notes confirms the co-existence and co-ontology of written and oral forms of poetry. Thus, for instance, he adduces a representation of the Muse on a pyxis from c. 445 BCE, where the Muse is giving a recital with book in hand (1963: 53 n. 8). Havelock needs to emphasize an identity between poetry and orality because his central argument (1963: 41) is that "the oral state of mind is still for Plato the main enemy." I think Havelock goes wrong in taking "orality" as a proxy for what Plato is criticizing. Some features of the oral universe align well with the targets of Platonic philosophical and cultural critique but this is an accidental rather than a necessary alignment.

23 See above n. 17. The verb *graphein* also describes the activity of the painter; the *Republic* includes some instances where that is the dominant meaning, but many where the passage could refer to both painting and writing. Most importantly, Socrates does describe mathematicians' generation of models with the verbs *plattein te kai graphein*. And remember that in the *Phaedrus* Socrates argues that writing is like painting (275d).

24 Lear (1997: 66–68) describes this as a psychological process of "externalization," "the process, whatever it is, by which Plato thought a person fashions something in the external world according to a likeness in his psyche. Then, for Plato the polis

is formed by a process of externalization of structures within the psyches of those who shape it. And more generally, *externalization is a basic psychological activity*. For Plato suggests that cultural products in general are externalizations" (emphasis in original). See also Burnyeat 1999.

25 Translation modestly modified.

26 Asmis 2005 [1992]: 341 agrees, as does Naddaff 2002: 28.

27 See also Asmis 2005 [1992]: 349 for a related analysis.

28 Plato was not by any means the first philosopher to introduce criticisms of poetry and its treatment of the gods: see Naddaff 2002: 32, 123. Also Asmis (2005 [1992]: 340) on Xenophanes' criticisms of the poets.

29 In "Envisaging the Body of the Condemned," (Allen 2000c: 134–135) I lay out the four thematic rules that Socrates lays down for good poetry in Books 2 and 3: (1) never tell stories that show the gods doing harm; (2) do not blame human unhappiness on the gods who are causes only of good; (3) do not depict the gods as changeable or deceitful; and (4) do not depict the after-life as a miserable place. Burnyeat (1999: 258–260) also identifies two additional rules, for him the fourth and fifth rules out of five: "(4) Heroes are admirable role-models for the young. So they never indulge in lamentation, mirth, or lying (save for high purposes of state), impertinence to their commanders or arrogance toward gods and men, sexual passion or rape, longing for food and drink, or greed for wealth; nor, *mutatis mutandis*, should any such thing be attributed to the gods (387c–391e). Finally (5) the moral argument of the *Republic* itself, when completed, will prove that it is justice, not injustice, that makes one happy. So no poet may depict a happy villain or a virtuous person in misery (392ac)."

Asmis (2005 [1992]: 347–349) also provides a good account of the poetic rules, but Naddaff gets only part of the story, identifying two "laws and patterns" (Naddaff 2002: 31). See also Irwin (2005 [1992]: 53), who relates the rules expressed in the *Republic* for poetry about the gods to the account of the gods in the *Timaeus* as being "entirely just and good, with no anger, jealousy, spite or lust."

Naddaff (2002: 11) makes another mistake worth flagging. She argues that there is no poetry at all in the original rustic utopian city and misidentifies the city of pigs with the luxurious city. In fact the "city of pigs" is Glaucon's label for Socrates' original utopia. Glaucon uses this label because the true utopia is, from his point of view, insufficiently luxurious. This error leads Naddaff to argue that "poetry is unessential to a healthy city." This is not the case at all. Instead, the healthy city is characterized by having a poetry consisting entirely of "hymns to the gods." This is true both of the original rustic utopia described in Book 3 (372b–373d) and of the utopia (607a) that results from purging the more luxurious city; in Book 10 Socrates says such a city will have nothing but hymns to the gods and encomia on the good. We must presume that these "hymns to the gods" would adhere altogether to the criteria for acceptable poetic practice that Socrates lays out in Books 2 and 3. The fact that there is poetry in the healthy, perfect utopia, whether the original rustic utopia or the purged luxurious utopia, is our most important clue that the argument of the *Republic* must be oriented toward distinguishing between two different kinds of aesthetic practice: one healthy and one not healthy.

30 See chapter 1, n. 31. See also Frank 2008.

31 For my use of "concepts," and "abstract concepts," and their relation to "Forms," see n. 5 above and appendix 1.

32 I owe this point to Reinhard 2006.

33 Naddaff (2002: 13–14) offers a similar reading.

34 Or Burnyeat (1999: 288): "The structure of *Republic* II–X is, in broad outline, a ring composition: poetry/city and soul/Forms/city and soul/poetry."

35 Socrates had ascribed a Homeric lineage to the concept of *eidôlon* (see n. 11 above); now he here ascribes a similarly Homeric lineage to the concepts of *eidôs* and *eikôn*: (*ho dê kai homêros ekalesen en tois anthrôpois eggignomenon theoeides te kai theoeikelon*). The line analogy will eventually explain the distinction among three concepts that might be easily confused: *eidôs*, *eikôn*, and *eidôlon*. More importantly, this passage on the constitution-painter emphatically assigns him the task of working with *eikones* and *eidê* and not with *eidôla*.

36 For a complementary argument, see Frank 2008.

37 The problem of what *mimêsis* means in the *Republic* has been the subject of long-standing controversy. In Books 2 and 3, Socrates distinguishes between mimetic and non-mimetic narrative where the former is the direct speech of drama or direct speech embedded in a narrative. In the criticisms of *mimêsis* in Books 2 and 3 the focus is on impersonation. In Book 10, however, where Socrates bans "as much of poetry as is mimetic," the concept of *mimêsis* is deployed much more broadly. It now picks out not only such texts as depend for their poetic effects on dramatic impersonation but all forms of representation. This shift in focus in the treatment of *mimêsis* has long been a basis for arguing that Book 10 was composed separately from the rest of the *Republic*. Thus Urmson (1997: 226 ff.) thinks that the Books 2–3 accounts of *mimêsis* and the Book 10 account are not coherent. He writes "the Book 3 distinction is simply irrelevant to Book 10." As he sees it, Books 2 and 3 take the immoral out of poetry, while Book 10 critiques poetry as such. This raises the question of what the relationship between the two critiques would be.

There are other problems also. Whereas Books 1–9 had developed an account of the tri-partite soul, Book 10 seems to revert to a bi-partite soul. Second, in introducing a Form for "couch," it introduces Forms for trivial things, which seems to contradict the earlier treatment of Forms. Third, the book introduces a God as the creator of the Form of couch, counter to arguments about the Forms in other dialogues. Lastly, Book 10 seems to operate with three cognitive realms – the realm of the Forms, the realm of the products of craftsmen who have looked to the Forms in producing their products, and the realm of representation, full of pictures and shadows of things like couches; this seems to contradict the use of four cognitive realms in the discussion of the line analogy. (See Naddaff 2002: 70–75, 106, for summaries of these problems and some attempts at solution. On the range of things for which there are Forms, see Fine 2003 [1999]a: 20; Nehamas 2003 [1999]: 176–178.)

As part of arguing for the overall coherence of the *Republic* including Book 10, Burnyeat offers convincing solutions to the problems of the switch to a bi-partite model of the soul, the use of a Form of a couch, and the introduction of a demiurge for the couch (1999: 246–248). Whereas earlier in the *Republic* Socrates explores "motivational conflicts" within the human soul that pit reason, desire, and spirit against one another, in Book 10, he explores "cognitive conflicts" "in which the reasoning part of the soul appears to be at variance with itself" (ibid.: 223 and 222–228). Why a Form of the couch? "Book X's positing of these two Forms indicates that Plato wants to claim there is an objectively correct answer to the question how the city should make use of couches and tables and all the other apparatus of civilized gatherings" (ibid.: 245). And why is the Form of the couch said to be created by a demiurge when the Forms are otherwise described as uncreated? Burnyeat draws on agricultural metaphors that Socrates uses to present the idea to connect the argument in Book 10 to the argument about the Forms in the *Timaeus*, where there are two different sets of Forms, uncreated Forms and others which grow out of the lives (including human life) created by the demiurge (ibid.: 246 ff.): "The moral end, and the agent who is to attain it, belong to the divinely arranged order of nature. God is thereby responsible for there being objective standards of correctness for the agent's use of the instruments of salvation, among which couches and tables have an important role to play" (ibid.: 248).

Burnyeat's solution to the *mimêsis* problem (1999: 288 ff.) is to argue that when, in the beginning of Book 10, Socrates bans so much of poetry as is mimetic (*poiêseôs … hosê mimêtikê*), he is picking out mimetic genres, particularly tragedy and comedy; Burnyeat bases this argument on a similar phrase in Book 3 that does pick out the genres of tragedy and comedy (394bc) and passages in the *Sophist* and *Statesman* that use a similar construction to identify kinds (*Soph.* 219a 10, 221e 6, 225b 13; *Polit.* 263e 9, 226a 1, 303e 10). He argues that in Book 10 Socrates does extend the ban on poetry but not by changing his definition of *mimêsis*. Instead, Socrates identifies mimetic poetry (tragedy and comedy, in which he includes Homer also) as oriented above all toward the production of pleasure; and all poetry aimed at pleasure is to be banned. *Mimêsis*, as Socrates discusses it in Books 2 and 3 and in Book 10, is primarily oriented toward pleasure.

This is surely right, but the one mistake in Burnyeat's argument is to gloss over the status of such poetry as is allowed in the ideal city with respect to its use of images. The good poetry will indeed be aimed at the truth rather than at pleasure; nonetheless, this good poetry (and other good cultural artifacts in the city) will have to be made out of the same materials as the poetry which was banned as *mimêsis* and as pleasure-seeking. How can this be justified? We need an explanation for how the image-making practice involved in producing good poetry is fundamentally different from that involved in producing bad poetry. Burnyeat does not provide this.

Asmis makes an attempt. Like Burnyeat, she offers a solution that depends on the idea of genre. She argues (2005 [1992]: 350) that when Socrates bans "mimetic poetry" (as opposed to *mimêsis*) in Book 10, he is banning "'indiscriminately imitative' or 'all-mimetic' poetry.' ... For 'mimetic' poetry is not just poetry that imitates, it is poetry that imitates anything at all." She continues (ibid.): "He returns to the problem of poetry [in Book 10] because the metaphysics and psychology that he developed in the meantime provide a new justification for the expulsion of mimetic poetry." Asmis's solution depends on distinguishing the objects of imitation of two different categories of poet. There are the bad poets and then the good ones, whom she describes thus (ibid.: 358): "The politically correct poet does not indeed look to the Forms; for if he did, he would be a creator of actual goodness in human beings – a lawgiver in fact. But it is open to him to take correct beliefs from the lawgiver, the user of his poems. Nor need one look for such instruction. Socrates' entire analysis of poetry in Books II and III is nothing other than an elaborate rule book, devised by the founders of the city for the instruction of the poets. Having correct beliefs, the poet is raised to the level of a craftsman, like the carpenter, the bridle maker, and all the other non-philosophical craftsmen in the new city. Like the rest, the poet has the position of serving the lawgiver. Instead of imitating humans as they are or appear to be, he creates images of humans as they should be, taking directions from the lawgiver, who looks toward the Forms."

But scholars have not yet noticed, to the best of my knowledge, that the line analogy establishes a distinction between *mimèsis* and a second form of image-making practice more closely bound to the truth. This second type of image-making practice is better thought of as "model-making." The burden of chapter 3 is to outline this critical distinction between two categories of image. This distinction is fundamental to making complete sense of the arguments about *mimèsis* in *Republic*.

3. The Philosopher as Model-Maker

1 On the line passage, see Annas 1997: 143–168; Bobonich 2004 [2002]: 58–66; Fine 2003 [1999]b; Mueller 2005 [1992]; Santas 2003 [1999]: 268–273.
2 There is some dispute in the literature as to whether the realm of the intellect should be assigned the top or bottom portion of the line, to the longer or the shorter portion. Those who think that it should be assigned the shorter portion see this as a way of symbolizing that the world of appearances is vaster than the world of the Forms, unified as they are under the Form of the good. Yet the evaluative language used in the passage consistently makes the realm of the intellect superior, and the image makes sense only if the three evaluative orders align with one another (superiority, position, length). Indeed, the parallels among the images of the sun, cave, and line indicate that all three images trace an upward ascent from the realm of the visible and of opinion to the realm of rationality. Most major recent interpreters of the line passage agree on this point: see Annas 1997: 148; Cooper 1997b; Fine 2003 [1999]b: 229 n. 26, 230. See also n. 9 below for further elaboration of this point.
3 On dialectic as a particular kind of cognitive practice, see Fine 2003 [1999]b: 237; Mueller 2005 [1992]: 184–190; Santas 2003 [1999]: 269–273.

4 Mueller (2005 [1992]: 184): "[A]lthough mathematicians make their arguments about images, 'they are not thinking about them, but about the things which resemble them … The things which they mold and draw … they use as images seeking to apprehend things which cannot be apprehended except by *dianoia*.' 516d6–511a1"; also at p. 185: "[Plato] thinks about mathematics as an attempt to understand the intelligible world by reasoning about sensible things rather than (as we might suppose) as an attempt to reason about the intelligible world using sensible things." See also Annas 1997: 150–152.

5 Mueller (2005 [1992]: 184) remarks: "There is some question about whether the illustration exhausts the content of the relevant section or whether there are nonmathematical instances of *dianoia*." In what follows, I will be arguing that there are indeed nonmathematical instances of *dianoia*. In Book 3, at 393a, Socrates has argued that with simple narrative (as opposed to *mimêsis*) the poet "does not attempt to direct our *dianoia* towards anyone else, or suggest that someone other than himself is speaking." In other words, poets, like mathematicians, engage *dianoia*. Here I agree with Fine, who sees all the images and analogies in the *Republic* as examples of the kinds of reasoning carried out in the realm of *dianoia* and writes (2003 [1999]b: 237, see also 236): "[Plato] places mathematics at L3 [*dianoia*] – it is the lower form of knowledge. Moreover it is just one example of L3 type reasoning – Plato's moral reasoning in the *Republic* is another example of it."

6 This is the only instance in the *Republic* in which Socrates uses the term *eikôn* to capture images, generally, including what he thenceforth consistently refers to as *eidôla*: forms of representation at three removes from the truth; here the distance from the truth that he assigns to this category of image is captured by the words *skia* and *phantasma*, "shadow" and "phantasm." These shadows and phantasms can represent moral as well as sensible objects. As Fine points out (2003 [1999]b: 233), shadows can include opinions about justice: "When Plato says that most of us are like the prisoners (are at L1), he does not mean that most of us literally see only images of physical objects. He means that our moral beliefs are relevantly like the prisoner's beliefs about physical objects; we are at L1 in our moral beliefs (not in our physical object beliefs), just as they are in L1 about their physical object beliefs. Thus, for instance, he talks about people who 'fight one another for shadows and wrangle for office as if it were a great good' (520c7–d1) – about people, that is, who take seeming goods to be real goods, and lesser goods to be greater goods than they are."

See also Annas (1997: 155) for the inclusion of moral objects in the category of shadows. Kraut (1997b: 203–204) puts it best: "Calling an act just is comparable to calling an image in a painting a tree: The image is not what a tree is, and it is correct to speak of it as a tree only if this means that it bears a certain relation to living trees; similarly, just acts, persons, and cities are not what justice is, and it is correct to call them just only if this means that they participate in the Form of Justice … It might be thought that for Plato knowledge of the Forms is valuable precisely because it is a means to some further goal. For example, he might claim that unless we study the Form of Justice, we are likely at some point to make errors in our judgment of which acts, persons, or institutions are just; and when we make errors of this sort, we will also make bad decisions about how to act."

I would differ from Fine, though, by insisting that there is no difference between being at L1 (in the realm of shadows and conjecture) with regard to physical and with regard to moral objects. Fine (2003 [1999]b: 233) thinks that the former are not relevant to understanding the true significance of L1. But she misses Socrates' focus on aesthetics. All aesthetic representation conveys moral judgments, as Socrates made clear in the image of the guardian children being put out to graze in a garden of symbols. Thus there is no difference between being at L1 about physical and about moral objects because physical objects are cognized with aesthetic judgments that contain moral evaluations.

7 Fine (2003 [1999]b: 232) thinks that we don't use this faculty much and that Plato is making a mistake to give it as much airtime as he does. "Plato might seem to be suggesting that one is at L1 if and only if one is confronted with an image of a sensible object – just as the objects analysis would have it. But if so, various difficulties arise. First, most of us don't spend much time looking at images and reflections of physical objects; nor will most people in the ideal city do so. Yet Plato says that most of us are at L1 (515a5); and that most people in the ideal city would be too (517d4–e2; 520c1–d1)."

She cites White 1979: 185–186 as taking the contrasting position "that most of us do spend a great deal of time looking at images of sensible objects in that we focus only on aspects or appearances of objects." Fine neglects how much human attention is captured by the aesthetic properties of objects, by stories, and by dream life.

8 On thinking without images and non-discursive thought, see Lloyd 1969–1970: 261–274; Mueller 2005 (1992): 189–190.

9 Scholars have often argued over whether the line represents a hierarchy of faculties or a hierarchy of objects cognized. This argument makes sense only if one neglects that the line image in fact represents two ordinal axes. There is a hierarchy of position on the line and also a hierarchy of comparative lengths. These two hierarchies are aligned with one another. Thus, the line differentiates modes of cognition both by differentiating cognitive faculties and by differentiating potential objects of cognition. I owe this observation about the symbolic meaning of the hierarchical order of the line and relative length of the sections to the philosopher J. A. Doyle.

For the debate see Fine 2003 [1999]a: 21–22. Fine (2003 [1999]b: 231) goes for a contents analysis as opposed to an objects analysis. Annas makes the mistake of thinking that the equality of the two middle sections of the line "suggests that Plato is not interested in having each section of the Line illustrate an increase in clarity over the one before" (1997: 149). This mistake arises from failing to see that the image is ordinal along two different axes or criteria. Similarly, Annas (1997: 150) recognizes that the line classifies both cognitive states and their objects but then (ibid.: 151), expresses uncertainty about "how the cognitive states are being classified – by their objects or by their methods." Santas (2003 [1999]: 272) presumes that the line makes its distinctions in terms of both "powers and objects." Socrates provides the basis for the confusion. At 477cd he says: "A capacity has no color or shape for me to see, nor any such property that I would normally refer to in other situations in order to distinguish one class of things from another in my own mind. The only element of a capacity I consider is what it is directed at and what its effect is. That is how I classify each capacity. Any capacity which is directed at the same object and has the same effect, I call the same capacity, and any capacity which is directed at a different object and has a different effect, I call a different capacity. How about you? Is that your method?"

10 Annas (1997: 149) is struck by the fact that Plato three times makes the point that mathematicians use the contents of the realm of belief as images, even though the objects in the realm of belief are originals for the images made in the lowest realm of conjecture.

11 On the relevant sort of shift of cognitive and intellectual attention entailed in cognizing material objects in themselves in the realm of belief and as images to be used in reasoning in the realm of *dianoia*, see Annas 1997: 148–152; Mueller 2005 [1992]: 189. Asmis (2005 [1992]: 345) usefully analyzes Diotima's account of the ascent "from an attraction to beautiful bodies, to an appreciation of beautiful souls and practices, to a contemplation of knowledge, and finally to a vision of beauty itself" in ways that reveal a close relationship between the ascent described by Diotima and the one mapped out by the divided line image. Those who are attracted to beautiful bodies may respond in either of two ways: by painting the particular body and producing an *eidôlon* of it, or by ascending from consideration of the particular body to an appreciation of beautiful souls and practices, the contemplation of knowledge, and a vision of beauty itself. Along this route they will consider the beautiful body as an *eikôn* and *paradeigma*. Asmis writes (ibid.): "Finally, the philosophically strengthened person has a vision of beauty itself and produces no longer 'semblances (*eidôla*) of goodness,' but true goodness, constituting a godlike immortality (212a)." But see Fine 2003 [1999]b: 217: "Knowledge does not consist in any special sort of vision or acquaintance but in one's ability to explain what one knows"; see also Fine 2003 [1999]b: 246.

12 See appendix 1 on the nature of the Form–paradigm relationship, which is a matter of the "participation" of the "model" or "paradigm" in the "Form," rather than of the "immanence" of the "Form" in the "model" or "paradigm."

13 On Forms for things like couches and houses, see Burnyeat 1999.

14 Similarly, in Book 6 a paradigm in the soul needs to be *enargês* (484c).

15 The most prominent examples of the argument that Book 10 does not continue the argument of the main line of the text include: Annas 1981: 37; Cornford 1945 [1941]: 314; Shorey's introduction to the *Republic*, 1930: lxi. Naddaff 2002: 2–3 summarizes this consensus and lays out her own argument against it. Also arguing in favor of continuity between Books 2 and 3 and Book 10 are Belfiore 1984; Ferrari 1989: 125; Janaway 1995; Monoson 2000; and Nehamas 1988: 215. Useful scholarship on this front also includes Frank, 2008.

The two strongest arguments for the coherence of the *Republic* are to be found in Burnyeat 1999 and Havelock 1963. See chapter 1, n. 27 on Havelock.

16 The earliest instances of *plattein* (and derived forms) based on a *TLG* search are: Hesiod (two); Simonides (one); Semonides (one); Damon (two); Parmenides (two); Empedocles (one); Xenophanes (two); Aeschylus (three); Sophocles (two);

Euripides (five); Hippocrates (thirteen); Herodotus (eight); Democritus (two); Aristophanes (five); Critias (one); Thucydides (one); Plato (fifty-eight); Xenophon (eight); Aesop (twelve). See appendix 3 for an account of my approach to word counts.

17 This question is typically taken as identifying an ontological difference but it might instead pose a question about which faculty the imitator uses: belief or thinking. If the question had the latter meaning, then Socrates would be asking whether the imitator is capable of making the cognitive shift that allows one to consider the material objects of the world not for themselves (i.e. as they appear to be) but insofar as they participate in the Forms (i.e. as they are or convey reality).

18 Others agree that knowledge of the truth is Plato's basic distinction between the poetry of the poets and that of the philosophers: Morgan 2000: 3; Naddaff 2002: 9. Naddaff eventually concludes (ibid.: 90): "The poet, because of his lack of knowledge, is an imitator, an imitator of images. The epistemological lack coincides with an ethical lack."

19 Translation is modestly modified. See Cooper 1997b for a helpful discussion of what *epistêmê* is in the *Republic* and Frank 2008 for a valuable discussion of this passage in particular.

20 Here I focus on what Burnyeat discusses as "cognitive conflict" "in which the reasoning part of the soul appears to be at variance with itself" in (Burnyeat 1999: 223, 222–228), although the images of the tragedians also mislead by tapping into the desires and triggering "motivational conflicts." See appendix 2.

21 Ibid.

22 Athenaeus, author of the second sophistic *Deipnosophists*, understood as well as anybody Plato's efforts to displace the poets and his claims for philosophy and turned the tables by mocking Plato with the same question Socrates here asks of Homer: "And as to the book of the *Laws* composed by him, and the *Republic* which was written before the *Laws*, what good have they done us? And yet he ought (as Lycurgus did the Lacedaemonians, and as Solon did the Athenians, and Zaleucus the Thurians), if they were excellent, to have persuaded some of the Greeks to adopt them ... And how can we consider Plato's conduct anything but ridiculous; since, when there were already three Athenian lawgivers who had a great name – Draco, and Plato himself, and Solon – the citizens abide by the laws of the other two, but ridicule those of Plato?" (Athenaeus 11.813, translation from http://digital.library.wisc.edu/1711.dl/Literature.DeipnoSub.)

For a brilliant account of Athenaeus' efforts in the *Deipnosophists* to develop an alternative to Platonic care of the self, see Paulas 2008.

23 See chapter 2, nn. 12–14.

24 The problems inherent in human cognition do not plague mathematical concepts alone. They also plague the domain of moral concepts. The prisoners in the cave are obliged to make their way through life only by assessing shadows of puppets. The puppets are held by puppet handlers operating behind them and out of view. Some of those puppet handlers may be philosophers who have returned to the cave after an encounter with the sun, where first they have trouble seeing but soon come to see fully. The puppet handlers work in the domain of the cave purely in the realm of opinion producing puppet versions of concepts, including of concepts like justice. True knowledge of justice, then, like knowledge of the good, is also

available to the would-be philosophers when they exit the cave. And if exiting the cave is indeed equivalent to climbing up the line of cognitive capacity, then knowledge of justice requires encountering "diagrams" of justice. What is the equivalent, in the domain of moral concepts, for mathematical diagrams in the domain of mathematical concepts? The answer is the kinds of images and stories that Socrates presents in order to help his interlocutors "see" justice.

25 Scholars have long debated whether city and soul are meant to be merely analogous, or actually equivalent (that is, isomorphic). I follow Lear 1997 in taking them as isomorphic.

26 In Socrates' analogy, the large nearby copy that helps one read a small, distant text, turns up as a matter of happy accident. Is the same thing possible when it is justice that we're trying to see? Only if, as Herodotean travelers who happen upon marvels, we should chance upon a truly just city. It's not impossible for a material instantiation of the abstract truth being pursued to turn up. But it's unlikely. Since we are unlikely to happen on a just city, Socrates will instead create the large copy, a word-picture that will become, in his terminology, a *paradeigma*. See appendix 1 for a discussion of the relationship between Forms and paradigms and of the idea that sensibles and paradigms "participate" in the Forms.

27 LSJ defines *hupograpsasthai* thus: "Write under orders, or from dictation; write under an inscription or add to it; sign; subscribe; write under, i.e. trace letters for children to write over (used in Plato *Prt.* 326d); trace in outline, sketch out; trace out laws as guides for action in *Laws* 734e; sketch, mark on a map."

28 The constitution-painter is therefore a writer of constitutions who is giving children, or the child-like, something to trace and imitate. And for those children, and the child-like, to read is to be able to see, or to take the patterns of what has been read into the soul. Socrates is explicit about this, asking: "Can you see any difference between those who are blind and those who are genuinely lacking in knowledge of everything that is? They have no clear pattern or model in their soul. They can't look at the reality the way painters do, making constant comparisons with it and observing it as closely as possible, and in this way establish rules about beauty, justice and goodness in everyday life – if they need establishing – or defend and preserve rules which already exist" (484c–d).

29 As I said in the Prologue, Plato's view of the quantities of social power available to be tapped by philosophers and other intellectuals through the careful use of language is optimistic in the extreme. The long-running disputes about the meaning of particular Platonic images and arguments is in itself evidence that readers don't all simply assimilate whatever it was Plato wanted his reader to assimilate. But at the same time that there are such long-running arguments, there are Platonic concepts that do seem to have worked their way into our vocabulary without much direct attention from us. A key instance would be the idea of the "plasticity" of the human psyche. See appendix 1 for examples of how scholars have taken that idea up without even particularly noting that they have done so.

30 Thus the images of the sun, the line, and the cave are all anticipated at earlier points in the dialogue such as this.

31 This analysis supplements the excellent reading by Jonathan Lear (1997: 68): "Plato decides first to look for justice writ large in the polis because, he says, he

will then be able to read the small print of the individual psyche. By now it should be clear that he is not relying on a mere analogy of polis and psyche, but on an isomorphism which must hold due to the way we function psychologically. Psyche and polis, inner world and outer world, are jointly constituted by reciprocal internalizations and externalizations; and the analogy is a byproduct of this psychological dynamic."

32 Translation modestly modified.

4. The Philosopher as Shadow-Maker

1 See Janaway (1995: 96, 101–102) on the principle of assimilation; and Lear (1997: 187, 189) on the process of internalization. See also Foucault (1978: 10–11) on "techniques of the self," "those intentional and voluntary actions by which men not only set themselves rules of conduct but also seek to transform themselves, to change themselves in their singular being." Havelock (1963: 45) provides the most intriguing analysis of the capacity of *mimêsis* to generate transformations of character; he argues that such power is strongest within the context of an oral culture where mnemonic necessities require one to forget oneself in order, for instance, to remember one's lines in a play: "Such enormous powers of poetic memorization could be purchased only at the cost of total loss of objectivity. Plato's target was indeed an educational procedure and a whole way of life."

2 Translation from Shorey, modestly modified.

3 At 395d Socrates remarks: "I think the decent man, when he comes in his narrative to some saying or action of a good man, will be prepared to report it as if he himself really were the person concerned. He will not be ashamed of an imitation of this sort. He will imitate the good man most when he acts in a responsible and wise manner, and will imitate him less, and less fully, when the good man is led astray by disease or passion, or by drunkenness or misfortune of some kind. When he comes to someone who is unworthy of him, I think he'll refuse to make any serious attempt to resemble one who is his inferior – except perhaps briefly, when the character is doing something good – both because he has had no training in imitating people like this, and because he resents shaping and modeling himself on the pattern of his inferiors. Inwardly, he treats behavior of this sort as beneath him – unless of course it's in jest."

This is like the passage in the Myth of Er, where Socrates argues that one should pattern one's life after the good, never the bad. See 618c–619a and also *Theaetetus* 176e–177a.

4 This is a particularly dramatic example of Socrates' success in convincing his interlocutors. This example tells against the hackneyed idea that Socrates never convinces anyone. Burnyeat (2003 [1999]) also observes that Socrates does successfully convince Glaucon in Book 10 of the *Republic*. Similarly, in *Theaetetus*, Theaetetus frequently professes himself convinced.

5 Homer called the heroes *theoeideis te kai theoeikeloi*; they participate in the forms and likeness of gods. Insofar as the heroes appear on the battlefield like gods, they

are like gods appearing among mortals; in the Homeric vocabulary, this also means that they appear vividly or *enargês*. The models produced by the constitution-painter are, like the models used by the mathematician in the line analogy, valued for their clarity. Importantly, this clarity is not representational. These models do not imitate the Forms or make them visible since an important point about the Forms is that they are imperceptible. Instead, these models, like divine heroes, convey emulation and in so doing both inspire further emulation and provide access to learning about the Forms. See also appendix 1.

6 See Frank 2005.

7 Havelock 1963: 145–164; Lear 1997: 63–65.

8 Importantly, the assimilation of the concepts as rules for action often proceeds by way of the psychic power of emulation. See Allen 2003.

9 I take the concept of poetic power (literally: lyric power) from von Hallberg 2008.

10 Naddaff (2002: 18) agrees.

11 Havelock 1963: 5–6, 145–165; Lear 1997: 80–82; von Hallberg 2008: 143–185; Asmis (2005 [1992]: 344) elaborates the Platonic criticism of poetry as acquiring its power by indulging a listener's cravings for pleasure.

12 Asmis 2005 [1992]: 355.

13 Cf. Naddaff 2002: 2. Asmis (2005 [1992]: 341) identifies Gorgias ("Encomium to Helen") as the source of a theory of language as imprinting rules for action on the soul of a listener: "A message is sent from speaker to a recipient who accepts it passively by a change in his soul."

14 For instance, see: Casebeer and Churchland 2003; Narvaez 2002; Narvaez 2008; Narvaez and Lapsley 2009; Nucci and Narvaez 2008; Shanks and St. John 1994. Even a cursory dip into the literature on cognitive psychology reveals that Plato's vocabulary of paradigms and patterns in the *Republic* remains a basic vocabulary for discussing human learning, whether metaphysical or moral.

15 Havelock (1963: 5) puts it thus: "Plato's target seems to be precisely the poetic experience as such. It is an experience we could characterize as aesthetic. To him it is a kind of psychic poison. You must always have your antidote ready." See also Lear 1997: 80. Also see Asmis (2005 [1992]: 347–348) and Naddaff (2002: 34 ff.) for related discussions of the noble lie, usefulness, and the idea of the *pharmakon*.

16 Kraut (2005 [1992]a: 12) writes: "Although Plato is ... in favor of giving extraordinary powers to rulers who themselves have a philosophical understanding of the human good, he is not unconcerned about the possibility that such power might be misused or arouse resentment." Cf. Socrates' argument at 342c–e: "'But surely, Thrasymachus, arts and skills control, and have power over, the objects of which they are the arts and skills.' He conceded this with great reluctance. 'In which case, there is no branch of knowledge which thinks about or prescribes, what is good for the stronger but only what is good for the weaker, for what is under its control.' He agreed to this too, in the end, though he tried to resist it. And when he did agree, I continued, 'Isn't it a fact that no doctor, to the extent that he is a doctor, thinks about or prescribes what is good for the doctor? No, he thinks about what is good for the patient. After all, it was agreed that a doctor, in the precise sense, is responsible for bodies; he's not a businessman. Isn't that what was agreed? ... And so, Thrasymachus, no one in any position of

authority, to the extent that he is in authority, thinks about or prescribes what is good for himself but only what is good for the person or thing under his authority – for whose benefit he himself exercises his art or skill. Everything he says, and everything he does, is said or done with this person or thing in mind, with a view to what is good and appropriate for the person or thing under his authority.'"

The relevant art in the *Republic* is poetics. All humans are under its control. Those who have poetic authority must exercise it for the benefit of those susceptible to it.

17 To see this, one must recognize that 414bc explicitly refers back to 389b, which itself explicitly refers back to 382b–d, where the term *eidólon* is used for the kinds of falsehood that are, in 414bc, to be employed in the noble lie.

18 Translation modified.

19 Cf. 433d where the rule that each should perform his own task is to be implanted (*empoiein*) in all children, women, slaves, free craftsmen, ruler, and ruled.

20 *Chrêstos* does, however, mean more than just "serviceable"; it has connotations of positive value, worthiness.

21 Thus Cooper (1997b, 19–20) writes: "It follows from what has been said so far that on Plato's account no one is just, strictly speaking, who does not have knowledge of what is best to do. True belief is not sufficient for an individual's justice in the *Republic*, nor, I think, though this is a more complicated question, for any other virtue of individuals. It is true that Plato conspicuously defines a city's courage (429a–430c) in terms of the deep-dyed belief (not knowledge) of the soldier-class in the correctness of the laws and institutions of the city they serve. But it is noteworthy that he denies this condition of belief makes the soldiers themselves brave, except in a qualified sense: it makes their city brave, but it gives them, as Socrates cautions, only 'civic bravery' (*politikê andreia*, 430c3), not bravery *tout court*. It makes them consistently do the things one expects of brave citizens – they are fearless and selfless soldiers and police officers – but they are far from having the philosopher's pervasive strength of character ... Similarly, the city's justice is defined as the condition in which each class sticks to its own social work (432d–435a), but this does not mean, nor does Plato anywhere suggest, that people who do stick to their social work thereby show themselves to be just. They do what is just, but whether they are just is obviously not settled by pointing to their behavior alone. 'Doing one's own social work' is presented only as a description of just action. It is not presented as part of the definition of the condition of justice itself – except, of course, the justice of a city, which is a different matter entirely ... Once these points are duly noted, one sees that Plato consistently restricts justice, as a virtue of individuals, to those who possess within themselves knowledge of what it is best to do and be."

The recognition that Plato was a pragmatist as well as a metaphysician allows for a resolution of the question of whether in the just city all individuals must also be just in being ruled by their own reason (as opposed to simply having a willingness to obey the reason of the philosopher-kings). See Williams (1997: 52–53) for an articulation of the problem. Plato the pragmatist would count those who obey the reason of the philosopher-kings as acting justly even if they themselves are not fully just. Moreover, Plato's pragmatist argument allows us to see that the element of *logistikon* in the city rules the spirited and epithumetic elements by means of well-constructed images. These elements of the city can assimilate images, in contrast to their inability to practice dialectic. If they are given the opportunity to assimilate philosophically correct images, then these non-rational elements of the soul and city will take in for their possessors all the elements of truth that they need in order to live justly. They will be able to participate in the rational elements of the city even through their non-rational faculties, and this will bring them very close to being fully just, as close as it is possible for them to be, which is all that Plato asks.

Lear's response to Williams is similar to my own. He writes (1997: 75 [see also 73 ff.]): "Plato does not believe the appetitive person has the virtue of temperance, but in a well-ordered polis, due to well-crafted internalizations, such a person will be disposed to temperance both inside and outside himself." I have extended Lear's answer by arguing that well-crafted internalizations in fact provide the spirited and epithumetic elements with the means of internalizing the contents of *to logistikon*; thus, through the use of images, even these elements of the soul can participate in *to logistikon*.

22 Naddaff (2002: 41) formulates Socrates' pragmatism in the *Republic* thus: "It doesn't necessarily matter to Socrates whether the stories told to the young are true or false; all that matters is whether they produce benefits or harm, health or illness."

23 On the obligation to do no harm, see chapter 2, n. 6.

24 Does this ethical obligation to write mean that, according to Plato, Socrates erred by not giving written expression to his philosophical ideas? Not if the power of symbols, and the knowledge of how to make them, were Plato's own discoveries, made after the death of his teacher, for then Socrates' choice would have been a matter merely of ignorance. Remember that even near his death, Socrates admitted to uncertainty about the meaning of his dream's injunction to cultivate the Muses and "make music." Lastly, it's worth noting that in the *Republic* the philosophers are obliged to return to the cave out of gratitude for the splendid education that their city has given them. Did Plato (thanks to the presence of Socrates in Athens for seventy years) receive an education that his teacher did not? Might their different obligations be understood on the basis of such a distinction?

25 The phrase "system of value" is from Allen 2000a, where I use it to describe the cluster of concepts that hold together the evaluative universe of Athenian political ethics.

5. What Plato Wrote

1 In the sixth century CE, the anonymous *Prolegomena to Platonic Philosophy* (ed. L. G. Westerink, Amsterdam, 1962) 15.36–40, "offer[ed]: as the last of seven reasons why Plato used the dialogue for his philosophy, the explanation that it 'keeps us attentive to his words through the different speakers and thus avoids us always having the same teacher, which is liable to make us nod off'" (Rihll 2003: 74). The fact that Plato wrote dialogues has been the source of much scholarly

controversy over the interpretation of these texts. Should they be interpreted, as Leo Strauss (1978 [1964]: 50) argues, like the dramas of Sophocles or Euripides or Shakespeare, where interpretation begins with the assumption that no character in the drama is a mouthpiece for the author? Or, as Richard Kraut argues, does Plato have aims that differ from a dramatist such that "he will have a reason that the dramatist lacks for using his main speakers as a mouthpiece for his own convictions" (2005 [1992]a: 25)? Both scholars agree that "Plato's aim in writing is to create an instrument that can, if properly used, guide others to the truth and the improvement of their souls," as Kraut puts it (ibid.). But neither scholar achieves a full account of the pedagogic possibilities inherent in written texts that use poetic tools and so neither, in my view, achieves a full account of how best to approach the interpretation of the dialogic form.

Plato's arguments for philosophical writing seem to me themselves to provide us with the resources for understanding how to interpret the dialogues as dialogues; these are the resources I hope to clarify in this chapter. In general, I think this issue is bedeviled by the relative weakness of philosophers' awareness of how literature functions psychagogically. Thus, the models for how the dialogues can work cognitively and intellectually are still, even after centuries of scholarly exploration, pretty thin. For instance, one common model is to propose that the purpose of dialogic writing is to "dramatize conflict between opposing characters and to give expression to competing philosophical ideas" (Kraut 2005 [1992]b: 26); another is that "the dialogue form [is] a device by which Plato avoids telling us everything he believes. According to this interpretation, one of Plato's aims in writing is to get his readers to think for themselves; and to accomplish this goal, he deliberately inserts fallacies, ambiguities, and other deficiencies into his works" (ibid.: 27). In fact, many weak dialogues have been written on the basis of these two models for understanding Plato's dialogic writing (Hobbes' dialogues would be an example).

To date, the best accounts of how Platonic dialogues function as a kind of intellectual work and argumentation are found in Coetzee, *Elizabeth Costello* (2003: ch. 1), and James Doyle, *Saying and Showing in Plato's* Gorgias (forthcoming a). Coetzee and Doyle both understand the Platonic dialogue (or some Platonic dialogues, at least) to be built upon an understanding of the relation between beliefs and human action that enables an exploration of ideas that is also always an exploration of human psychology, and an exploration of the degree to which any given human individual can lay hold of the reality of things ("of being") by means of the particular and flawed instrument of his own psyche – the only instrument each of us has for accessing the reality of things. Irwin (2005 [1992]: 73–78) moves in this direction. He argues that Plato developed his literary methods out of pre-existing literary traditions for displaying arguments in conflict but then developed the genre to show what it means to come to be rationally convinced and "to show how such conviction is possible." His account does not, however, look directly at Plato's arguments about writing and poetry and, instead, like the efforts of most scholars to answer the question of why Plato wrote, is speculative.

2 Several epigrams are attributed to Plato. See, for instance, Diog. Laert. 3.30.

3 Diogenes Laertius knew this. In addition to reporting Socrates' expostulation that the *Lysis* was nothing but lies and to identifying Plato as a *politikos* in his writing, he also believed that Plato wrote to provide reminders. He reported (3.27): "He used also to wish to leave a memorial of himself behind, either in the hearts of his friends, or in his books." But Yunis (2003b: 190) argues that Plato wrote, and wrote dialogues specifically, to "encourage critical reading while avoiding the interpretive problem of the absent author"; by the end of his article (ibid.: 212), however, he softens his line to say that Plato's dialogic structure gives readers the "option" of avoiding the absent author. This is correct.

4 This argument about the different genres of dialogue Plato might have written provides a new way of categorizing the dialogues. We don't need to say whether a dialogue is early or late in order to call it Socratic. We can now understand that the production of reminders of Socrates is simply one genre out of several that Plato's dialogues may deploy. If anything, the explicitness at the opening of the *Theaetetus* about its status as a reminder of Socrates underscores the fact that Plato had generally taken the genre in other directions, writing not to provide reminders but to produce either theoretical models or noble lies.

I would argue, then, that what we think of as the Socratic dialogues are, in essence, those where the genre Plato has chosen to foreground is that of either the reminder or the noble lie about philosophy. And the dialogues that we do not call Socratic are those where Plato has chosen to foreground the genre of the theoretical model that provides access to the truth. This approach to categorizing dialogues as Socratic or non-Socratic need not map onto chronologies of early and late. Instead, this approach reflects choices of genre not only available to Plato but also fully theorized by him as recorded in the *Republic*.

Notably, those dialogues that the scholarly consensus identifies as late on stylometric criteria (*Timaeus, Critias, Sophist, Statesman, Laws*) are also characterized by three important changes in Plato's literary style: (1) Socrates does not appear or plays a minor role "in five of the six dialogues often classified as late" (Kraut 2005 [1992]b: 16); (2) The final six dialogues are characterized by a significant reduction in the frequency of "objectionable" hiatus (Brandwood 2005 [1992]: 101–102), a stylistic technique advocated by Isocrates. (Of the late middle dialogues, the *Phaedrus* has indications of a shift over the course of its writing to a style involving intentional avoidance of objectionable hiatus.); (3) Also, after the *Republic*, Plato seems to abandon reported dialogue and the use of the "he said" device; he abandons it explicitly at the beginning of *Theaetetus*, but he's already taken that approach in the *Parmenides*.

With these three major shifts – the change in the use of the character Socrates; the self-conscious effort to adhere more closely to the stylistic norms advocated by Athenian prose writers like Isocrates; and the abandonment of the marks of reported discourse – it seems clear that Plato was differentiating his literary project, in his final works, from that which had come before. Morgan (2005 [1992]: 232–233) proposes: "It is possible then that there is a shift in the dialogues. That shift may be either from a historically attentive portrait to one that employs Socrates as a Platonic mouthpiece or from an earlier to a later Platonic perception of Socrates." Did he switch from an effort to produce noble lies to an effort to produce, simply, reminders, whether of Socrates' philosophy (in the *Theaetetus*) or of his own (in *Timaeus, Critias, Sophist, Statesman, Laws*)?

5 Kraut's instincts lead him nearly to this conclusion (2005 [1992]a: 26–27): "Plato begins his career as a writer in order to give expression to the philosophy and way of life of Socrates. His purpose in doing so is not purely historical; rather, he regards Socrates as a model of wisdom and insight, and he sets down his portrait of Socrates so that he and others will have an enduring reminder of this remarkable man." Morgan (2005 [1992]: 232) reaches a related conclusion: "Socrates is Plato's model of the philosopher and the philosophical life." But see Hobbs (2000: 158–162, 235–249) on the pedagogic inadequacy of the figure of Socrates as a role model.

6 Gill 1973: 25–28. In his production of reminders, Plato appears to have practiced just the types of imitation that Socrates recommends at 399a–c and 539b–d. See also n. 3 above.

7 At 500c, though, Socrates does describe the man whose mind is truly fixed on eternal realities as endeavoring to imitate the eternal order and to make himself as much like it as possible. He asks, "Do you think it is possible not to imitate the things to which anyone attaches himself with admiration?"

  And two passages do apply the word *mimeomai* to Plato's (but not Socrates') practice. Thus, at 539b–d, Socrates remarks that while younger men like to imitate "confuters," older men will "not share this craze" but will "choose to imitate the one who consents to examine the truth dialectically rather than the one who makes a jest and sport of mere contradiction, and so he will himself be more reasonable and moderate, and bring credit rather than discredit upon his pursuit."

  Also, in the Book 3 discussion of musical modes, Socrates argues that the two modes that should be left in use for imitation are those that convey the sounds of a courageous man bearing up in battle and of a moderate man persuading others through discourse (399a–c).

8 Asmis 2005 [1992]: 362 n. 23: "At 396c5–e2, Socrates specifies that the poet must imitate good characters most of all when they act prudently and less when they err, and that the poet will imitate unworthy characters only briefly when they do something worthwhile. Socrates does allow that 'for fun' (*paidias charin*, 396e2) a poet may occasionally imitate someone unworthy."

  Fine agrees that Plato constructs his images to accord with his philosophical principles for the right use of images (2003 [1999]b: 236): "The *Republic* is peppered with images used self-consciously to illustrate something about the Forms: the Sun, Line, and Cave are cases in point. Similarly, Plato partially explains the nature of justice in the soul through the analogies of health and of justice in the city; he uses the analogy of the ship to illustrate the nature of democracy and so on. So the *Republic*'s moral reasoning satisfies (a) [at L3 (in the domain of *dianoia*) one uses sensibles as images of Forms, although one is thinking of Forms, not of sensibles; at L4 one thinks of Forms directly, not through images of them]; it also satisfies (b) [at L3 one proceeds from a hypothesis to various conclusions; at L4 one proceeds from a hypothesis to unhypothetical first principles (510b) – that is to (a definition of, and perhaps also further propositions about) the Form of the good.]"

Thrasymachus compares Socrates to an old woman telling stories (349e).

9 For thorough readings of the Myth of Er, see Annas 1981; Halliwell 1988; Naddaff 2002; Zuckert 2009: 378–384.

10 Plato knows how to put the same point in argumentative terms rather than in the form of a myth or fiction. He does this in the *Theaetetus*, where Socrates says to Theodorus: "My friend, there are two patterns set up in the world. One is divine and supremely happy; the other has nothing of God in it, and is the pattern of the deepest unhappiness. This truth the evildoer does not see; blinded by folly and utter lack of understanding, he fails to perceive that the effect of his unjust practices is to make him grow more and more like the one, and less and less like the other. For this he pays the penalty of living the life that corresponds to the pattern he is coming to resemble" (176e–177a).

11 Nussbaum 1986; Williams 1981.

12 On these conceptual revisions, see Allen 2000a, ch. 9. The conceptual changes provide progress for the citizens in their grasp of ethical principles: see Bobonich 2004 [2002].

13 Gill 1993: 71; Havelock 1963; Paulas 2008.

14 The *Laws* makes this idea explicit at 817a–d. On that passage, Asmis (2005 [1992]: 338) writes: "The tragic poets approach the lawmakers and ask, May we bring our poetry to your city? The lawmakers reply that they, the lawmakers, are 'poets,' too, rivals and competitors in making the 'most beautiful drama.' Their drama is the state, an 'imitation of the most beautiful and best life.' If the tragedians can show them dramas that agree with theirs, they will be allowed to perform; otherwise not."

Naddaff (2002: 5) puts it thus: "It is within this context [of the institution of ostracism] that Nietzsche understands the writer Plato's rivalry with the poets or, as Nietzsche phrases it, the 'immense desire to step into the shoes of the overthrown poet ... and inherit his fame,'" citing Nietzsche in "Homer on Competition" (*Homers Wettkampf*). See on this point ibid.: 5–10. Asmis (2005 [1992]: 360) also agrees and (364 n. 39) cites Nussbaum (1986: 227) who suggests "that the *Phaedrus* may be the first example of the 'philosophical poetry' now proposed by Plato."

15 His analysis of linguistic efficacy went beyond the theory of language articulated in the *Republic* to include study, in other dialogues, of the effects on the establishment of values of psychological phenomena like maternal proximity, paternal charisma, and the fear of death. See my "Last Words" (Allen 2003); Naddaff (2002: 39) also notices the psychological importance of this last theme.

16 The idea of "orienting ideals" is captured well by Lear's analysis of the processes of internalization and externalization. He writes, for instance (1997: 69): "Plato's point (at 435e) is not that a spirited polis, say, is spirited simply in virtue of having spirited citizens, but in having spirited citizens who are successful in shaping the polis in their image ... If a just polis is an externalization of the just citizens who shape it, it would be reasonable to work one's way backwards down this externalization to learn about the psyches of these citizens."

6. How Plato Lived

1 See Nightingale (1995: 11) for Plato's approach to creating and defending "a new and quite peculiar mode of living and thinking [which] alone, he claimed, deserved the title of 'philosophy.'" Also Naddaff 2002: 68.

2 I owe my attention to this passage to Irami Osemi-Fripong.

3 This point echoes the view in the *Phaedrus* that once a discourse is written down it circulates everywhere (*kulindeitai pantachou*) reaching both those with understanding and those without (275e).

4 Kraut (2005 [1992]a: 22–23) provides a good summary of the arguments made on this point. The fundamental mistake made by those who want to draw a strong distinction between Plato's "written" and "unwritten" doctrines is a failure to understand the diverse ways in which Plato thought writing could function. See chapters 2–4.

5 See chapter 2, n. 16. See also Mueller (2005 [1992]: 171–173), on the modes of intellectual apperception thought to characterize Platonic academic study; Morgan (2005 [1992]: 234, 239) on the shift from silent study to ecstatic apperception; also Ackrill 2003 [1999]: 140–141; Fine 2003 [1999]: 7 n. 21; Lloyd 1969–1970: 261–274. Fine (2003 [1999]: 217) writes: "Knowledge does not consist in any special sort of vision or acquaintance but in one's ability to explain what one knows"; Mueller writes (2005 [1992]: 189): "Socrates' way of speaking about the abandonment of sensibles in dialectical argument was taken by the Neoplatonists to involve reference to a mysterious 'nondiscursive' thought, which, among other things, violates Aristotle's dictum (*On the Soul* 431a16–17) that 'the soul never thinks (*noein*) without an image (*phantasma*). Nothing in the *Republic* seems to me to justify this Neo-Platonist reading although one cannot preclude the possibility that Plato had something of this sort in mind."

6 In defense of the coherence of Plato's written and unwritten doctrines, Kraut (2005 [1992]b: 22–23) correctly makes the important point that Aristotle looks to Plato's dialogues for information about what Plato thought; Aristotle, who was in a position to know, thought that the written and unwritten material cohered. Irwin (2005 [1992]: 88 n. 82) agrees.

7 On this dialogue, see Ackrill 2003 [1999]; Barney 2001.

8 See the *Theaetetus*. See also Ackrill 2003 [1999]: 136–137. On the problem of contraries, see Nehamas 2003 [1999]: 191.

9 Mueller (2005 [1992]: 187) also makes the point that the *Republic* focuses specifically on cognition through images.

10 I owe this phrase to Richard Kraut.

11 What are these sparks? Ackrill (2003 [1999]: 139) reviews the different dialogues in which Plato provides accounts of our "capacity to conceive universals of which we have met no actual perfect instance (*Phaedo* 73c–77a), ... our capacity to see logical connections (*Meno* 80d–86b), ... our capacity to seize the universal in the particular (*Phaedrus* 249b–c)." He adds: "[Plato's] Anamnesis is the forerunner of Locke's doctrine of innate ideas and of more recent theories of innate grammatical programmes."

12 This phrase is taken from Ackrill (2003 [1999]: 141).

13 The letter attributes to Plato a desire to "implant" a philosophical way of life in others (327b) and distinguishes between broader and narrower communication. The former is *enargôs* (as Socrates' images aspire to be) while the latter is "riddling" (*ainittomenoi*) (332d). On implanting a way of life, see also: 327e, 328a, 330b, 331e, 339e, 340d.

14 See Cooper (1997b: 24–26) for a similar account of the philosophical life.

15 Vlastos (1997: 209) agrees: "I don't take [Plato] to be making the implausibly strong claim that the love of abstract objects by itself guarantees just behavior or the emotional discipline that characterizes the just person. Rather, his weakened and more plausible claim is that one will be in the best position to lead a life dominated by the love of Forms if one trains the non-rational components of one's soul to serve one's love of philosophy. It is this weaker claim that lies behind his portrayal of the philosopher as the paradigm of human justice. By putting oneself into the best position to lead the philosophical life, one develops the intellectual and emotional skills that we look for in a completely just person."

7. The Case for Influence

1 I mean this metaphorically, not in the literal sense that Plato conceived of his writing project as a form of scientific experiment. According to Y. L. Too, Isocrates was "the ancient author who more than any other establishes writing as a medium of political expression and activity" (1995: ch. 4). I am making the argument that Plato contributed just as much to that project.

2 See Allen (2006a) for a full account of the arrival of the term *prohairesis* in Athenian politics and the basis for dating Aristotle's lectures on rhetoric to 355 BCE. Dinarchus' extant speeches contain only the verb *proaireô*. I have not included Demades in this analysis since his one remaining speech is considered spurious.

3 Allen 2006a.

4 Translation modified.

5 This delay is not a problem for the argument but, to the contrary, a good indication that Plato's written texts, as opposed to his oral performances, carried his influence into politics.

6 The speaker of the speeches *Against Aristogeiton* I and II, in the Demosthenic corpus, refers to his effort as allied to Lycurgus' prosecution. Because the speeches are attributed to Demosthenes, historians have therefore argued that Demosthenes was allied to Lycurgus in this prosecution. But the rhetorical anomalies in these speeches – their extensive Platonism, which differs greatly from the rest of the Demosthenic corpus – cast significant doubt, in my view, on the case for their authorship by Demosthenes. Dionysius of Halicarnassus similarly thought that these speeches could not be by Demosthenes (Butcher 1887: 221). If Demosthenes was not the author of these speeches, then the case for his routine collaboration with Lycurgus is weakened. Burke 1977 makes the case for routine collaboration between Lycurgus and Demosthenes; in this and the following chapter, I take issue with that view.

7 The material in this and the following paragraph derives from Allen 2000a: chs. 3–8, ch. 10; 2000b.

8 This is also true of Xenophon so the rejection of anger is in all likelihood a Socratic idea in its origins; but Plato elaborates and develops the view extensively across his dialogues.

9 Allen 2000a: 71.

10 The earliest instances of *kolasis* are found in Empedocles, Fr. 115, line 18; Pherecydes Hist., *Fragmenta*, Fr. 103b line 7; Hippocrates et Corpus Hippocraticum, *Epistulae*, *Epistle* 17, line 133; Thuc., 1.41.25; Plato, *Apol.* 26a7; *Prot.* 323e2, 326d8; *Rep.* 380b4; *Laws* 764c3, 777b3, 794c1, 849a7, 853c2, 881b1, 932c2, 934b5, and *Def.* 416a33.

Also, of uncertain date: Aesop, *Fabulae*, *Fable* 1, version 1, line 22; *Fable* 1, version 2, line 23; *Fable* 208, version 1, line 8.

11 By the end of the fourth century, *aniatos* appears in the sophist Gorgias (fr. 11a, line 224), Plato (twenty instances), Aristotle and the Aristotelian corpus (eighteen instances), the medical writers (two instances), the orators (four instances, see n. 12 below), and one instance each in Pindar, Theophrastus, and Hecateus.

The distribution of the word *thêrion* in major late fifth- and fourth-century prose authors is as follows: Herodotus (thirty-three instances, of which none is metaphorical); Thucydides (no instances); Plato, *Laws* (twenty instances, of which fifteen are metaphorical or comparative), *Republic* (sixteen instances, of which fifteen are metaphorical or comparative); other Platonic texts (forty instances); Xenophon, *Cyropaedia* (thirty-five instances, of which none is metaphorical); other Xenophon texts (thirty-nine instances); Isocrates (six instances, of which all are metaphorical or comparative); Aristotle, *Politics* (thirteen instances), *Nic. Eth.* (fourteen instances).

There are also fourteen instances in the Hippocratic corpus, thirty-two in Ctesias, and one in Thrasymachus Frag. 10, line 4.

12 Aeschines: *thêrion* (2.20, 2.34, 2.146, 3.156, 3.182); *aniatos* (3.114, 31.156); Dinarchus: *thêrion* (1.50, 2.10, 3.19, Oration 68, Fr. 2, line 4); Demades: *thêrion* (On the Twelve Years 42; Fr. 114, line 8); author of *Against Aristogeiton* I: *thêrion* (8, 20, 31, 65, 58, 95); *aniatos* (95, three instances); Demosthenes: *thêrion* (18.322, 24.143); *aniatos* (18.324). Also the word *thêrion* appears in several spurious Demosthenic speeches: [35].8, [34].52, [43].83, [58].49, [61].21, and in the spurious Lysianic funeral oration: [2]. 19. *Aniatos* also appears in Antiphon 2.4.12 but is not used to characterize the wrong-doer or his acts.

13 See Allen 2000a: 323, for a table of the relative frequency of penal words within each orator.

14 Antiphon, Andocides, and Lysias constitute a first generation of orators, who lived too early for the question of whether they were taught by Isocrates or Plato to be relevant. The second generation includes Isaeus, Demosthenes, Lycurgus, Aeschines, Dinarchus, Demades, and Hyperides. The pseudo-Plutarchan *Lives of the Orators* claims that Isaeus was taught by Lysias; that Aeschines was "said to be taught" by Socrates and Plato or by Leodamas; that Lycurgus was taught by Plato and Isocrates; that Demosthenes was "said to be taught" by Isaeus, Isocrates, and Plato; that Hyperides was taught by Plato and Isocrates (at the

same time as Lycurgus) (see also Athenaeus xii, 552d); and that Dinarchus studied with Theophrastus, student of Aristotle, and Demetrius of Phaleron.

The most confusing case is that of Demosthenes. Plutarch, in his *Demosthenes* (5.5) claims with an air of authority that Demosthenes studied with Isaeus, not Isocrates, more skeptically cites Hermippus (floruit end of third century BCE) as saying, on the basis of an anonymous source, that Demosthenes had studied with Plato, and also asserts that it was said that Demosthenes had mastered the rhetorical systems of Isocrates and Alcidamas secretly. Demosthenes was also said to have studied with Aristotle (A. H. Chroust, "The *Vita Aristotelis* of Dionysius of Halicarnassus (1 Ep. Ad Amm. 5)," cited in Cooper [2000: 245]). What are we to make of these claims of the biographers?

Craig Cooper (2000: 224–245) explains the claim that Demosthenes had studied with Plato as having arisen in a first-century CE battle between philosophers and rhetoricians in Rome (reported on by Cicero) over which camp would dominate the Roman educational world; each camp claimed Demosthenes for themselves, the philosophers doing so by attributing his education to Plato and, later, Aristotle. The claims made about Demosthenes' teachers are, in other words, the least likely to be accurate.

What other evidence can be brought to bear on the question? Given the intense hostility between Isocrates and Plato (see Rowe 2002; Irwin 2005 [1992]: 66–67), it is unlikely that any of these orators studied extensively with both. Pseudo-Plutarch may get the teacher–student relations right with the order in which the author lists the teachers for those orators who were said to have multiple teachers. If the teacher named first for each orator was the main teacher, then Lycurgus, Aeschines, and Hyperides would be identified as having studied mainly with Plato while Demosthenes would be identified as having studied mainly with Isaeus. My own interpretation of the rhetorical patterns of argument and vocabulary to be found in the orators would confirm pseudo-Plutarch's identification of Lycurgus, Aeschines, and Hyperides as students of Plato while also confirming doubt about the claims that Demosthenes studied with him.

The remaining question is whether Demosthenes did in fact study with Isocrates. The evidence against this attribution is that Demosthenes uses somewhat less hiatus avoidance (an Isocratean stylistic technique) than other fourth-century orators (Milns 2000: 215; Badian 2000: 11) and that two of Demosthenes' early enemies, Androtion and Timocrates, were students of Isocrates. But there are a few unusual words that Demosthenes shares with Isocrates: *phenakizein, philanthrôpia*, and *pseudologia* in particular.

15 For instance, he says: "If you vote against this man, you will not only chastise [*kolasete*] him, but also turn young men toward virtue [*ep' aretên*]" (10). And he warns that if the jury fails to convict Leocrates, citizens will begin to think that shamelessness, treachery, and cowardice constitute the noblest types of action (*to kalliston*, 110). And at eight points in his lengthy passage of quotation, Lycurgus tells his jurors that they should learn from the paradigms that he is presenting to them (100, 101, 102, 107, 111, 124, 128, 129). Other orators do use this term but not with this frequency.

16 For a full account of Lycurgus' Platonism as well as an overview of the literature on the subject, see Allen 2000b, which focuses on his speech. On the Lycurgan era generally, see Mitchel 1965; he too (p. 192) notes the "Platonic influence" on Lycurgus.

17 Translation modified.

18 Words related to *mimeó* appear in Plato's texts with a frequency that overshadows any other author prior to the end of the fourth century: Herodotus (three instances); Thucydides (three instances); Aristophanes (twelve instances); Plato (297 instances); Isocrates (thirty-nine instances); Xenophon (thirty-two instances); Aristotle (160 instances); Aesop (twelve instances). There are also a handful of instances in Pindar, Aeschylus, Xenophanes, Empedocles, Parmenides, and Pythagoras, among others. Lycurgus uses the term five times in his single speech, a frequency per speech that exceeds his colleagues; their total usage is as follows: Demosthenes (seventeen instances); Aeschines (nine instances); Andocides (two instances); pseudo-Lysias (three instances); Lysias (one instance); Hyperides (one instance).

19 See Allen 2006a for a full account of how the orators use *prohairesis*.

20 See Rhodes (1978), Sawada (1996: esp. 57–59, 80–81) and Wallace (1989: 132–133) for general discussion of how the concept of "parties" has been approached at different periods in Athenian historiography. On the problem of the "pro-" and "anti-Macedonian" language, see Cawkwell 1963a: 127 n. 4.

21 There are different ways of formulating the basic consensus that existed among Athenian politicians. For instance, Cawkwell (1963a: 120) writes: "The real motive of those who wanted peace in 346, both Philocrates with his principal abettor Demosthenes, and Eubulus and Aeschines, was to try to keep Philip out of Greece itself." Cawkwell (1963c: 49–50) describes how all leading politicians came to support the Peace of Philocrates. Buckler (2000: 143) writes: "The decisive difference between [Aeschines and Demosthenes] ... is whether in 339–338 Athens should have supported Philip against Thebes, which was Aeschines' position, or Thebes against Philip, Demosthenes', which the Athenians endorsed ... [Aeschines' case is that ...] Athens by its prestige would have led the Amphictyons against the sacrilegious, resolved the dispute and prevented Philip from intervening in Greece" (3.128–129).

22 For instance, Sawada 1996.

23 Rhodes 1978.

24 Badian 2000: 26–28.

25 Badian 2000: 19: "By the early 350s the international scene had completely changed."

26 On who the enemy was, see Ryder 2000: 45–47.

27 When one looks beyond the pro- and anti-Macedonian language in the historical scholarship, one finds a fair degree of unanimity on the formulation of the actual policy dispute as having to do with whether Athens worked for its pre-eminence within the order established by Philip or against that order. See, for instance, Cawkwell 1963b: 209; Cawkwell 1963c: 52–53, 67; Mitchel 1965: 193.

28 Cawkwell 1963a: 123–127, 131–134; 1963b: 206; 1963c: 51–52. Cawkwell writes (1963b: 206): "From 344 on [Demosthenes'] speeches show his constant

efforts to discredit Philip. All that Philip did was represented as a breach of either the letter or the spirit of the Peace. With Hegesippus he sought the rejection of the proposals to amend the Peace: Hegesippus was responsible for the amendment about Amphipolis, which virtually brought, as he must have known it would bring, the negotiations with Philip to a stalemate, but Demosthenes in the *Second Philippic*, had played his part in the same affair by urging his countrymen not to trust Philip. The aim of all this *diabolê* was to break up the Peace and resume the war, and Demosthenes was the leader of what was freely called the war-party, *hoi poiountes ton polemon* (Dem. 9.6)."

29 Jaeger 1986 [1944].

30 Isocrates' *Antidosis* is the important text here.

31 There are some minor overlaps with distinctive terms in Demosthenes' vocabulary (*phenakizein, philanthrôpia, pseudologia*), but little beyond this. For Isocrates' influence on Demosthenes' speeches, see Mesk, 1901: 209–212; Jaeger 1986 [1944]: 126; de Romilly 1958: 94; Rowe 2002: 155–156. Cawkwell (1963c, esp. 63–65, 63 n. 89) argues for the influence of both Isocrates and Xenophon on the politician Eubulus, from whom we have no extant speeches. And see Laistner 1930: 129–131.

32 Burke (1977) correctly identifies these three speeches of 330 BCE as part of a single political moment. The other speech that shares some of the anomalous rhetorical features marking the speeches of 330 BCE was Aeschines' earlier speech, *Against Timarchus* (c. 345 BCE), and it too was an important battle in Aeschines' ongoing war with Demosthenes. One scholar has identified *Against Timarchus* as initiating the concern with *paideia* in late fourth-century Athenian politics (Fisher 2001: 53–66; see also Fisher 2007).

More recently, Rowe (2002) has made an argument about a "culture war" in Athens that pitted a Platonizing Demosthenes against Isocrates. I think he is wrong. He takes too seriously the biographers' claims that Demosthenes was educated by Plato and tries to make the case that Demosthenes, as a student of Plato, was one of Isocrates' most ardent enemies. But see n. 14 above for the weakness of the biographers' claims on this point.

Also, Rowe's other evidence is thin. He analyzes Demosthenes' *Against Androtion* as making a target of Isocratean-trained politicians because Demosthenes complains "about a clique that controls the council" (ibid.: 151–152). Even if the relevant clique had all been trained by Isocrates, that fact does not in itself mean that Demosthenes is complaining about Isocrates' teaching as such; cliques are an irritant to a politician seeking influence regardless of the basis for that cliquishness. One would, for instance, need more evidence before concluding that a complaint about a clique of Yale-educated politicians was a complaint about Yale as such.

Similarly, Rowe (2002: 158 ff.) connects Demosthenes' *Against Timocrates* to Plato's *Laws*, but he produces a list of intellectual points of contact between Plato and Demosthenes that does not distinguish Platonic from conventional Athenian ideas; indeed Rowe himself concedes as much.

33 Translation modified.

34   There are only six speeches that directly quote poetry; the other three are the speeches that constitute the political battle between Aeschines and Demosthenes in 345–343 BCE: *Against Timarchus*, *On the False Embassy*, and *On the Embassy*. Perlman (1964) provides a deft reading of how each of these three orators uses poetry: he explains the extensive quotation in *Against Leocrates* and *Against Timarchus* as necessitated by the fact that in each case the prosecutor had a weak legal case and he argues, correctly in my view, that Demosthenes uses poetry mainly to mock Aeschines. Buckler (2000: 138) also notices Aeschines' extensive quotation but thinks Aeschines does this "to counter his enemy's feeble disparagement of his voice and public presence."

35   Translation modified.

36   For "sun," confirmed via *TLG* search. Lycurgus Fr. 6.19.7, does refer to the priest of the sun. And only Demosthenes invokes the earth (*ô gê!*) alongside the gods.

37   See Notopoulos 1942.

38   Translation modified.

39   Aeschines' argument is also a class-based criticism of Demosthenes' non-aristocratic social position.

40   "Solon," Aeschines argues, "was a man capable of law giving [*nomothêtêsai dunatou*] and experienced at poetry and philosophy [*kai peri poiêsin kai philosophian diatetriphotos*]" (3.108). And later he argues: "You see standing beside me the benefactors of the state: Solon, who equipped the democracy with the best of laws, a philosopher and a good lawgiver, begging you soberly [*kosmêsanta tên dêmokratian, andra philosophon kai nomothetên agathon, sôphronôs, hôs prosêkon autoi, deomenon humôn*] (3.257).

41   For *sophistês*, see chapter 1, n. 3. The earliest instances of *philosophia*, up to the time of Plato, are: Aeschylus (one instance); Herodotus (none); Thucydides (none); Hippocrates (one instance); Philolaus (two); Gorgias (one); Critias (one); Plato (147); Isocrates (fifty-five); Xenophon (four).

42   Plato calls Solon *nomothetês* at *Rep.* 599e, *Phaedrus* 278c, and *Symp.* 209d. These are exactly the three texts that others of Aeschines' remarks indicate he was familiar with. Instances of *nomothetês* (in all forms) in Plato, historians, and the orators: Herodotus (none); Thucydides (one); Critias (three); Plato (165); Xenophon (two); Aeschines (thirty-three); Demosthenes (twenty-one); Lysias (eight); Isaeus (three); Antiphon (one); Lycurgus (one). Although Demosthenes' number of uses is close to Aeschines', his corpus is at least five times the size of Aeschines' corpus.

43   Andocides 1.83–84.

44   The first instance of the term *nomothetês* appears in Thucydides 8.92.2 in the plural. Aeschines uses the singular thirty-two times in his three speeches. Leaving these instances aside, in oratory there are thirty-six instances of the plural use and thirty-one of the singular. Demosthenes uses the singular seven times, though it appears an additional eleven times in speeches spuriously attributed to him.

45   Also, Aeschines uses words like *daimôn*, *kosmos*, and verb forms deriving from the adjective *orthos*; he refers to the "venerable Cephalus, famous as the truest representative of democracy" (3.194), perhaps indicating a fourth-century

interpretation of the *Republic*? He also discusses musical education and the production of *paradeigmata* for young men.

46 Is it possible that the fact that we have only one speech from Lycurgus and three from Aeschines, when we have fifty some from Demosthenes, reflects precisely this difference in political approach?

47 For the history of the Areopagus, including the question of composition, see Wallace 1989; Cawkwell 1988.

48 Allen (2000a) initiated the argument that in Athens the judgment of the demos took precedence over the law so that Athens was a "state of judgment" or lived under "the rule of judgment" rather than the "rule of law." Lanni 2008 makes the strongest available case for the argument that Athens cannot be identified as a "rule of law" system. Ober 2009 develops a helpful compromise between the "rule of judgment" view and the "rule of law" view. He argues that the Athenians tacked between prioritizing the law, when they wished to stabilize political norms, and prioritizing judgment, when they wished to allow for sufficient flexibility within their political order.

49 On *eunoia* in Athenian political rhetoric, see Boyle 2007 and de Romilly 1958. The Athenians may have introduced the office of *nomothetês* in the mid-fifth century (Cawkwell 1988), but if so they did not use it. The board of ten *nomothetai* was introduced only at the very end of the fifth century. The word is modeled on the older *thesmothetai*, an office which the Athenians did have in the archaic period. The earliest instances of the word *nomothetês* in the literary record appear in Thucydides (8.97.2) and in three fragments from Critias. Then there is an overabundance of the term in Plato. See n. 42 above.

50 The view he expresses here is good evidence that his primary influence is not Isocrates who didn't care about the differences among regime types. On Isocrates' "political philosophy," see helpfully, Wallace 1989: 158–173.

51 See chapter 3, n. 16 for the earliest instances of *plattein* including those in Plato. There are fifty-eight instances in Plato; the next highest frequencies are in Herodotus (eight instances) and Xenophon (eight instances). The only oratorical texts in which *plattein*, meaning "to fashion," is used more than once are: Aes., *On Embassy* (four instances); Demades, *On the Twelve Years* (two); Dem., *Philip I* (two), *On the Crown* (four), *False Embassy* (three), *Against Stephanus 1* (five); Isocrates, *Evagoras* (two).

52 Diog. Laert. 3.26. See Prologue, nn. 17, 18, and 19 for a full list of comic jokes about Plato. Similarly, Athenaeus remarked (11.508b): "Plato seems to have written laws not for real humans, but for ones molded [*diaplattomenois*] by him." John Paulas drew my attention to this passage and suggests that *diaplattomenois* might well be translated as "thoroughly Platonified."

53 Translation modified.

54 Theophrastus is another example of a Platonist who took on the project of developing "types" of man. On Plutarch's Platonism and use of the comparative method, see Liebert 2009a and 2009b.

55 I hope the evidence offered is by now sufficient to refute the suggestion of Rowe (2002) that it was Demosthenes who took Platonic positions.

56 These three speeches were related by more than political strategy. As Perlman (1964: 170) points out, Demosthenes' uses of poetic quotation in *On the Embassy* "are cleverly connected with Aeschines' accusations against Demosthenes in *Against Timarchus*." In other words, in the speech of 343 BCE Demosthenes is not only prosecuting Aeschines but also answering Aeschines' earlier attack on Timarchus.

57 The word is used by Thucydides, for instance, to designate violent revolution. See, for instance, Thuc. 1.58, 1.97, 2.73, 3.72, 3.82, 4.76, 4.108.

58 Plut. *Dem.* 24.2.

8. Culture War Emergent

1 Cawkwell 1963c on Eubulus; see also Badian (2000: 20–25, 30), on Androtion, Eubulus, and Demosthenes. Cawkwell (1969: 164) considers whether there was a reality behind the claims about corruption and concludes that it is impossible to say.

2 Cawkwell 1963c: 55–56, citing Harpocration s.v. *theôrika*.

3 On the dating of this law, see Cawkwell 1963c: 48.

4 On the ideology of election as opposed to allotment, see Wallace 1989: 149–150, 176.

5 Dem. 3.10 ff.; Dem. 1.20; cf. Dem. [59].4–6.

6 For all the details in this paragraph, see Dem. 4.16, 21–27, 36, 47; and also Dem. 1.19–20; 2.13, 27–31; 3.33–35; 14.14–15. See Ryder (2000: 51, 54–55, 77) on Demosthenes' criticisms of reluctance to serve and his proposals for military reform. Demosthenes was effectively making the opposite argument from Xenophon who argued (*Hipparchicus* 9.3 ff.) that the cavalry should consist at least one fifth of mercenaries the better to maintain full strength.

7 Ibid.

8 For naval reform, see Dem. 14. For reform to the cavalry and infantry, see Dem. 4. For the consistency of his views, see passages cited in n. 6 above.

9 The spurious *Fourth Philippic* puts in Demosthenes' mouth the equivalent to a slogan. He is fighting indifference and laziness (*rhaistônê kai rhaithumia*) ([10].7). This author has correctly identified the main theme in Demosthenes' speeches from the beginning of his career to the end: The Athenians are lazy and idle; they choose the pleasant path rather than the difficult path; they need instead to be energetic (*prothumos*). For the theme of the contrast between ease and difficulty see, 1.10 (*ameleia*); 1.15 (*errathumêkotos*); 2.25 (over-reliance on *elpis*); 3.18, 3.30–34 (*rhaithumian*); 4.12 (the Athenians lack *paraskeuais*); 5.10 (over-reliance on *elpis*); 6.2, 5, 27 (*rhaistônê*); 8.32 (*rhaithumous*); 8.36, 46 (*rhaithumia*); 9.5 (*rhaithumias, ameleias*); 9.35 (*malakizometha*); 11.16–17, 14.8, 17.29 (*malakian, eklusin*). For the exhortation to *prothumia*: 1.5; 2.27; 3.14; 14.14–15. Recognizing Demosthenes' consistency in how he frames the political choices of the Athenians provides evidence against the argument that his policy reflects no consistent political stance in the 350s and early 340s.

10 On Demosthenes' regular position on the losing side before 348 BCE, see Cawkwell 1962: 377.

11 Eubulus' allies included Aeschines, Lycurgus, Meidias, Phocion, and Hegesileos. On his allies, see Cawkwell 1963c: 48–49. In 343 BCE when Aeschines defended himself against Demosthenes, he described himself as on trial for "Eubulus' policies" (*ta Euboulou politeumata*) (Aes. 2.8). In the 330s Lycurgus would build on Eubulus' foundations and pick up the policy and building projects that had been interrupted by the renewed war with Philip between 340 and 338 BCE. See chapter 9.

12 This seems to have led some scholars to credit him with inventing the Stratiotic Fund to support military operations but as Cawkwell (1962) shows, this is incorrect; the fund and its treasurer probably existed for much of the fourth century. The issue in Demosthenes' day was whether to devote surpluses to this fund instead of to the Theoric Fund: see Dem. 19.291; 1.19–20; 3.10. For a good account of the sort of agenda that focused on the internal strengthening of Athens, see Cawkwell 1963c: 55 ff.

13 The power of investigation was called *apophasis*; on the 50 drachmae limit, see Allen 2000a: 40–45; cf. 102–103. According to Wallace, Hansen dates the introduction of *apophasis* from the Areopagus to 355 BCE or shortly thereafter (because of Isocrates' *Areopagiticus* in 355 BCE), in Wallace 1989: 115. [Dem.] 59.79–83 relates an incident involving the Areopagus' investigation of Theogenes, which took place in latter half of 350s, and so would seem to confirm this dating. Wallace (1989: 111) agrees that the Areopagus acquired a more active role in religious oversight, beginning around 355 BCE. This is confirmed by a decree from 352 BCE (*IG* ii^2: 204) in which the Areopagus "was granted in perpetuity supervision over the *hiera orgas*" and "the other holy precincts of Athens." But Wallace prefers a later date for a more general power of *apophasis*. He dates its arrival to 343 BCE on the grounds that the various cases for which we believe it to be used all occurred around then and in order to connect the cases in the late 340s with cases where the Areopagus executed citizens in the early 330s.

But while the prosecutions emerging from these cases occurred around 343 BCE, in at least one case, that of the General Proxenos, the act of wrong-doing which was the subject of the case had occurred earlier, in 346 BCE, so Demosthenes' decree may already have been in place by then. Also, in 346 or 345 BCE, the Areopagus "appeared before the demos to express its disapproval of Timarchus' measures concerning buildings on the Pnyx" (Wallace 1989: 122) (Aes. 1.81–84). Indeed, Buckler (2000: 141) dates Demosthenes' decree to 346 BCE.

Lastly, it's important to recognize that Dinarchus' description in 323 BCE of Demosthenes' decree is tendentious (1.62–63). Dinarchus makes it out that Demosthenes' decree even allows the Areopagus to execute; in doing so, he refers to the case of Antiphon. Since he is prosecuting Demosthenes for treason, it makes sense that he would put a negative spin on Demosthenes' actions. When in 330 BCE Demosthenes himself had described the same case of Antiphon, he very carefully made the point that all the Areopagus did was investigate before handing the wrong-doer over to the assembly for punishment (Dem. 18.132–133). In other words, there is no reason to associate Demosthenes' decree with the power that the Areopagus developed in the early 330s to execute citizens; as a result, there is no reason to try, as Wallace does, to move the dating of the decree later in order to put it in closer proximity to the executions of the early 330s. It makes more sense to follow Hansen's dating: Demosthenes' decree expanded the Areopagus' powers with *apophasis* in the mid-350s. For that matter, Demosthenes was chosen *hieropoios* (temple overseer) to the Semnai, a role linked to the Areopagus, earlier than 348–346 (Dem. 21.115); his relationship to this body was already strong by then.

Then we would need to recognize that a second expansion of the Areopagus' powers, beyond investigation and to execution, occurred in the early 330s. We don't know who would have been responsible for that expansion but Demosthenes' care in 330 BCE to describe his role in a case where the Areopagus limited itself to the investigation phase suggests that it was not he.

See also Plut. *Dem.* 14.5.

14 Lyc. 1.52; cf. 1.12; Aes. 3.252–253; cf. 3.20. See n. 13 above for Demosthenes' view of this extended authority.

15 *SEG* 12.87; Cawkwell (1969: 169 n. 2) provides an overview of the dating of this law, as well as a review of the epigraphical evidence.

16 For a review of the ideology and politics around the Areopagus, see Wallace 1989: 131–206. My argument differs from his because I do not see Demosthenes as endorsing the use of the Areopagus to execute. See n. 13 above.

17 Badian 2000: 35: "Even after the first *Philippic*, Demosthenes shows no particular concern about Philip who had been seizing Athenian possessions ever since 357." Cf. Ryder 2000: 46–48, 52–53; Cawkwell 1963b: 128.

18 On Oreus, Eretria, Megara, see Brunt 1969; on Elis, see Dem. 19.295, 260, 294; Dem 10.10. On Demosthenes' overstatement, see Cawkwell 1963b: 203–205.

19 See Dem. 6, 8, 9, and 11, and the spurious speeches by his associates, [Dem.] 7 and 13.

20 On the events around the treaty, see Cawkwell 1963b: 204–205; Ryder 2000: 60–71; Buckler 2000: 115–140, 151.

21 For scholarly answers to this question, see Ryder 2000: 63–70. Cawkwell (1963a: 128) makes the interesting suggestion that an ideology of pan-hellenism may have tempted people into believing Philip's promises; he could have triggered that ideology by proposing to lead a war against Persia from as early as the late 350s.

22 As Ryder (2000: 58) puts it, "The negotiation of the peace-treaty concluded between Athens and Philip in spring 346 and its immediate consequences during that summer form the crucial episode in Demosthenes' political career. By the end of it Demosthenes had reached an assessment of Philip's ambitions in Greece that was not going to change over the rest of the king's life."

23 On the consequences of the speech-order on the first embassy, see Ryder 2000: 62.

24 Cf. Plato, *Seventh Letter* 340d. In addition, four testimonia associate the word with Hippias the Sophist of Elis (Diels–Kranz Fr. 2, line 2, Fr. 5a, line 3, Fr. 11, line 19, Fr. 12, line 6); two of those are actually in Platonic texts.

25 Too often scholars want to explain the conflicts between Demosthenes and Aeschines as being merely a matter of inexplicable personal antagonism; thus

Buckler (2000: 148) concludes his discussion of Demosthenes and Aeschines by referring to the "vitriol of the two men for each other."

26 There are two instances of *akosmia* in Plato and thirty-six instances of *akolastos*. Otherwise, before the end of the fourth century, there are the following instances of *akosmia*: Euripides (one), Sophocles (one), Gorgias (one), Empedocles (one), Ocellus (one), Aristotle (five), Aesop (one). *Akolastos* is a more common word, appearing (before the time of Aristotle) in the texts of a wide-range of intellectuals: Herodotus, Hippocrates, Euripides, Sophocles, Idomeneus, Aristophanes, Alexis, Megasthenes, Chamaeleon, Zeno, Nicolaus, Aristoxenus, Philolaus, Critias, Diotogenes, Ephorus, Xenophon, Dicaearchus, and Dinon. There is one instance in Herodotus and there are three in Xenophon. This search did not include uses of comparative and superlative forms of the adjective.

Eukosmia is rare in oratory. It appears in Isocrates' *Areopagiticus* of 355 BCE: 7.37, *eukosma* in Demosthenes 19.255, and *eukosmia* in [Dem.] 25.10.

27 Aes. 1.136–159; 2.166 (*dikaios erôs, sôphrôn kai ennomos erôs*); Plato, *Symp.* 188d5; (*erôs sôphrôn kai dikaios*); Democritus, *Fragments*, 73, line 1 (*dikaios erôs*); Plato, *Rep.* 403a; Xenophon, *Symposium* 1.10 (*sôphrôn erôs*). Cf. Plato, *Phaedrus* 230–234, 241, 244; Euripides, *Hippolytus* 359.

28 See appendix 3 for a chart of the use of *miso-* compounds in Athenian literature. The compounds are relatively rare. Most writers did not use them to invent new types of hater. Instead a few basic kinds were repeatedly invoked: *misotyrannos*, *misodêmos*, and *misoponêros*. Three authors appear to have enjoyed developing *miso-* compounds: Aristophanes, Plato, and Aeschines. Aristophanes uses the compounds to make fun of their use (see particularly *Wasps* 1165 and *Peace* 662). He is, in other words, using these compounds with tongue in cheek. Only Plato and Aeschines seem to take them seriously and to develop their usage. These coinages, like *mnêmonikos*, must reflect a Socratic usage.

9. Culture War Concluded

1 Philochorus *F. Gr. Hist.* 328F56a.

2 As a consequence, in 335 BCE, both Lycurgus and Demosthenes were on the list of Athenian politicians whom Alexander demanded be turned over for execution. Thanks to the intervention of the pro-Macedonian politician Demades, both were spared. See Arrian *Anabasis* 1.10; Plut. *Dem.* 23.4, *Phoc.* 17.2.

3 On Demosthenes' activities after Chaeronea: Dem. 18.248–249; Aes. 3.24, 3.159; Plut. *Dem.* 21; [Plut.] *Mor.* [*Ten Orators*] 845f; 851b; cf. Tod no. 196. See also Cawkwell 1969; Harris 1994. On his role as *sitônês*, see Moreno 2007: 335. Also, late in 338/7 BCE Demosthenes proposed a decree, which was passed, for the tribes to elect commissioners to improve the fortifications; he was chosen as commissioner by his tribe and he gave a hundred *minai* to the work (Aes. 3.17, 24, 27–31; Dem. 18.111–119; [Plut.] *Mor.* [*Ten Orators*] 845f–846a, 851a). On Demosthenes' request to be elected *eirênophulax*, see Sealey 1993: 207; Harris 1994; Ryder 1976; Cawkwell 1963c: 55 ff.

On Lycurgus' activities, see Mitchel 1965: 196–198; Mitchel 1970; Mitchel 1975; Burke 1977; Humphreys 1985. Demades was treasurer of the Stratiotic Fund in 334/3 and collaborated with Lycurgus (Mitchel 1962).

4 Sealey (1993: 196): "Early in 339/8 on the proposal of Demosthenes they suspended work on the dockyards and the arsenal and they decreed that the large revenues, hitherto assigned to the theoric fund, should be directed to military purposes. Philochorus reports this" (citing Philochorus *F. Gr. Hist.* 328F56a). Cf. Cawkwell 1963c: 57. On Lycurgus' activities, see Burke 1977: 336; Mitchel 1965: 196–198; Mitchel 1970; Mitchel 1975; Humphreys 1985; Sawada 1996: 74–76.

5 See chapter 8, n. 14.

6 For the term *kosmêtai*, we have the following instances before the end of the fourth century: Homer (one), Plato (three), Xenophon (one), Aeschines (one), Aristotle and Aristotelian Corpus (two). The Platonic instances are *Laws* 755c2, 772a4, 844a1. For *sôphronistai*, we have Hippocrates (one), Thucydides (three), Plato (one), Aristotle and Aristotelian Corpus (three), Aristoxenus (one), Clearchus (two), Lycophron (one), and Demosthenes (one). The Platonic instance is at *Republic* 471a7. The Demosthenic instance is at 19.28 and is used to criticize Aeschines: "God forbid that Athens should ever be in such evil case as to require an Aphobetus or an Aeschines to be *sôphronistai* to the young."

7 On the *ephêbêia* generally, see Lyc. Fr. 20; Wallace 1989: 195–196; Sealey 1993: 211–212; Mitchel, 1965: 202–204; see also Mitchel 1961 and 1975. For Plato's program, see *Laws* 760b–763b, cf. 765d; 801d, 951e.

8 The question of the grain supply from Byzantium, which Demosthenes had long been involved in securing, was among the strategic issues at stake in the conflict with Philip. See Sealey 1993: 201; Ryder 2000: 49; Buckler 2000: 120; Moreno 2007.

9 Diod. 17.8.5; Plut. *Dem.* 23.1. See Sealey 1993: 202–204; Cawkwell 1963b.

10 Diod. 17.3.2; Cawkwell 1969; Worthington 2000: 99. Aeschines attacks Demosthenes for his policy with Persia at 3.156, 173, 239, 259.

11 Sealey 1993: 212–219.

12 The other speech is Lysias 22, *Against the Grain-Dealers* (386 BCE). I leave out trials arising from official scrutiny (*dokimasia*) and cases dealing with public finance or political bribery, for which the city generally appointed prosecutors, as in Hyp. 1 and Din. 1.

13 Worthington (2000b: 101) agrees that "Leocrates' crime was not great."

14 [Plut.] *Mor.* [*Ten Orators*] 843d; Lyc. 1.53; Dem. 18.88; Aes. 3.25–253.

15 Seven years later, when Demosthenes was tried on bribery charges, the accusation that he had traitorously fled Athens after the Battle of Chaeronea was repeated; this was clearly a charge with durability. See Din. 1.12.

16 Burke 1977. See also Sawada (1996: 61 and nn. 19 and 20) who provides a thorough review of the controversy over who reinitiated the suit as well as a very thorough argument in favor of Demosthenes. In addition to taking up and expanding Burke's point about Aeschines' relative weakness, she investigates (1996: 68) Dem. 18.308, which was used by Cawkwell 1969 to support the idea that Aeschines reinitiated the case. She rightly shows that this passage does not provide evidence for this. People who reject the view that Demosthenes reopened

the case include Cawkwell 1969; Worthington 2000: 96–97, 110 n. 31; Harris 1995: 140–142, 173–174.

17 Sawada (1996: 73, 80) also misses this so once she has identified Demosthenes as the politician responsible for reinitiating the Ctesiphon case, she is at a loss to explain his action in terms of political strategy; as a consequence, she argues that his motivation is purely personal; he simply wanted to do Aeschines in and saw a chance to do it. This is implausible. When Worthington (2000b: 96–97) rejects her argument that Demosthenes had reinitiated the suit, he can do so because she has failed to provide an adequate explanation for why he would have done so. I hope in this section to have advanced the case for Demosthenes' reinitiation of the suit precisely by providing an answer to the "why" question; my answer focuses wholly on political strategy.

18 See chapter 7.

19 Scholars dispute whether Agis' war with Macedon ran from spring to autumn of 331 BCE (Badian 1967) or from summer 331 to spring 330 (Cawkwell 1969: 170–173; Bosworth 1975). Sealey (1993) follows Badian. My view is that Cawkwell and Bosworth have the stronger arguments here, and Sealey does acknowledge their strength (1993: 315 n. 85). At any rate, the difference does not affect my argument. Whatever the case, Agis arrived in Athens in 331 BCE to seek the city's support for his revolt (see Sealey 1993: 205–207).

20 Ibid.

21 The primary sources on this question offer apparently conflicting evidence. Most scholars seem to have chosen a single source on which to base their view of what Demosthenes did at this time, rather than looking for an answer that makes sense out of as many pieces of the evidence as possible. Thus Cawkwell (1969: 176, cf. 179) asserts: "Demosthenes supported the policy of keeping out," citing Aes. 3.165 ff.; Sealey (1993: 206) writes: "It is not known what Demosthenes did during the rising of Agis. Prosecuting Ktesiphon a year later, Aischines said that Demosthenes made strange speeches, whirled around on the speaker's platform, and professed to have brought the Lakonians together and to have persuaded the Thessalians and Perrhaibians to secede. This utterance of Aischines may be distortion or invention; it is certainly not informative. The most likely conclusion is that Demosthenes did little or nothing, as is indeed asserted by Deinarchos (1.35)."

In contrast, Burke (1977: 336: 25) thinks that Demosthenes initially supported the uprising. But the sources yield more information than scholars have recognized.

22 Cawkwell 1969: 176.

23 Demades was treasurer of the Stratiotic Fund in 334/3 and collaborated with Lycurgus (Mitchel 1962). On this episode of the 50 drachmae payout, see [Plut.] Mor. [Ten Orators] 818e–f; see Burke 1977: 336; Sawada 1996: 65.

24 On the wage rate, see Allen 2000a: 41.

25 [Plut.] Mor. [Ten Orators] 843d–3; see Sawada 1996: 65–66.

26 Mitchel 1970: 179. But see Sawada 1996: 65–66 for a counter case. I think Sawada underestimates the sense of political emergency that affected Athenian politics during this episode. I take the rhetorical intensity of the three speeches of

330 BCE as a sign that political intensity was at a pitch similar to 346–344 BCE after the embassies and the signing of the Peace of Philocrates. Also, as we shall see, the language Aeschines quotes from Demosthenes' contributions to the debates supports the argument that a major distribution from the theoric fund had just occurred.

27 See n. 21 above.

28 See chapter 8 n. 9 for the consistency of Demosthenes' campaign against "enervation" and related problems.

29 Burtt 1954: 10.

30 Cawkwell 1961: 76–77, citing Athenaeus 509a–b. [Dem.]17.10, 17.15 alludes to this in Cawkwell's opinion. See also Paus. 7.17.7.

31 If Philip won, democracy would die, Demosthenes argued in 8.2, 14, 18, 60; 9.3, 6–19.

32 Indeed, the League of Corinth set up by Philip guaranteed the existing constitutions of member cities.

33 For a summary of the contrast between how Philip treated Thebes and how he treated Athens, see Sawada 1996: 63. Cawkwell (1963a: 131) similarly sees the failure of Demosthenes' predictions to come true at an earlier moment as the basis for his brief fall from political authority in 344/3 BCE. Once Philip had taken the pass at Thermopylae, he had not marched forward. See also Sawada (1996: 82), who argues, citing M. Ostwald ("The Athenian Legislation against Tyranny and Subversion," *Transactions and Proceedings of the American Philological Association* 86, 1955: 123–125) that Philip wasn't anti-democratic.

34 *SEG* 12.87. Translation from Wallace 1989: 179.

35 While most scholars accept Demosthenes' explanation, Worthington (2000b: 93), sides with Aeschines and thinks that was just a pretext for getting out of town. See Aes. 3.26; [Plut.] *Mor.* [*Ten Orators*] 851a–b; Dem. 18.248; Din. 1.78.

36 Worthington 2000: 94: "Agis' war of 331–330 and the Crown trial in 330 seem to have been turning-points for Demosthenes' public profile."

37 Diod. 18.8.3–6; Plut. *Dem.* 28–30, *Phoc.* 29, 33.

38 Worthington (2000b: 106–107) reviews the evidence on the level of disfranchisement.

39 Badian 2000: 16.

40 On the *nomophulakes*, see Williams 1985: 182. On Demetrius' reforms and their ideological significance, see Wallace 1989: 201–206; this citation includes a discussion of the dating of the *nomophulakes*. It is possible that the *nomophulakes* had been established a decade or two earlier, but an earlier date of establishment would not actually affect the argument. The earliest possible establishment of this new position would have been in the 330s, which would only confirm that Platonic ideas were actively circulating then, as the speeches of Lycurgus and Aeschines indicate that they were.

There were, however, also other examples of this position: in Elis (Thuc. 5.47.9), in Keos (see H. Bengston, *Die Vertraege der grieschisch-roemischen Welt* ii² [Munich and Berlin, 1962]), and in Cyrene (*SEG* 9.1). See Wallace 1989: 263–264 n. 35. There is also a suggestion, based on a remark in Philochorus (*F. Gr. Hist.* F64b), that a board of seven *nomophulakes* was set up in Athens in the mid-fifth century but if so the scholarly consensus is that they did not last long at that time. See Cawkwell 1988.

41 And like the Nocturnal Council in the *Laws*, this was a body that knew something about philosophy; it is reported to have called three philosophers before it (Menedemos of Eretria, Asklepiades of Phlious, and Kleanthes) to investigate whether they had any proper livelihood (Athenaeus 168a; Diog. Laert. 7.168–169). All three were rewarded, instead of being punished, with 10 drachmae apiece. The dates for the episode for the first two philosophers would have been earlier than 322; the date for Kleanthes is during the period of Demetrius of Phaleron (see Wallace 1989: 120).

42 Diog. Laert. 5.38; Athenaeus 13.610–611.

43 Plut. *Dem.* 30; [Plut.] *Mor.* 550f.

44 Jones 1999: 229, citing Diog. Laert. 5.38; Pollux *Onomastikon* 9.42 Bekker (pp. 368–369); Athenaeus 13.610–611.

45 Ibid.

46 On Demosthenes' statues for the Bosporan "unworthies," see Din. 1.41–43; on the statues established by Lycurgus, see [Plut.] *Mor.* [*Ten Orators*] 841f.

Epilogue

1 Pocock 1989 [1971]: 104.

Appendix 1

1 See chapter 2 n. 14 and chapter 3 n. 6.

2 See Naddaff (2002: 15–17), Fine (2003 [1999]a: 11, 15, 18, 27), and Irwin (2003 [1999]: 145, 146, 148–149) as examples of scholars who pick up the importance of this and related terms (e.g. *tupos*) but do not stop to analyze them.

3 Also Irwin 2005 [1992]: 67; Havelock 1963: 3; Kraut 1997b: 213.

4 See chapter 4 nn. 5 and 8 on "emulation."

References

Greek texts

Aeschines, "Against Timarchus," "Against Ctesiphon." In C. D. Adams, trans., *Aeschines*. Cambridge, MA: Harvard University Press, 1919.

Aristotle, *Rhetoric*. In J. H. Freese, trans., Aristotle, vol. 22. Cambridge, MA: Harvard University Press, 1926.

Demosthenes, "On the Crown." In C. A. Vince and J. H. Vince, trans., *Demosthenes*. Cambridge, MA: Harvard University Press, 1926.

Diogenes Laertius, *The Lives and Opinions of Eminent Philosophers*, trans. R. D. Hicks. Cambridge, MA: Harvard University Press, 1925.

Lycurgus, "Against Leocrates." In J. O. Burtt, trans., *Minor Attic Orators*, vol. 1. Cambridge, MA: Harvard University Press, 1941.

Plato, *Phaedo*. In H. N. Fowler, trans., *Plato*, vol. 1. Cambridge, MA: Harvard University Press, 1966.

Plato, *Phaedrus*. In H. N. Fowler, trans., *Plato*, vol. 9. Cambridge, MA: Harvard University Press, 1925.

Plato, *Timaeus, Critias, Cleitophon, Menexenus, Epistles*, ed. G. P. Gould. Cambridge, MA: Harvard University Press, 1989.

Plato, *The Republic*, ed. G. R. F. Ferrari, trans. Tom Griffith. Cambridge: Cambridge University Press, 2000.

Plato, *Republic*, Books 1 to 5, trans. P. Shorey. Cambridge, MA, Harvard University Press, 1930.

Plato, *Republic*, Books 6 to 10, trans. P. Shorey. Cambridge, MA: Harvard University Press, 1935.

Plato, *Republic 10*, trans. S. Halliwell. Warminster, UK: Aris & Phillips, 1988.

[Plato] *Seventh Letter*, trans. G. R. Morrow. In J. M. Cooper, ed., *Plato: Complete Works*. Indianapolis, IN: Hackett Publishing, 1997.

[Plato] *Seventh Letter*. In R. G. Bury, trans., *Plato*, vol. 7. Cambridge, MA: Harvard University Press, 1966.

Plato, *Theaetetus*. In M. Burnyeat, ed., *The* Theaetetus *of Plato*, trans. M. Levett. Indianapolis, IN: Hackett Publishing Company, 1990.
Pollux, Julius, of Naucratis, *Onomasticon*, ed. I. Bekker. Berlin: Nicolai, 1846.
Xenophon, *Memorabilia*. In E. C. Marchant, trans., *Xenophon*, vol. 4. Cambridge, MA: Harvard University Press, 1923.

I have in some instances modified the translations derived from these sources. Endnotes indicate where that has occurred. I have used the Morrow translation of the *Seventh Letter* and the Shorey translation of the *Republic* once each, as indicated in an endnote. For those texts, it is otherwise the Bury and Griffith translations that are cited.

General

Ackrill, J. L. 2003 [1999]. "Language and Reality in Plato's Cratylus." In Fine, ed., *Plato 1: Metaphysics and Epistemology*, 125–142.
Allen, D. S. 2000a. *World of Prometheus: The Politics of Punishing in Democratic Athens*. Princeton, NJ: Princeton University Press.
Allen, D. S. 2000b. "Changing the Authoritative Voice: Lycurgus' *Against Leocrates*." *Classical Antiquity* 19 (1): 5–33.
Allen, D. S. 2000c. "Envisaging the Body of the Condemned: The Power of Platonic Symbols." *Classical Philology* 95 (2): 133–150.
Allen, D. S. 2003. "Last Words." Lecture given at the University of Southern California, November.
Allen, D. S. 2006a. "Platonic Quandaries: Recent Scholarship on Plato." *Annual Review of Political Science* 9: 127–141.
Allen, D. S. 2006b. "Talking About Revolution: On Political Change in Fourth-Century Athens." In S. Goldhill and R. Osborne, eds., *Rethinking Revolutions through Ancient Greece*. Cambridge: Cambridge University Press, 183–217.
Annas, J. 1981. *An Introduction to Plato's* Republic. New York: Oxford University Press.
Annas, J. 1997. "Understanding and the Good: Sun, Line, and Cave." In Kraut, ed., *Plato's* Republic: *Critical Essays*, 143–168.
Asmis, E. 2005 [1992]. "Plato on Poetic Creativity." In Kraut, ed., *The Cambridge Companion to Plato*, 338–364.
Badian, E. 1967. "Agis III." *Hermes* 95: 178–184.
Badian, E. 2000. "The Road to Prominence." In Worthington, ed., *Demosthenes: Statesman and Orator*, 9–44.
Barney, R. 2001. *Names and Nature in Plato's* Cratylus. New York: Routledge.
Belfiore, E. S. 1984. "A Theory of Imitation in Plato's *Republic*." *Transactions of the American Philological Association*. 114: 121–46.
Bobonich, C. 2004 [2002]. *Plato's Utopia Recast: His Later Ethics and Politics*. Oxford: Oxford University Press.
Bosworth, B. 1975. "The Mission of Amphoterus and the Outbreak of Agis' War." *Phoenix* 29: 27–43.

Boyle, B. P. 2007. "The Athenian Courtroom: Politics, Rhetoric, Ethics." Unpublished PhD dissertation, University of Chicago.

Brandwood, L. 2005 [1992]. "Stylometry and Chronology." In Kraut, ed., *The Cambridge Companion to Plato*, 90–120.

Brunt, P. A. 1969. "Euboea in the Time of Philip II." *Classical Quarterly* 19 (2): 245–265.

Buckler, J. 2000. "Demosthenes and Aeschines." In Worthington, ed., *Demosthenes: Statesman and Orator*, 114–158.

Burke, E. M. 1977. "'Contra Leocratem' and 'de Corona': Political Collaboration?" *Phoenix* 31 (4) (winter): 330–340.

Burnyeat, M. F. 1999. "Culture and Society in Plato's *Republic*." In G. B. Peterson, ed., *The Tanner Lectures of Human Values*. Salt Lake City: University of Utah Press, 217–324.

Burnyeat, M. F. 2003 [1999]. "Knowledge is Perception: *Theaetetus* 151D–184A." In Fine, ed., *Plato 1: Metaphysics and Epistemology*, 320–354.

Burtt, J. O., trans. 1941 /1954. *Minor Attic Orators*. Vols. 1 and 2. Cambridge, MA: Harvard University Press.

Butcher, S. H. 1887. "Review of Weil's *Demosthenes*." *Classical Review* 1 (8): 218–221.

Cartledge, P. 2002. *The Greeks: A Portrait of Self and Others*. 2nd edn. Oxford: Oxford University Press.

Cartledge, P. 2009. *Ancient Greek Political Thought in Practice*. Cambridge: Cambridge University Press.

Casebeer, W. D. and P. S. Churchland. 2003. "The Neural Mechanisms of Moral Cognition: A Multiple-Aspect Approach to Moral Judgment and Decision-Making." *Biology and Philosophy* 18 (1) (January 1): 169–194.

Cawkwell, G. L. 1961. "A Note on Ps. Demosthenes 17.20." *Phoenix* 15 (2) (summer): 74–78.

Cawkwell, G. L. 1962. "Demosthenes and the Stratiotic Fund." *Mnemosyne* 15 (4): 377–383.

Cawkwell, G. L. 1963a. "Demosthenes' Policy after the Peace of Philocrates. I." *Classical Quarterly* 13 (1): 120–138.

Cawkwell, G. L. 1963b. "Demosthenes' Policy after the Peace of Philocrates. II." *Classical Quarterly* 13 (2): 200–213.

Cawkwell, G. L. 1963c. "Eubulus." *Journal of Hellenic Studies* 83: 47–67.

Cawkwell, G. L. 1969. "The Crowning of Demosthenes." *Classical Quarterly* 19 (1): 163–180.

Cawkwell, G. L. 1988. "ΝΟΜΟΦΥΛΑΚΙΑ and the Areopagus." *Journal of Hellenic Studies* 108: 1–12.

Coetzee, J. 2003. *Elizabeth Costello*. New York: Viking Press.

Cooper, C. 2000. "Philosophers, Politics, Academics: Demosthenes' Rhetorical Reputation in Antiquity." In Worthington, ed., *Demosthenes: Statesman and Orator*, 224–45.

Cooper, J. M. ed. 1997a. *Plato: Complete Works*. Indianapolis, IN: Hackett Publishing.

Cooper, J. M., 1997b. "The Psychology of Justice in Plato." In Kraut, ed., *Plato's Republic: Critical Essays*, 17–30.

Cornford, F. M., trans. 1945 [1941]. *The Republic of Plato*. New York: Oxford University Press.

de Romilly, J. 1958. "*Eunoia* in Isocrates or the Political Importance of Creating Good Will." *Journal of Hellenic Studies*. 78: 92–101.

Derrida, J. 1989. "La Pharmacie de Platon." In *Phèdre/Platon*, trans. with introduction and notes by Luc Brisson. Paris: Flammarion.

Devereux, D. T. 2003 [1999]. "Separation and Immanence in Plato's Theory of Forms." In Fine, ed., *Plato 1: Metaphysics and Epistemology*, 192–214.

Doyle, J. (forthcoming a). *Saying and Showing in Plato's* Gorgias.

Doyle, J. (forthcoming b). "Socratic Methods."

Edmunds, L. 2006. "What Was Socrates Called?" *Classical Quarterly* 56 (2): 414–425.

Euben, J. P. 1997. *Corrupting Youth: Political Education, Democratic Culture, and Political Theory*. Princeton, NJ: Princeton University Press.

Ferrari, G. R. F. 1987. *Listening to the Cicadas: A Study of Plato's* Phaedrus. Cambridge: Cambridge University Press.

Ferrari, G. R. F. 1989. "Plato and Poetry." In G. Kennedy, ed., *Cambridge History of Literary Criticism*, vol. 1. Cambridge: Cambridge University Press, 92–148.

Fine, G., ed. 2003 [1999]a. *Plato 1: Metaphysics and Epistemology*. New York: Oxford University Press Inc.

Fine, G. 2003 [1999]b. "Knowledge and Belief in *Republic* 5–7." In Fine, ed., *Plato 1: Metaphysics and Epistemology*, 215–246.

Finley, M. 1985. "Censorship in Classical Antiquity." In *Democracy Ancient and Modern*, 2nd edn. New Brunswick, NJ: Rutgers University Press, 142–172.

Fisher, N., trans. 2001. *Aeschines: Against Timarchos*. Oxford: Oxford University Press.

Fisher, N. 2007. "Lykourgos of Athens: Lakonian by name, Lakoniser by policy?" In N. Birgalias, K. Burasalis, and P. Cartledge, eds., *The Contribution of Ancient Sparta to Political Thought and Practice*. Athens: Alexandria Publications, 327–344.

Ford, A. 2002. *The Origins of Criticism: Literary Culture and Poetic Theory in Classical Greece*. Princeton, NJ: Princeton University Press.

Foucault, M. 1977. *Discipline and Punish: The Birth of the Prison*, trans. A. Sheridan. New York: Pantheon Books.

Foucault, M. 1978. *The History of Sexuality*, trans. R. Hurley. New York: Pantheon Books.

Foucault, M. 1994 [1971]. *The Order of Things: An Archaeology of the Human Sciences*. New York: Vintage Books.

Frank, J. 2005. *A Democracy of Distinction: Aristotle and the Work of Politics*. Chicago: University of Chicago Press.

Frank, J. 2007. "Wages of War: On Judgment in Plato's *Republic*." *Political Theory* 35: 443–67.

Frank, J. 2008. "Vying for Authority in Plato's *Republic*." Paper presented at the American Political Science Association Annual Meeting, August 28–31, Boston, MA.

Freud, S. 1957–1981. *The Complete Psychological Works of Sigmund Freud*. Translated from the German under the general editorship of James Strachey, in collaboration with Anna Freud, assisted by Alix Strachey and Alan Tyson. London: Hogarth Press.

Gaiser, K. 1980. "Plato's Enigmatic Lecture *On the Good.*" *Phronesis* 25: 5–37.

Gill, C. 1973. "The Death of Socrates." *Classical Quarterly* 23: 25–28.

Gill, C. 1993. "Plato on Falsehood—Not Fiction." In C. Gill and T. P. Wiseman, *Lies and Fiction in the Ancient World.* Exeter: Exeter University Press, 38–87.

Habermas, J. 2001. *The Liberating Power of Symbols: Philosophical Essays,* trans. P. Dews. Cambridge, MA: MIT Press.

Hansen, M. H. 1995. *Sources for the Ancient Greek City-State.* Copenhagen: Kgl. Danske Videnskabernes Selskab.

Harris, E. M. 1994. "Demosthenes Loses a Friend and Nausicles Gains a Position: A Prosopographical Note on Athenian Politics after Chaeronea." *Historia: Zeitschrift für Alte Geschichte* 43 (3): 378–384.

Harris, E. M. 1995. *Aeschines and Athenian Politics.* New York: Oxford University Press.

Harris, W. V. 1991. *Ancient Literacy.* Cambridge, MA: Harvard University Press.

Hattam, V. and J. Lowndes. 2007. "The Ground Beneath Our Feet: Language, Culture, and Political Change." In Skowronek and Glassman, eds., *Formative Acts: American Politics in the Making,* 199–219.

Havelock, E. A. 1963. *Preface to Plato.* Cambridge, MA: Harvard University Press.

Hirschman, A. O. 1977. *The Passions and the Interests.* Princeton, NJ: Princeton University Press.

Hobbs, A. 2000. *Plato and the Hero: Courage, Manliness, and the Impersonal Good.* Cambridge: Cambridge University Press.

Humphreys, S. 1985. "Lycurgus of Butudae: An Athenian Aristocrat." In J. W. Eadie and J. Ober, eds., *The Craft of the Ancient Historian: Essays in Honor of Chester G. Starr.* Lanham, MD: University Press of America, 199–252.

Irwin, T. H. 2003 [1999]. "The Theory of Forms." In Fine, ed., *Plato 1: Metaphysics and Epistemology,* 143–170.

Irwin, T. H. 2005 [1992]. "Plato: The Intellectual Background." In Kraut, ed., *The Cambridge Companion to Plato,* 51–89.

Jaeger, W. 1986 [1944]. Paideia: *The Ideals of Greek Culture. The Conflict of Cultural Ideals in the Age of Plato,* vol. 3. Oxford: Oxford University Press.

James, W. 1997 [1907]. "What Pragmatism Means," "Pragmatism's Conception of Truth." In L. Menand, ed., *Pragmatism: A Reader.* New York: Vintage, 93–131.

Janaway, C. 1995. *Images of Excellence: Plato's Critique of the Arts.* Oxford: Clarendon Press.

Janaway, C. 2006. "Plato and the Arts." In H. H. Benson, ed., *A Companion to Plato.* Chichester, UK: Wiley-Blackwell, 388–400.

Jones, N. F. 1999. *The Associations of Classical Athens: The Response to Democracy.* Oxford: Oxford University Press.

Kahn, C. H. 1998. *Plato and the Socratic Dialogue: The Philosophical Use of a Literary Form.* Cambridge: Cambridge University Press.

Keynes, J. M. 2006 [1936]. *General Theory of Employment, Interest, and Money.* New Delhi: Atlantic Publishers & Distributors (P) Ltd.

Kraut, R. 1997a. *Plato's* Republic: *Critical Essays*. Lanham, MD: Rowman & Littlefield Publishers, Inc.

Kraut, R. 1997b. "The Defense of Justice in Plato's *Republic*." In Kraut, ed., *Plato's* Republic: *Critical Essays*, 197–222.

Kraut, R., ed. 2005 [1992]a. *The Cambridge Companion to Plato*. New York: Cambridge University Press.

Kraut, R. 2005 [1992]b. "Introduction to the Study of Plato." In Kraut, ed., *The Cambridge Companion to Plato*, 1–50.

Krentz, P. 1982. *The Thirty at Athens*. Ithaca, NY: Cornell University Press.

Kuhn, T. S. 2000. *The Road Since Structure: Philosophical Essays, 1970–1993, with an Autobiographical Interview*, ed. J. Conant and J. Haugeland. Chicago: University of Chicago Press.

Laistner, M. L. W. 1930. "The Influence of Isocrates's Political Doctrines on Some Fourth Century Men of Affairs." *Classical Weekly* 23 (17) (March 10): 129–131.

Lakoff, G. 1987. *Women, Fire, and Dangerous Things: What Categories Reveal About the Mind*. Chicago: University of Chicago Press.

Lakoff, G. 2004. *Don't Think of an Elephant: Know Your Values and Frame the Debate*. White River Junction, VT: Chelsea Green Publishing Company.

Lakoff, G. and M. Johnson. 1980. *Metaphors We Live By*. Chicago: University of Chicago Press.

Lanni, A. 2008. *Law and Justice in the Courts of Classical Athens*. New York: Cambridge University Press.

Lear, J. 1990. *Love and Its Place in Nature: A Philosophical Interpretation of Freudian Psychoanalysis*. New York: Farrar, Straus, and Giroux.

Lear, J. 1997. "Inside and Outside the *Republic*." In Kraut, ed., *Plato's* Republic: *Critical Essays*, 61–94.

Liebert, H. 2009a. "Between City and Empire: Political Ambition and Political Form in Plutarch's *Parallel Lives*." PhD dissertation, University of Chicago.

Liebert, H. 2009b. "Plutarch's Critique of Plato's Best Regime." *History of Political Thought* 30 (2009): 251–71.

Lloyd, A. C. 1969–1970. "Non-Discursive Thought: An Enigma of Greek Philosophy." *Proceedings of the Aristotelian Society* 70: 261–274.

Mara, G. M. 1997. *Socrates' Discursive Democracy: Logos and Ergon in Political Philosophy*. Albany: State University of New York Press.

Mesk, J. 1901. "Demosthenes und Isokrates." *Wiener Studien* 23: 209–12.

Milns, R. D. 2000. "The Public Speeches of Demosthenes." In Worthington, ed., *Demosthenes: Statesman and Orator*, 205–223.

Mitchel, F. W. 1961. "The Cadet Colonels of the Ephebic Corps." *Transactions and Proceedings of the American Philological Association* 92: 347–357.

Mitchel, F. W. 1962. "Demades of Paeania and $IGII^2$ 1493, 1494, 1495." *Transactions and Proceedings of the American Philological Association* 93: 213–229.

Mitchel, F. W. 1965. "Athens in the Age of Alexander." *Greece & Rome* 12 (2): 189–204.

Mitchel, F. W. 1970. *Lykourgan Athens: 338–322*. Cincinnati: University of Cincinnati Press.

Mitchel, F. W. 1975. "The So-Called Earliest Ephebic Inscription." *Zeitschrift für Papyrologie und Epigraphik* 19: 233–243.

Monoson, S. S. 2000. *Plato's Democratic Entanglements: Athenian Politics and the Practice of Philosophy*. Princeton, NJ: Princeton University Press.

Moreno, A. 2007. *Feeding the Democracy: The Athenian Grain Supply in the Fifth and Fourth Centuries* BC. Oxford Classical Monographs. Oxford: Oxford University Press.

Morgan, K. 2000. *Myth and Philosophy from the Presocratics to Plato*. Cambridge: Cambridge University Press.

Morgan, M. L. 2005 [1992]. "Plato and Greek Religion." In Kraut, ed., *The Cambridge Companion to Plato*, 227–247.

Morgan, T. J. 1999. "Literate Education in Classical Athens." *Classical Quarterly* 49 (1). New Series: 46–61.

Mueller, I. 2005 [1992]. "Mathematical Method and Philosophical Truth." In Kraut, ed., *The Cambridge Companion to Plato*, 170–199.

Naddaff, R. A. 2002. *Exiling the Poets: The Production of Censorship in Plato's Republic*. Chicago: University of Chicago Press.

Nails, D. 2002. *The People of Plato: A Prosopography of Plato and Other Socratics*. Indianapolis, IN: Hackett Publishing Company, Inc.

Narvaez, D. 2002. "The Expertise of Moral Character." Paper presented at Whitehouse Conference on Character and Community. June 19, 2002, Washington, DC. http://www2.ed.gov/admins/lead/safety/character/narvaez.pdf.

Narvaez, D. 2008. "Human Flourishing and Moral Development: Cognitive Science and Neurobiological Perspectives on Virtue Development." In Nucci and Narvaez, eds., *Handbook of Moral and Character Education*, 310–327.

Narvaez, D., and D. Lapsley, eds. 2009. *Moral Personality, Identity and Character: An Interdisciplinary Future*. New York: Cambridge University Press.

Nehamas, A. 1988. "Plato and the Mass Media." *The Monist*. 71: 214–234.

Nehamas, A. 2003 [1999]. "Plato on the Imperfection of the Sensible World." In Fine, ed., *Plato 1: Metaphysics and Epistemology*, 171–191.

Nightingale, A. 1995. *Genres in Dialogue: Plato and the Construct of Philosophy*. Cambridge: Cambridge University Press.

Notopoulos, J. A. 1942. "Socrates and the Sun." *Classical Journal* 37 (5): 260–274.

Nucci, L. P., and D. Narvaez, eds. 2008. *Handbook of Moral and Character Education*. New York: Routledge.

Nussbaum, M. C. 1986. *The Fragility of Goodness: Luck and Ethics in Greek Tragedy and Philosophy*. Cambridge: Cambridge University Press.

Ober, J. 1998. *Political Dissent in Democratic Athens: Intellectual Critics of Popular Rule*. Princeton, NJ: Princeton University Press.

Ober, J. 2009. *Democracy and Knowledge: Innovation and Learning in Classical Athens*. Princeton, NJ: Princeton University Press.

Paulas, J. 2008. "Athenaeus and the Advantages of Philology." Unpublished PhD dissertation, University of Chicago.

Penner, T. 2005 [1992]. "Socrates and the Early Dialogues." In Kraut, ed., *The Cambridge Companion to Plato*, 121–169.

Perlman, S. 1964. "Quotations from Poetry in Attic Orators of the Fourth Century BC." *American Journal of Philology* 85: 155–172.

Pocock, J. G. A. 1989 [1971]. *Politics, Language, and Time: Essays on Political Thought and History.* Chicago: University of Chicago Press.

Popper, K. R. 1945. *The Open Society and Its Enemies.* London: G. Routledge & Sons, Ltd.

Reinhard, D. 2006. "Playing Dead: The Poetics of Hades in Homer and Sophocles." Unpublished PhD dissertation, University of Chicago.

Rhodes, P. J. 1978. "On Labelling Fourth-Century Politicians." *Liverpool Classical Monthly* 3: 207–211.

Rihll, T. E. 2003. "Teaching and Learning in Classical Athens." *Greece & Rome* 50 (2). Second Series (October): 168–190.

Ritter, C. 1888. *Untersuchungen über Platon: Die Echtheit und Chronologie der Platonischer Schriften.* Stuttgart, Germany: Kohlhammer.

Rocco, C. 1997. *Tragedy and Enlightenment: Athenian Political Thought and the Dilemmas of Modernity.* Berkeley and Los Angeles: University of California Press.

Rowe, G. O. 2002. "Two Responses by Isocrates to Demosthenes." *Historia: Zeitschrift für Alte Geschichte* 51 (2): 149–162.

Ryder, T. T. B. 1976. "Demosthenes and Philip's Peace of 338/7 BC." *Classical Quarterly* 26 (1): 85–87.

Ryder, T. T. B. 2000. "Demosthenes and Philip II." In Worthington, ed., *Demosthenes: Statesman and Orator*, 45–89.

Santas, G. 2003 [1999]. "The Form of the Good in Plato's *Republic*." In Fine, ed., *Plato 1: Metaphysics and Epistemology*, 247–274.

Sawada, N. 1966. "Athenian Politics in the Age of Alexander the Great: A Reconsideration of the Trial of Ctesiphon." *Chiron* 26: 57–84.

Scott, D. 2003 [1999]. "Platonic Recollection." In Fine, ed., *Plato 1: Metaphysics and Epistemology*, 93–124.

Sealey, R. 1955. "Athens after the Social War." *Journal of Hellenic Studies* 75: 74–81.

Sealey, R. 1993. *Demosthenes and His Time: A Study in Defeat.* Oxford: Oxford University Press.

Sewell, W. H., Jr. 1994. "Ideologies and Social Revolutions: Reflections on the French Case." In Skocpol, ed., *Social Revolutions in the Modern World*, 169–198.

Sewell, W. H., Jr. 2005. *Logics of History: Social Theory and Social Transformation.* Chicago: University of Chicago Press.

Shanks, D. R. and M. F. St. John. 1994. "Characteristics of Dissociable Human Learning Systems." *Behavioral and Brain Sciences* 17 (3): 367–447.

Skinner, Q. 2005. "On Intellectual History and the History of Books." *Contributions to the History of Concepts* 1 (1): 29–36.

Skocpol, T., ed. 1994. *Social Revolutions in the Modern World.* Cambridge: Cambridge University Press.

Skocpol, T., ed. 1998. *Democracy, Revolution, and History.* Ithaca, NY: Cornell University Press.

Smith, S. D. 1990. "The Pursuit of Pragmatism." *Yale Law Journal* 100 (2) (Nov.): 409–449.

Strauss, L. 1978 (1964). *The City and Man*. Chicago: University of Chicago Press.

Tarnopolsky, C. H. 2010. *Prudes, Perverts, and Tyrants: Plato's* Gorgias *and the Politics of Shame*. Princeton, NJ: Princeton University Press.

Taylor, C. C. W. 1997. "Plato's Totalitarianism." In Kraut, ed., *Plato's* Republic: *Critical Essays*, 31–48.

Thomas, R. 2009. "Writing, Reading, Public and Private 'Literacies': Functional Literacy and Democratic Literacy in Greece." In W. A. Johnson and H. N. Parker., eds. *Ancient Literacies: The Culture of Reading in Greece and Rome*. New York: Oxford University Press, 13–45.

Too, Y. L. 1995. *The Rhetoric of Identity in Isocrates: Text, Power, Pedagogy*. Cambridge: Cambridge University Press.

Urmson, J. O. 1997. "Plato and the Poets." In Kraut, ed., *Plato's* Republic: *Critical Essays*, 223–234.

Vlastos, G. 1991. *Socrates: Ironist and Moral Philosopher*. Cambridge: Cambridge University Press.

Vlastos, G. 1997. "A Metaphysical Paradox." In Kraut, ed., *Plato's* Republic: *Critical Essays*, 181–196.

von Hallberg, R. 2008. *Lyric Powers*. Chicago, University of Chicago Press.

Wallace, R. W. 1989. *The Areopagos Council to 307* BC. Baltimore, MD: Johns Hopkins University Press.

Wallach, J. R. 2001. *The Platonic Political Art: A Study of Critical Reason and Democracy*. University Park: Pennsylvania State University Press.

Walzer, M. 2002. *The Company of Critics: Social Criticism and Political Commitment in the Twentieth Century*. New York: Basic Books.

West, C. 1989. "Prophetic Pragmatism: Cultural Criticism and Political Engagement." In West, *The American Evasion of Philosophy: A Genealogy of Pragmatism*. Madison: University of Wisconsin Press, 211–242.

White, N. P. 1979. *A Companion to Plato's* Republic. Indianapolis, IN: Hackett Publishing Company.

Williams, B. 1981. *Moral Luck: Philosophical Papers, 1973–1980*. Cambridge: Cambridge University Press.

Williams, B. 1997. "The Analogy of City and Soul in Plato's *Republic*." In Kraut, ed., *Plato's* Republic: *Critical Essays*, 49–60.

Williams, J. M. 1985. "Athens without Democracy: The Oligarchy of Phocion and the Tyranny of Demetrius of Phalerum, 322–307 BC." Unpublished dissertation, Yale University.

Wolpert, A. 2001. *Remembering Defeat: Civil War and Civic Memory in Ancient Athens*. Baltimore, MD: Johns Hopkins University Press.

Worthington, I., ed. 2000. *Demosthenes: Statesman and Orator*. London: Routledge.

Yunis, H. 2003a. *Written Texts and the Rise of Literate Culture in Ancient Greece*. Cambridge: Cambridge University Press.

Yunis, H. 2003b. "Writing for Reading: Thucydides, Plato, and the Emergence of the Critical Reader." In Yunis, *Written Texts*, 189–212.

Zuckert, C. H. 2009. *Plato's Philosophers: The Coherence of the Dialogues*. Chicago: The University of Chicago Press.

Further Reading

Allen, D. S. 2003. "Burning *The Fable of the Bees*: Cultural Poetics and the Incendiary Authority of Nature." In L. Daston and F. Vidal, eds., *The Moral Authority of Nature*. Chicago: University of Chicago Press, 74–99.

Allen, D. S. 2004. *Talking to Strangers*. Chicago: University of Chicago Press.

Annas, J. 2003. *Plato: A Very Short Introduction*. Oxford: Oxford University Press.

Ausland, H. W. 1997. "On Reading Plato Mimetically." *American Journal of Philology* 118 (3) (autumn): 371–416.

Ball, T. 2006. "Must Political Theory Be Historical?" *Contributions to the History of Concepts* 2 (1): 7–18.

Benoit, W. L. 1991. "Isocrates and Plato on Rhetoric and Rhetorical Education." *Rhetoric Society Quarterly* 21 (1) (winter): 60–71.

Block, J. 2007. "Agency and Popular Activism in American Political Culture." In Skowronek and Glassman, eds., *Formative Acts: American Politics in the Making*, 52–74.

Bowra, C. M. 1938. "Plato's Epigram on Dion's Death." *American Journal of Philology* 59 (4): 394–404.

Boys-Stones, G. R. 2003. *Metaphor, Allegory, and the Classical Tradition*. Oxford: Oxford University Press.

Chroust, A.-H. 1967. "Plato's Academy: The First Organized School of Political Science in Antiquity." *Review of Politics* 29 (1): 25–40.

Clemens, E. 2007. "Retrospective: Formative Action and Second Acts." In Skowronek and Glassman, eds., *Formative Acts: American Politics in the Making*, 363–377.

Darnton, R. 2005. "Discourse and Diffusion." *Contributions to the History of Concepts* 1 (1): 21–28.

de Romilly, J. 1992. "Isocrates and Europe." *Greece & Rome* 39 (1). Second Series (April): 2–13.

Ellis, J. R. 1976. *Philip II and Macedonian Imperialism*. London: Thames & Hudson.

Gabrielsen, V. and J. Lund, eds. 2007. *The Black Sea in Antiquity. Regional and Interregional Economic Exchanges.* Aarhus: Aarhus University Press.

Geuss, R. 2008. *Philosophy and Real Politics.* Princeton, NJ: Princeton University Press.

Hammond, N. 1994. *Philip of Macedon.* Baltimore, MD: Johns Hopkins University Press.

Hidalgo, O. 2008. "Conceptual History and Politics: Is the Concept of Democracy Essentially Contested?" *Contributions to the History of Concepts* 4 (2): 176–201.

Johnson, W. A. and H. N. Parker, eds. 2009. *Ancient Literacies: The Culture of Reading in Greece and Rome.* New York: Oxford University Press.

Kerferd, G. B. 1963. Review of *Anonymous Prolegomena* to Platonic Philosophy by L. G. Westerink. *Classical Review* 13 (3): 347.

Koselleck, R. 2006. "Conceptual History, Memory, and Identity: An Interview with Reinhart Koselleck." Interview by Javiér Fernández Sebastián and Juan Francisco Fuentes, *Contributions to the History of Concepts* 2 (1): 99–127.

Laclau, E. 1994. *Making of Political Identities.* London: Verso.

Lane, M. S. 2001. *Plato's Progeny: How Plato and Socrates Still Captivate the Modern Mind.* London: Gerald Duckworth & Co. Ltd.

Lear, G. 2006. "Plato on Learning to Love Beauty." In G. Santas, ed., *The Blackwell Guide to Plato's Republic.* Malden, MA: Blackwell Publishing Ltd., 104–124.

Lear, G. 2007. "Permanent Beauty and Becoming Happy in Plato's *Symposium.*" In J. Lesher, D. Nails, and F. Sheffield, eds., *Plato's Symposium: Issues in Interpretation and Reception.* Cambridge, MA: Harvard University Press, 96–123.

Leslie, K. 2006. "Plato, Aesop, and the Beginnings of Mimetic Prose." Research article (June 5) http://caliber.ucpress.net/doi/abs/10.1525/rep.2006.94.1.6.

Lofberg, J. O. 1925. "The Date of the Athenian Ephebêia." *Classical Philology* 20 (4): 330–335.

Lynch, J. P. 1972. *Aristotle's School: A Study of a Greek Educational Institution.* Berkeley: University of California Press.

McQueen, E. I. 1978. "Some Notes on the Anti-Macedonian Movement in the Peloponnese in 331 BC." *Historia: Zeitschrift für Alte Geschichte* 27 (1): 40–64.

Merlan, P. 1954. "Isocrates, Aristotle and Alexander the Great." *Historia: Zeitschrift für Alte Geschichte* 3 (1): 60–81.

Neserius, P. G. 1933. "Isocrates' Political and Social Ideas." *International Journal of Ethics* 43 (3) (April): 307–328.

Ober, J. 1985. *Fortress Attica: Defense of the Athenian Land Frontier 404–322 BC. Mnemosyne* Supplement 84. Leiden: E. J. Brill.

O'Sullivan, L.-L. 1997. "Athenian Impiety Trials in the Late Fourth Century BC." *Classical Quarterly* 47 (1): 136–152.

Palonen, K. 2005. "The Politics of Conceptual History." *Contributions to the History of Concepts* 1 (1): 37–50.

Richter, M. 2005. "More than a Two-way Traffic: Analyzing, Translating, and Comparing Political Concepts from Other Cultures." *Contributions to the History of Concepts* 1 (1): 7–20.

Roebuck, C. 1948. "The Settlements of Philip II with the Greek States in 338 BC." *Classical Philology* 43 (2): 73–92.

Rosen, S. 1988. *The Quarrel between Philosophy and Poetry: Studies in Ancient Thought*. New York: Routledge, Chapman & Hall, Inc.

Sachs, D. 1997. "A Fallacy in Plato's *Republic*." In Kraut, ed., *Plato's Republic: Critical Essays*, 1–16.

Saunders, T. J. 2005 [1992]. "Plato's Later Political Thought." In Kraut, ed., *The Cambridge Companion to Plato*, 464–492.

Saxonhouse, A. W. 1994. "The Philosopher and the Female in the Political Thought of Plato." In N. Tuana, ed., *Feminist Interpretations of Plato*. University Park: The Pennsylvania State University Press, 67–86.

Saxonhouse, A. W. 1995. *Fear of Diversity: The Birth of Political Science in Ancient Greek Thought*. Chicago: University of Chicago Press.

Sellars, J. 2003. "Simon the Shoemaker and the Problem of Socrates." *Classical Philology* 98 (3) (July): 207–216.

Sheingate, A. 2007. "The Terrain of the Political Entrepreneur." In Skowronek and Glassman, eds., *Formative Acts: American Politics in the Making*, 13–31.

Shorey, P. 1933. *What Plato Said*. Chicago: University of Chicago Press.

Skinner, Q. 2007. "Intellectual History, Liberty and Republicanism: An Interview with Quentin Skinner." Interview by Javier Fernández Sebastián, *Contributions to the History of Concepts* 3 (1): 103–123.

Skowronek, S. and M. Glassman, eds. 2007. *Formative Acts: American Politics in the Making*. Philadelphia: University of Pennsylvania Press.

Skowronek, S. and M. Glassman. 2007a. "Formative Acts." In Skowronek and Glassman, eds., *Formative Acts: American Politics in the Making*, 1–9.

Stalley, R. F. 1990. "Review, Plato *Republic* Book 10." *Classical Review* 40 (1) (April) New Series: 11–12.

Sullivan, J. 2003. "Demosthenes' Areopagus Legislation: Yet Again." *Classical Quarterly* 53 (1): 130–134.

Tilly, C. 1998. "Where Do Rights Come From?" In Skocpol, ed., *Democracy, Revolution, and History*, 55–72.

Walzer, M. 1998. "Intellectuals, Social Classes, and Revolutions." In T. Skocpol, ed., *Democracy, Revolution, and History*. Ithaca, NY: Cornell University Press, 127–142.

Index

abstraction, 36, 41, 53, 72, 74
Academy, 5, 13, 86, 122, 138, 147, 162;
  date of opening, 166
Ackrill, J. L., 168, 190, 191
action, actuality, 20, 49, 54, 60, 68, 157
Adeimantus, 11, 49, 166
Adonis, Garden of, 26, 28
Aeschines, 91–94, 97–107, 109, 111,
  112, 115–123, 125–129, 132,
  134–139, 160, 167, 192–204
Aeschylus, 103, 124, 140, 158, 179,
  194, 196
Aesop, 15–16, 180, 192, 194, 201
aesthetics, 162, 178
after-life, 34–35, 61; reincarnation, 35,
  75; see also Hades, underworld
Against Aristogeiton I and II, 93,
  191–192
Against Ctesiphon, 93, 99–100, 106,
  108, 120–121, 127
Against Demosthenes, 92, 133,
  198–199
Against Leocrates, 92, 98–99, 106, 108,
  121, 128–129, 132–133, 135, 196
Against Stephanus 1, 197
Against Timarchus, 104–105, 120,
  195–196, 198
agency, 91–92
agent of change, 143, 169

Agis III, king of Sparta;, 128–130, 133,
  203, 204; appeal to Athens, 130, 203;
  Demosthenes' response to, 129, 132
akolasia, 92, 120, 201
akosmia, 120, 201
akrasia, 113; see also weakness of will
Alexamenes of Teos, 167
Alexander the Great, 2, 119–120,
  124–125, 129, 133, 137, 201
Alexis, 163, 201
allegory, 52, 75, 89, 105, 139; of the
  cave, 30, 39, 44, 85, 148–149, 156,
  176, 180, 181, 188; of the soul,
  171; of the sun, 30, 39, 84, 153, 156,
  171, 176, 181, 188; see also
  analogy
Allen, D. S., 161–163, 169, 173, 183,
  185, 189, 191–192, 194, 197, 199,
  203
alliances, political, 95, 123, 127, 130,
  145, 162, 199
alliteration, 146
ameleia, 198
American political development
  studies, 162
amnesty, 12, 166
Amphiareion, 124
Amphipolis, 95, 96–97, 195
Amphis, 163